Biosocial
Criminology

A Primer

Kevin M. Beaver

Florida State University

KENDALL/HUNT PUBLISHING COMPANY
4050 Westmark Drive   Dubuque, Iowa 52002

Interior Image Credits:

Biology illustrations - Pages 52, 54, 56, 57, and 63, © Kendall/Hunt Publishing.
Brain cross-section - Page 124, Source: National Institute on Alcohol Abuse & Alcoholism, National
Institutes of Health
Line-art illustrations and diagrams created by the author.

Cover Images:

Shadow image © Phase4phtography, 2008. Used under license of Shutterstock, Inc.
Finger print © BruceRolft, 2008. Used under license of Shutterstock, Inc.
Cracked Glass © Regisser, 2008. Used under license of Shutterstock, Inc.

Copyright © 2009 by Kendall/Hunt Publishing Company

ISBN 978-0-7575-5876-4

Printed in the United States of America
10 9 8 7 6 5

Table of Contents

Author's Note

Biosocial criminology is an emerging perspective that has gained traction in the past few years. Unfortunately, even though more and more students are becoming interested in learning about the genetic, biological, and neurological foundations to antisocial behaviors most criminology programs do not offer classes in biosocial criminology. As a result, most undergraduate and graduate criminology students earn their degrees with very little, if any, exposure to the biosocial correlates to crime and delinquency. Without a background in the biosocial criminological literature, and lacking a full appreciation of how to conduct biosocial research, most newly-minted PhDs turn their attention to more accessible research avenues. The purpose of this book is to provide those who are interested in biosocial criminology a concise introduction to this perspective.

Many people were instrumental in shaping this book into its current form (although all errors are mine and mine alone). To begin with, I would like to acknowledge my project coordinator, Ryan L. Schrodt, my acquisitions editor, Eric Flesvig, for their encouragement and help while writing this book. A special thanks is in order for my fellow biosocial researchers, including Matt DeLisi, Michael G. Vaughn, Anthony Walsh, and John Paul Wright. Working with such a great group of collaborators has most certainly sharpened my thinking about biosocial criminology. I am also deeply grateful to Travis C. Pratt for writing the Foreword to this book. In addition, I would like to thank my graduate students, Brian B. Boutwell and J.C. Barnes, for reading and commenting on many of the chapters.

And last, but certainly not least, I would like to acknowledge my gorgeous wife, Shonna, who has supported me in every aspect of my life. And to my two darling children, Brooke and Jackson, who are the center of my universe. The three of you mean more to me than you will ever know.
Thank you.

Dedication

This book is dedicated to my beautiful wife, Shonna, and
to my two adorable children, Brooke and Jackson.

Beginning
Quote

"Believe those who are seeking the truth. Doubt those who find it."

—Andre Gide.

Foreword

Theories of criminal behavior can become either popular or marginalized to the periphery of the discipline of criminology for a variety of reasons. Ironically enough, many of these reasons have little or nothing to do with a theory's scientific merit. Indeed, some theories catch the attention of criminologists because they provide puzzles for scholars to decipher, thus making their work "interesting" to other scholars and to the field at large. Other theories find their way into the discipline because they specify propositions that can be easily tested—even better if they can be assessed using data drawn samples of easily accessible undergraduate students—and can therefore result in peer-reviewed publications (the currency of the academy that can lead to tenure and promotion). Still other theories may enjoy a position of popularity among scholars simply because they are merely consistent with the prevailing social and professional context of the time. The alternative, of course, is that others may be pushed to the side for ideological reasons because we might find the policy implications of the theory unsettling.

These reasons notwithstanding, certain theories have gathered criminologists' allegiance because they have the weight of scientific data on their side. To be sure, systematic reviews of the criminological literature have revealed high levels of support for certain theoretical perspectives (e.g., self-control and social learning theories) while highlighting the absence of support for others (e.g., deterrence/rational choice theory). The underlying assumption of these efforts, however, is that empirical data should play a role in the choice concerning which theories criminologists choose to either accept or reject (a proposition that, unfortunately, has less general support in the field than one might think).

Yet data can be a tricky thing. New theories of criminal behavior are often developed either in concert with, or following, the availability of new data sources. One of the most notable examples of this phenomenon can be seen in the effects of the new developments in survey methodology that came along in the 1960s. As scholars began to view students and members of the community as prime sources of criminological information, an explosion of refinements to survey techniques took place. As a result, the unit of analysis shifted away from examining social aggregates like neighborhoods, cities, and beyond (the favored foci of macro-level theories like social disorganization, subcultural, and anomie theories) toward a more explicit focus on individual-level dynamics that may explain variation in offending behavior. On the heels of these developments came a host of longitudinal datasets (e.g., the National Youth Survey; the National Longitudinal Survey of Youth; the Glueck's data from Boston), which have fueled the rise of individual theory and research concerning continuity and change in offending over the life-span. Taken together, these trends have brought us perspectives like social bond/social control, social learning, and life-course theories—paradigms that remain dominant in the field today.

We may be entering a new phase of criminological thought as a result of, at least in part, the availability of new data that have revived the biosocial perspective— the subject of this extremely ambitious book by Kevin Beaver. As Beaver is quick to note, biological discussions of criminal behavior have largely been relegated to the dustbin of criminological thought. Such thinking was marginalized initially for legitimate reasons because of a lack of scientific rigor and an explicitly racist motive among certain theorists, yet a sustained disdain has remained for a biologically informed version of criminological thought primarily as the result of the intellectual constraints associated with sociological criminology. Just as important, however, is the role that data limitations have traditionally placed on the biosocial paradigm: the absence of data on genetic and biological indicators that can be examined directly.

Enter now Kevin Beaver's book and the research contained within it. Much of the work he presents here is rooted in datasets from the biological and health sciences, and others like the National Longitudinal Study of Adolescent Health (Add Health). These datasets contain a rich amount of information on health and biological indicators that have traditionally been absent from the kinds of surveys that sociological criminologists like to dispense to their college classrooms. Put simply, it was easy for criminologists to dismiss the effects of biological and genetic factors on criminal behavior when they were simply ignoring them in their research designs. Now, with the availability of this new data, scholars can integrate these concepts into existing criminological models, and challenge other models that may explicitly deny biosocial influences.

That is a key contribution of Kevin Beaver's book. Not only does it trace the theoretical history of the biosocial paradigm (demonstrating the harmful consequences of the sociological stranglehold on criminology), but it brings to bear cutting edge social scientific research from a genetic/biological standpoint and clearly shows its relevance for criminology. Indeed, this book challenges certain criminological orthodoxies concerning the relationships between a number of "traditional" risk factors (e.g., peers, parents, communities) and criminal/deviant behavior. In a field where the working assumption is that empirical data should guide our thinking about criminal behavior, a large body of evidence is emerging that clearly shows that an entire class of previously ignored criminogenic risk factors need to be seriously considered.

In the end, the strength of this book is that Beaver isn't attempting to topple traditional criminological thought, but to rather shake it up sufficiently so that it will be forced to recognize the genetic and biological roots to human behavior. That Beaver can communicate this level of complexity without the crutch of using complex language makes this book even more of a rare contribution to the field. We'll all be challenged and we may not all fully agree, but we're all going to have to take notice.

Travis Pratt
Arizona State University, October 2008

Why Biosocial Criminology?

Introduction

During the past two decades or so there has been tremendous scientific interest in studying and understanding the human brain and the human genome. Thousands of studies have been published attempting to uncover how the brain works, the functions of different regions of the brain, and how specific parts of the brain contribute to the development of certain disorders. Similarly, the successful completion of the Human Genome Project (HGP) has provided researchers with a detailed roadmap into the genetic origins of life. The HGP has also spawned a wealth of research attempting to tie particular genes to different types of behaviors, to different diseases, and to almost every other imaginable human characteristic. At no other time in history has so much scientific progress been made in terms of learning about the development of human behaviors. And the overwhelming majority of this work was produced by molecular and behavioral geneticists, neuroscientists, psychologists, and psychiatrists; not by criminologists and certainly not by sociologists.[1]

The scientific revolution that has occurred recently has passed the field of criminology by. Where research has shown that the brain is associated with certain behavioral disorders, criminologists have looked the other way; where research has shown that certain genetic variants are associated with certain types of antisocial behaviors, criminologists have pretended not to hear; and where research has shown that all human characteristics are due to nature *and* nurture, criminologists have argued that only nurture matters. Environmental conditions, according to most mainstream criminologists, are the only factors that could possibly cause a person to engage in crime. Criminologists have arrived at such a conclusion by ignoring mounds of methodologically rigorous interdisciplinary research and by writing their own mythical story on what causes criminal and delinquent behaviors. What's even worse is that these mythical accounts are often pawned off as factual, with students being required to learn, memorize, and regurgitate the materials as if they were axiomatic laws.

The discipline of criminology has come to a crossroad where it must decide to continue down the current path or to make a sharp turn and begin to traverse down a different route. If criminology continues in the current direction, and focuses only on the environmental underpinnings to human behavior, then it is setting itself up to be an inconsequential and disposable discipline. If criminology decides to change directions, and begins to focus on both the environmental and genetic basis to human behavior, then it will align itself with many other more established disciplines, disciplines that have made worthy contributions to the understanding of behavior. This latter direction is the one that is currently being pursued by biosocial criminologists and it is the one that will be described in great detail in the forthcoming chapters. In order to understand why biosocial criminology is such a new perspective, and why so few criminologists have had much exposure to this perspective, we first must explore the dominance of sociological criminology.

The Dominance of Sociological Criminology

Any serious student of criminology needs to be well-versed in all of the different factors that may ultimately lead to crime and delinquency. Unfortunately this simply is not the case within the criminological community. Criminologists know a lot about a little—that is, they are well-schooled on the social origins of crime, but are woefully ignorant about all other potential causes of crime. To understand why, it is first necessary to recognize that most criminologists were trained as sociologists. As students, they learned about the ways in which families, neighborhoods, subcultures, peers, and other social institutions mold and shape all types of human behavior, including criminal and delinquent behaviors. At the same time, they were taught very little biology, and the biology that they were exposed to was taught by sociologists who put their own simplistic, archaic, and outdated spin on the biology-behavior connection. Think about this: most faculty members who teach criminology courses completed more than nine sociology classes during their graduate education, but less than one biology course.[2]

What does this mean? It means that criminologists are well-informed about the social environment and how it may relate to criminal behaviors, but they know virtually nothing about biology—and the biology that they do know is likely incorrect. So it is probably not too much of a surprise that when criminologists are asked to explain and study crime, they fall back on their strong background of sociology and identify social and environmental factors as particularly important in the etiology of offending behaviors.[3] It is also probably not too surprising to learn that they speak very little about how biology could relate to criminal behaviors. And when they do discuss biology, they typically fall back on what they were taught by sociologists—that is, that biology does not matter. This situation is understandable; after all, criminologists are experts in sociology and thus when confronted with questions about the causes of crime, they use their intimate knowledge of social factors to explain criminal behaviors.

It is unfortunate that criminologists do not receive even a minimum amount of formal education in biology. Even worse, however, is that some criminologists are proud of their biological ignorance.[4] In class, they mock biology; in writings, they censor biology; behind closed doors, they snicker about researchers who study biology; and in public, they argue that any scholar who studies biology should be equated with a racist, a sexist, a fascist, or any other -ist that can be conjured up.[5] It is these criminologists who have done a disservice to the criminological academy and who have done more to prevent the accumulation of knowledge than to advance it. Matthew Robinson (2004, pp. ix-x) added to this view when he argued that "the biological sciences have made more progress in advancing our understanding about behavior in the past 10 years than sociology has made in the past 50 years."[6] If Robinson is correct, then it is unfortunate that students are taught very early in their academic careers that studying biology is not valued. But the antagonism with biology does not end there: many students who decide to go against the grain and pursue the biological underpinnings to human behavior are informally purged from criminology and sociology academic programs.

Let us take a step back so we can digest and reiterate what has just been discussed. First, most criminologists have never taken a biology class and thus know virtually nothing about biology. Second, many criminologists not only know very little information about biology, but they also are adamantly opposed to biological explanations of human behavior. Much more will be spoken about this later in the chapter. Third, current criminology students are taught virtually nothing about the role that biology may play in the development of offending behaviors. This lack of biological knowledge is passed from teacher-to-student, such that criminology students graduate without knowing anything about the role that biology plays in crime and delinquency. This cycle continues to repeat itself over time and across generations and today it remains deeply entrenched within most criminology programs. The difficulty with breaking this cycle is that there are relatively few programs that offer a class on biosocial criminology and there are relatively few faculty members who could teach such a class. This book is designed to overcome these obstacles by exposing undergraduate and graduate students, sociologically-trained criminologists, and laypersons alike to biological concepts and by showing how these concepts can be used in biosocial criminological theory and research.

Is Criminology a Science?

Is criminology a science? The answer to this question, especially among criminologists and students of criminology, is an obvious "yes"; however, for other social commentators, the answer to this question is not so obvious and may be teetering more toward "no" than toward "yes".[7] In order to shed some light on the answer to this question, let us begin by defining science and examining how scientific knowledge is typically accrued. In its most general terms, science can be thought of as the state of knowledge accumulation based on the scientific method. To understand this definition, we need to provide an in-depth explanation of what is meant by the scientific method.

The scientific method is a detailed step-by-step process employed for acquiring knowledge about a particular phenomenon (e.g., crime). At its most basic level, the scientific method can be thought of as being comprised of three interlocking steps. The first step entails making a series of educated predictions, also known as hypotheses, about the way two or more entities are related. For example, in criminology, we often make predictions about whether a particular social factor, such as delinquent peers, is associated with some type of delinquent outcome, such as smoking marijuana. There are three different hypotheses that could be advanced: 1) adolescents who are exposed to delinquent peers are more likely to smoke marijuana than are adolescents who are not exposed to delinquent peers; 2) adolescents who are exposed to delinquent peers are less likely to smoke marijuana than are adolescents who are not exposed to delinquent peers, and; 3) adolescents who are exposed to delinquent peers are just as likely to smoke marijuana as are adolescents who are not exposed to delinquent peers. The first two hypotheses make directional claims (more or less likely to use marijuana), while the third hypothesis claims that there is no relationship between delinquent peer exposure and marijuana use. This latter hypothesis is referred to as a null hypothesis, because the association between delinquent peers and marijuana use is assumed to be nonexistent.

All three of these hypotheses could, in theory, be supported, although most people would probably lean towards assuming that the first hypothesis is the most likely. The scientific method, however, requires that we do not rely on our hunches, instincts, or intuitions but rather that we test these competing hypotheses. Testing hypotheses is the second step in the scientific method and there are multiple ways to test hypotheses. We could interview people, we could observe people, or we could read case studies; but the most widespread way of testing hypotheses is by collecting and analyzing data using quantitative statistical techniques.[8] (The precise statistical methodologies used by biosocial researchers will be discussed in detail in Chapter 7.) With this approach, a sample of people is asked questions that are of interest to the researcher. Using the current example, adolescents would be asked about their use of marijuana and their exposure to delinquent friends. This information would then be entered into a statistical software program where researchers could analyze the data. Based on the analyses, the researcher would be able to conclude which of the three hypotheses is supported. The use of data analysis techniques to test competing hypotheses provides a more objective way of assessing the veracity of each hypothesis than simply relying on hunches or intuitions.

The third step in the scientific method is to decide, based on the results of the statistical test, which of the hypotheses is supported. Then the supported hypothesis can be evaluated in light of the existing pool of studies that has also examined this particular topic. In the current example, perhaps the test revealed support in favor of hypothesis #1. If so, then this finding would be added to a large body of research showing that exposure to delinquent peers is a potent risk factor for using illegal drugs. It is only by using the scientific method that knowledge about a particular relationship (in this case, the relationship between delinquent peers and marijuana use) can begin to accumulate.

The results of any individual study cannot tell us for certain the "truth" about reality. For instance, in the previous example we may have found support in favor of hypothesis #1, but another study may have revealed support in favor of hypothesis #3. That is why scientific knowledge accumulates incrementally, and that is also why replication studies are needed to test the same hypotheses.

But, when most of the evidence begins to accumulate in favor of one hypothesis or another, then researchers begin to feel more comfortable with assuming that that hypothesis is reflective of reality. The scientific method also allows researchers to rule out (or falsify) factors that are unrelated to crime and explanations that are not tenable. For example, there is not any empirical research supporting Cesare Lombroso's view that the size and shape of a person's head are independent causes of criminal involvement. As a result, no longer do criminologists believe that the origins of crime are found in the nooks and crannies of the skull.

The scientific method thus promotes the accumulation of knowledge by 1) stating hypothesis; 2) objectively testing those hypotheses, and 3) deciding which hypothesis is supported based on the results of step #2. The trick for the advancement of knowledge for a particular phenomenon is to examine any and all hypotheses. If a researcher comes along and proposes that crime is the result of wearing blue jeans, most of us would immediately laugh and tell the researcher to quit wasting their time exploring this idea. It seems obvious that the type of pants a person wears has no bearing on their odds of engaging in crime. However, let us pretend that this researcher is adamant that wearing blue jeans is a cause of crime. How would we settle the dispute between those who agree with the researcher versus those who disagree with the researcher? Relying on our own intuitions would not be scientific; for reasons that are entirely obvious we *could* be incorrect. The most objective way to test the possible connection between wearing blue jeans and criminal involvement is to use the scientific method by collecting and analyzing data. Perhaps we could interview people and ask them if they have ever committed a crime and, if they had, what they were wearing. In that way, we would be able to examine the relationship between wearing blue jeans and engaging in crime. More than likely we would find no relationship between blue jeans and crime, but using the scientific method would be the appropriate, objective way of assessing the hypothesis. We use the scientific method because sometimes our intuitions are wrong, and what once seemed intuitively obvious may turn out to be incorrect. It was not too long ago when it seemed intuitively obvious that the world was flat and that the earth was the center of the universe.

The scientific method is the gold standard for examining different hypotheses about the causes of crime and delinquency. The scientific method is also employed to help settle disputes over the causes of crime. For example, let us pretend that three different criminologists have three different views on what causes crime: one argues that neighborhoods are the strongest cause of crime, one argues that peers are the strongest cause of crime, and one argues that families are the strongest cause of crime. Which view is correct? Who should be believed? The most common way of answering these questions is to use the scientific method. For the most part, this is how criminologists proceed when debating ideas, when testing theories, and when examining the causes and correlates of crime.

The rules of the game, however, seem to change anytime the word "biology" is spoken within the criminological community; no longer is the scientific method the tool of choice for evaluating ideas, but rhetoric, propaganda, and scare-tactics are often used instead. To see how criminologists use these different strategies to deal with biological explanations to crime, let us revisit the scientific method. Recall that the first step in the scientific method is stating hypotheses. It is here, at the first step, where criminologists often begin to invoke different tactics to stave off biological explanations to crime. Instead of testing all hypotheses, many criminologists argue that examining hypotheses that link biology to crime is a dangerous enterprise and that these types of hypotheses should never be explored. Moreover, students pursuing their degrees are sometimes told by their professors that they cannot write papers that deal with the biology-behavior hypothesis. This is particularly disheartening given that college is the time and the place when criminology students should be encouraged to explore all issues related to crime, and when no hypotheses should be off-limits. Unfortunately scholarly ideas are censored in many academic criminological programs across the nation.

The biology-behavior connection is even viewed with trepidation at some scholarly journals.[9] Typically, at least within criminology journals, all manuscript submissions are sent out to be evaluated by reviewers. These reviewers then provide comments and feedback as to whether the paper should be published in the journal. Editors play a central role in the journal submission process because they choose the reviewers and they ultimately make the decision of whether the study should be published. Some editors, however, hold anti-biology views and thus are less likely to accept an article for publication when biology is shown to matter in the genesis of antisocial behaviors. The first step in the scientific method is thus censored by some faculty members and by some journal editors when the hypotheses deal directly with biology.

The second step in the scientific method is testing the hypotheses, which usually entails some type of quantitative methodological approach. The major problem with testing hypotheses linking biology and crime is that there is not much data available that can be used to test these types of hypotheses. Typically criminological and social science datasets only contain information about social environments, not about biological factors. What this means is that criminologists who are interested in the biological basis to crime are often unable to test their ideas because of a lack of data. And if they cannot test their hypotheses, then they cannot engage in the scientific method, and if they cannot engage in the scientific method, then their ideas may be attacked vehemently by sociological criminologists.

Even those criminologists who do have access to biologically sensitive data, and who do test their hypotheses, are not necessarily in the clear. Remember that in order for a study to be published, it must be sent out to reviewers who ultimately judge the scientific merits of the study. Most criminology reviewers, however, have very little knowledge of biology and yet are still asked to evaluate studies that link biology to crime. That is akin to asking a veterinarian to perform heart surgery on a human; they simply are not qualified, just as most criminology reviewers are not qualified to review biosocial research. What is even worse is that some reviewers despise biology and thus evaluate the paper based on their own ideological views rather than on the scientific merit of the paper. The end result is that biologically based studies are typically evaluated by reviewers who 1) know nothing about biology and/or 2) are strong opponents to biological research. All of these factors line up to make it very difficult for criminologists to publish studies that examine the association between biological factors and criminal involvement.

Keep in mind that the third step in the scientific method is deciding which hypothesis is supported. It is also at this step that researchers can look to see how the findings from one study fit with the findings generated from previous research. Sociological criminologists often dismiss any study showing an association between biology and crime as unimportant, unethical, or wrong. Moreover, when looking to the extant research, many criminologists are guilty of selectively overlooking research supporting the biology-behavior connection and focusing only on sociologically informed research. As a result, many criminologists have a warped view of the relative effects of environmental factors and biological factors in the development of offending behaviors.

With this background, let us return to the original question of whether criminology is a science. On the one hand, yes, criminology is definitely a science when it comes to examining the link between different environmental conditions and criminal involvement. On the other hand, criminology is probably not a science when it comes to examining non-environmental factors (e.g., biological factors) and how they relate to criminal involvement. Criminology needs to rectify this problem, but unfortunately many criminologists do not view biology as important to the study of crime and oppose any and all biological explanations to crime. Below we will discuss why criminology, as a discipline, cannot survive and be taken seriously without biology.

Why Criminology Needs Biology

A growing number of criminologists concede that criminal behaviors are partially the results of biological factors, but maintain that they will focus only on the environment and leave the study of biology to researchers from other fields. While this seems like a plausible balance to strike, there are at least four different reasons why such logic is flawed, each of which will be discussed in detail below.

Standard social science methodologies (SSSMs). Virtually all criminological research employs standard social science methodologies (SSSMs) to test hypotheses linking social factors to criminal behaviors. This is especially true for family-based studies that are interested in determining whether certain family socialization processes (e.g., abuse and neglect) are associated with delinquent involvement.[10] In SSSMs, one person (typically an adolescent in criminological research) from each household is included in the sample (i.e., the sample that is ultimately analyzed to evaluate the hypotheses). Questions may then be asked about the youth's grades, their peer relationships, their family life, their personality traits, and their involvement in delinquent behaviors. The responses to the questions could then be analyzed to test different hypotheses about the correlates to delinquency.

Let us use an example to explore SSSMs in greater detail. Suppose that we were interested in determining whether there is a relationship between being physically abused and engaging in serious violence (e.g., assaults). Using SSSMs, we would ask questions to the respondent about whether they were physically abused by their parents and how frequently they had been in a physical fight during the past year. Once we had included an adequate number of people in our sample, let's say one hundred, we could then analyze the data to see if there is a relationship between abuse and fighting. Essentially we would be testing the model depicted in Figure 1.1. If abused persons were more likely to engage in physical fighting than non-abused persons, then we would probably conclude that being abused is a risk factor for physical fighting. The logic seems impeccable and this is the exact same process that has been used for almost every single study ever published in a criminology journal.

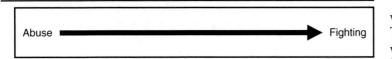

Figure 1.1
Hypothetical relationship between physical abuse and serious fighting using an SSSM.

There is a major problem with this approach, however. To understand that problem, we need to introduce some basic statistical concepts and terminology. When criminologists assess the relationship between two variables (a variable is any entity that can vary or that can be different from person-to-person) they often use a statistic called the correlation coefficient, which is symbolized with an "r". The correlation coefficient is a way of measuring the direction and magnitude of the relationship between two variables. The correlation coefficient can take on any value between -1 and $+1$. Values that are close to -1 depict a strong negative relationship between the two variables, while values that are negative and not as close to -1 indicate weaker negative relationships. Negative relationships mean that when values on one variable increase, values on the other variable decrease. The relationship between verbal IQ and the number of serious violent offenses committed is a good example of a negative relationship; when verbal IQ increases, the number of serious violent offenses committed decreases. Correlation coefficients that are positive are interpreted very similarly to negative correlation coefficients; values close to $+1$ indicate a strong positive relationship, while values farther away from $+1$ represent weaker positive relationships. Positive relationships mean that as values on one variable increase so too do the values on the other variable. The relationship between the number of alcoholic beverages consumed and the number of times that a person falls down exemplifies a positive relationship. Correlation coefficients that are close to 0 mean that there is not a relationship between the two variables.

Correlation coefficients are used frequently in social science research to determine whether two variables are related. Just because two variables are related does not necessarily mean that values on one variable are causing values on the other variable. (This is akin to the statement that correlation does not equal causation.) All that a correlation coefficient can tell us is whether there is a relationship, the direction of the relationship (positive or negative), and the strength of that relationship. It is always possible that another variable, one that we did not take into account, is driving the relationship between the two variables. The classic example is the relationship between ice cream sales and the violent crime rate, which is shown in Figure 1.2. As ice cream sales increase, the violent crime rate increases as well. There is a correlation between these two variables, but does that mean that ice cream sales cause crime to increase? Absolutely not; instead there is another factor that is causing ice cream sales to increase and this same factor is also causing crime rates to increase. That factor is temperature, where people eat more ice cream during the summer months and their daily activities place them in greater proximity to criminals. Figure 1.3 shows the interrelationships among these three variables.

In statistical jargon, ice cream sales would correspond to the independent variable, the violent crime rate would correspond to the dependent variable, and temperature would correspond to the

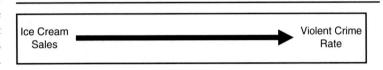

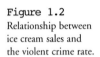

Figure 1.2
Relationship between ice cream sales and the violent crime rate.

confounding variable (it confounds the relationship between ice cream sales and crime rates). Additionally, when a relationship between two variables is observed, but then disappears when a third confounding variable is taken into account, the relationship is said to be spurious. In the current example, the association between ice cream sales and the violent crime rate is spurious because when temperature is taken into account the relationship between the independent and dependent variables vanishes.

It is important to point out that criminological research can never rule out the possibility that the relationship between two variables is spurious. But it does help to know that not all variables represent potential confounders that could render the relationship spurious. The only time when a variable could be a confounder is when it is related to both the independent variable and the dependent variable. If a variable is only related to the independent variable or only to the dependent variable, then the effects of this variable do not need to be taken into account. For example, let us pretend that poverty rates are associated with violent crime rates, but that they are unrelated to ice cream sales. As Figure 1.4 shows, including the poverty rate does not make the relationship between ice cream sales and crime rates evaporate and thus the poverty rate would not be considered a confounding variable in this association. Remember that the only time that an omitted variable can potentially be a confounding variable is when it is related to both the independent

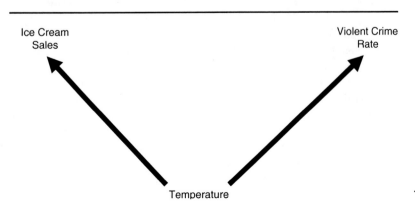

Figure 1.3
A spurious relationship between ice cream sales and the violent crime rate after taking into account temperature.

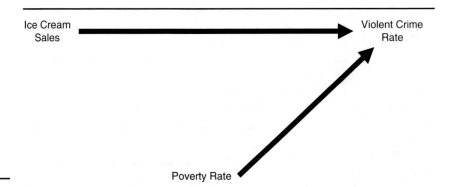

Figure 1.4
Hypothetical
relationship between
ice cream sales and
the violent crime
rate after taking
into account the
poverty rate.

and dependent variables. Importantly, when the omitted variable is related to both the independent and dependent variables, then the effects of this variable must be taken into account or the relationship could perhaps be spurious.

We can now use the information presented above to discuss one of the major methodological shortcomings with SSSMs. If we return to the example depicted in Figure 1.1 we see that there is a relationship between abuse and fighting, where persons who were abused were more likely to engage in physical fighting. Recall that this model was tested with an SSSM, where only one child per household is included in the sample. Be sure to bear in mind that just because two variables are correlated does not mean that one is causing the other; it is always possible that a third confounding variable is causing both. In this example, a potentially confounding variable is genetic factors.

Think about this: parents who are physically abusive are predisposed to act violently. If these predispositions are just moderately influenced by genetic factors, and if these genetic factors are passed from parent-to-child, then the child would also be predisposed to act violently. As a direct result, it could be the case that genetic factors, not socialization factors, account for the correlation between abuse and fighting. This association, in other words, is spurious because the genetic factors that predispose parents to act aggressively (i.e., to be abusive) are passed to the child, which predisposes the child to act aggressively (i.e., to engage in fights frequently). Figure 1.5 portrays this possibility. It is probably easier to think about spurious relationships with the previous example using ice cream sales, the violent crime rate, and temperature. If we superimpose this previous example on our new example, then abuse would correspond to ice cream sales, fighting would correspond to the violent crime rate, and temperature would correspond with genetic factors. In either case, after including the confounding variable, genetic factors (temperature), the relationship between abuse (ice cream sales) and fighting (the violent crime rate) disappears. What this means is that the independent variable (abuse) does not have a causal effect on the dependent variable (fighting).

Let us use another example to make this point clear. Suppose that an adolescent had a father, a grandfather, and a great-grandfather who all died from heart attacks when they were in their late thirties. Heart attacks that occur this early in life are largely due to genetic factors. As a result, the adolescent would be at great risk for

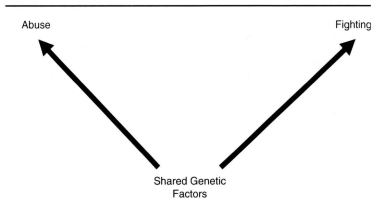

Abuse   Fighting

Shared Genetic
Factors

Figure 1.5
A hypothetical
example of spurious
relationship between
physical abuse and
serious fighting after
taking into account
genetic factors.

having a heart attack as well. It would be silly to argue that socialization processes accounted for the association between the father having a heart attack and their child also being at risk for a heart attack. The same is true for aggression. Abusive parents are likely to have children who are also aggressive not necessarily because of socialization processes but because of genetic factors that are transmitted from parent-to-offspring. Of course, it could be the case that both socialization processes and genetic factors account for the relationship between abuse and fighting, but criminological research rarely examines the genetic perspective.

This leads us directly to the major flaw with SSSMs: the inability to control for genetic factors. Any researcher who uses an SSSM is unable to take into account the effects that genetic factors have on the relationship between the independent and dependent variables.[11] (The reason for why this is the case will be explored fully in Chapter 2. Briefly, when only one child per household is included in the sample then it is impossible to take into account genetic effects.) This is akin to examining the relationship between ice cream sales and the violent crime rate without being able to take into account the effects of temperature. This is a very serious drawback to SSSMs because any research (using SSSMs) that has been published examining the correlation between environmental conditions (primarily family-level variables) and child outcomes *could* be spurious. Given that over 99 percent of all criminological research uses SSSMs, the entire body of family socialization research *could* be incorrect; the relationships could be spurious relationships accounted for by the confounding effects of genetic factors. This bears repeating: any study that uses an SSSM to investigate whether socialization variables (e.g., parental socialization) have an effect on a person's behaviors or personality traits could be spurious because unmeasured genetic factors could be confounding the relationship. *Moreover, all research that uses SSSMs assumes that the effect of genetic factors on the outcome measure (e.g., delinquency, or antisocial personality traits) is zero.* If this assumption is incorrect, then the research findings flowing from SSSMs may be wrong because of spuriousness. And, as will be discussed in the next chapter, the empirical evidence indicates beyond a shadow of a doubt that all behaviors are at least partially the result of genetic factors, and some have strong genetic origins. The only way to circumvent this problem of genes-as-confounders is to employ research designs that can take into account genetic factors. Still, SSSMs continue to be the dominant research design within criminology.

Skeptics of biosocial research may be quick to point out that while the logic of this argument is correct there simply is not any empirical evidence to support this view. They are correct in that there is not much evidence to support this argument, but that gap in the literature is due to the fact that very little criminological research has ever tested the possibility that genetic effects are confounding variables. Why? Because most criminologists deny that genetic factors matter to the study of crime and because most criminologists only use SSSMs. The few studies that have examined this possibility (using the scientific method) have revealed that genes are indeed confounders. Let us explore one of these studies in detail.

One of the most influential criminological theories is Michael Gottfredson and Travis Hirschi's general theory of crime.[12] These theorists argue that low levels of self-control are the cause of crime, delinquency, and analogous behaviors. Substantial empirical evidence has accrued in favor of this hypothesis.[13] As a result, there has been great interest in identifying the factors that cause variation in levels of self-control. According to Gottfredson and Hirschi, parental socialization techniques, including parental monitoring, parental recognition of their child's transgressions, and parental discipline, cause the emergence of self-control. Research examining Gottfredson and Hirschi's parental socialization thesis has found some support for it.[14] The problem, however, is that all of these studies employed SSSMs, which means that the correlation between parental socialization and child levels of self-control could be spurious owing to the effects of unmeasured genetic factors.

A study conducted by John Wright and Kevin Beaver, however, addressed the confounding effects of genes when examining the correlation between parental socialization techniques and levels of self-control.[15] They tested for an association between parental socialization and low self-control in two ways. First, they employed an SSSM and found that measures of parental socialization were associated with levels of self-control, a finding that supported Gottfredson and Hirschi's thesis. Second, they estimated the association between parental socialization and levels of self-control after taking into account genetic factors. The results of these models indicated that there was not a correlation between parental socialization and self-control, meaning that genetic factors rendered the relationship spurious.

The research by Wright and Beaver provided the first criminological evidence showing that genetic factors may account for relationships between parental socialization and antisocial outcomes. Research from other fields, however, also tends to reinforce the findings reported by Wright and Beaver—that is, genetic factors account for some, if not all, of the association between parenting factors and child outcomes.[16] Even with this information in hand, criminologists continue to conduct research using SSSMs and they continue to pretend that genetic factors are unrelated to the etiology of criminal behaviors. Perhaps the most serious problem, however, is that some criminologists continue to think that it is entirely acceptable to focus only on environmental factors and to leave the study of genetic factors to other fields. As the above discussion made clear, this line of reasoning leaves researchers who use SSSMs open to the serious criticism that any and all relationships that they discover are spurious. Simply controlling for genetic factors would ward off such attacks and make criminological research much more informative, much more believable, and much more scientific.

The nature of nurture. The second key reason why criminologists need to study both environmental and biological influences is because of what is called the "nature of nurture."[17] To understand what is meant by the nature of nurture it is first necessary to understand that there is an underlying assumption among most criminologists that variables can be neatly divided into those that are social and those that are biological. For example, some of the main social variables studied by criminologists include delinquent peers, parental management techniques, and neighborhood-level influences. Little, if any, thought is given to the possibility that social environments are influenced by genetic factors; this even seems a little absurd to suggest. Yet it is important to realize that most environments are partially the result of genetic factors. How this could be the case will be discussed in Chapter 3, but a quick example will help to show that this is possible.

Take, for example, delinquent peers, a staple variable among sociological criminologists. Most criminologists would feel comfortable in assuming that exposure to antisocial friends has to do with social processes, not biological ones.[18] Likewise, many criminologists, especially social learning theorists, would also feel comfortable in assuming that adolescents who associate with delinquent peers will be socialized to become delinquent.[19] After all, this seems like a reasonable perspective to take. The problem, however, is that research has found that genetic factors are strongly implicated in the formation of delinquent peer groups.[20] Friendship networks are formed on the basis of shared interests, shared talents, shared backgrounds, shared behaviors, and shared personality traits. There are, in other words, high levels of similarity among friends. Adolescents who enjoy sports tend to hang out with other athletes; adults who enjoy drinking alcohol tend to associate with others who also drink; parents who are wealthy tend to affiliate with other wealthy parents; and so it goes. All of the dimensions that are similar between friends are at least partially due to genetic factors. The fact that people befriend others on these genetically influenced dimensions necessarily translates into meaning that the formation of peer groups also has genetic origins. Genetic influences have also been found on measures of the family environment, parenting, mate choice, and a host of other variables that are typically assumed to capture purely social effects.[21]

When criminologists argue that they are focusing only on how social factors relate to criminal outcomes, they are making the incorrect assumption that the variables included in their analyses are purely social. Nothing could be further from the truth; almost all variables are biosocial and due to the effects of the environment *and* biology; it is not one or the other, it is both. This is a far cry from the nature versus nurture debate, where researchers argued whether nature (biology) or nurture (the environment) was the dominant force in shaping human development. Within criminology, however, the nature versus nurture debate is alive and well. In virtually every other discipline, save sociology, the nature/nurture distinction is a dead issue, and has been for some time. These disciplines have been informed by mounds of research showing that virtually all human characteristics are due to nature and nurture acting in complex ways to structure human development.

When criminologists argue that they will focus only on environmental correlates to crime, they are assuming that environmental measures are not contaminated with biological influences. This assumption is not tenable and thus whether they know it or not most criminologists are engaging in biosocial research.

Keeping pace with the hard sciences. The third reason that criminology needs to examine the effects of environmental and biological variables is so that it can keep pace with the hard sciences, such as molecular genetics and neuroscience. The findings from hard science research are highly influential, much more so than the findings of criminological research. Take, for example, the consumption of research by non-academics. Highly rated television shows, such as *60 Minutes*, and nationally accredited magazines, such as *Time*, often feature stories about cutting-edge research, research that is almost exclusively from the hard sciences. Other media outlets, such as the nation's leading news websites, have links that cover the latest breaking scientific research. Once again, virtually all of this research is derived from hard science studies.[22]

On the one hand, this state-of-affairs is understandable; much of the hard science research deals with issues that are of utmost concern, such as the latest cancer treatments. But, on the other hand, one of the most fundamental issues affecting American citizens is crime.[23] Public opinion surveys show that a sizeable portion of the public views crime as a major social issue, with more than 40 percent of Americans indicating that they are fearful to walk alone in their neighborhood at night.[24] Why then is criminological research so infrequently covered by the media? Numerous factors feed into this answer; it is probably due in part to the fact that criminological research is not cutting-edge, it does not adequately capture reality, and it ignores biological influences.

Criminologists may quibble with the insinuation that studying biology would ultimately lead to more media coverage and more influence with the public. Obviously studying biology is not a panacea, but it is important to note that when criminological research is covered by the media it often deals with the association between biology and crime. For example, in 2002, a team of researchers led by Avshalom Caspi reported a relationship between a variant of a specific gene and involvement in antisocial behaviors.[25] The results of this study were covered extensively by major media outlets and, as a result, much of the public (i.e., non-academics) were informed of this important finding.

As discussed above, if scientific disciplines are judged in part by how their research influences persons outside of the academic community, then the hard sciences leave criminology in their dust. But what about among academics–is criminological research taken seriously by researchers outside of the field of criminology? This is a difficult question to answer, but one way to examine this question objectively is by looking at how many times articles are cited. In general, the most influential studies are cited frequently, while those that are not as influential are cited rarely, if ever. Most scholarly journals have an impact factor score, which essentially relays how many times, on average, each study in that journal is cited. Journals with higher impact factors generally are equated with being more prestigious and influential. Among criminology journals, almost all have impact factors less than two, meaning that on average most studies published in these journals are cited less than two times. Only one criminology journal—*Criminology*—has an impact factor that is greater than two.[26]

How do the impact factors for criminology journals compare to those of other disciplines? The short answer is that there is no comparison: the journals from almost every other discipline have much higher impact factors. For example, the two leading genetics journals—*Nature Genetics* and *Nature Reviews Genetics*—have impact factors greater than 22, while the two leading psychology journals—*Psychological Review* and *Annual Review of Psychology*—have impact factors greater than 11. When evaluating the scholarly influence of different disciplines via impact factors, criminology ranks near the bottom.

Perhaps even more surprising than the low impact factors for criminological journals is that criminologists are punished when they do publish in non-criminological journals, even though these scholarly outlets may be much more influential. All of this seems a bit crazy, but listen to this: from time to time, reports are published that rank the top criminologists and top criminology programs in the world.[27] The ranking systems vary from study to study, but typically criminologists are ranked by how many articles they have published or how many times their research has been cited. The main problem is that usually only articles that are published in criminology journals count in the ranking.[28] This is true even if the study dealt with criminology but was published, say, in a non-criminology journal. Hypothetically speaking, a criminologist could publish a criminology study in one of top journals in the world—like *Science* [29]—and yet that article would never count in their favor. Although most criminologists only publish their work in criminology journals, the fact that non-criminology journal articles are excluded from most ranking systems speaks to the disciplinary bias of criminologists. Perhaps if criminology returned to its interdisciplinary roots and valued research from other fields, it would be able to keep pace with the hard science research.

Informing public policy. The fourth reason that criminologists need to focus on environmental and biological factors is so that they can be more influential in the shaping of public policy. On first glance, it might appear somewhat odd and counterintuitive to think that just by exploring the biological basis to behavior that criminology will have more of an impact on public policy. After all, much of the controversy swirling around the study of biology by criminologists is the potential for dangerous and oppressive policies to be signed into law. This concern, while understandable on the surface, is completely unfounded for at least three reasons. First, criminologists have very little clout when it comes to influencing public policy, even when it comes to policies that are directly relevant to crime. To think that this will change if criminologists explore the biology-behavior connection is misguided.

Second, criminologists who oppose biological research draw attention to the atrocities of the past century when eugenics and forced sterilization laws were used to restrict reproduction among certain groups, such as minorities. The underlying assumption here is that biological researchers were the only people behind the enactment of such laws. This simply is not true and instead it is interesting to learn that it was liberal and radical sociologists, not just conservative biologists or geneticists, who whole-heartedly supported the eugenics movement.[30] Sociologists viewed eugenics as progressive, as a way of contributing to the advancement of society, and as way of stamping out the social problems that plagued society. It is even possible, as Matt Ridley points out, that Hitler's thinking that ultimately culminated in the atrocities carried out by the Nazi regime was shaped by the writings of Karl Marx, not by Charles Darwin.[31]

Of course sociologists no longer support eugenics, but neither do geneticists, biologists, or biosocial criminologists. So why do criminologists continue to argue against biological research on the grounds that it could lead to a new eugenics movement? And why do they not argue that liberal thinking could be used to unintentionally support oppressive policies? The answers to these questions probably center on the fact that most criminologists were taught (by sociologists) that geneticists were the only proponents to eugenics. There is nothing to gain from pointing fingers, but what is important to realize is that both liberal thinking as well as genetic research was used to enact eugenics laws and movements. To saddle biological research with the blame of eugenics is to turn a blind eye to other culprits as well. The important point is that any idea or piece of research can be used for evil purposes if it is twisted and shaped to do so. Sociological research is no exception.

Third, biosocial research is often viewed as only being capable of contributing to evil, dangerous, and oppressive policies. Is it not possible that biosocial research could conceivably lead to progressive policies? Most criminologists would answer this question with a resounding, "No!" Let us explore this issue in a little greater detail to show why criminologists are way off the mark.

Within criminology there is a liberal-based view towards punishment, where the overwhelming majority of all criminologists favor the limited use of punitive sanctions. Nowhere is this type of liberal thinking more evident than on debates about the death penalty. Taken as a whole, most criminologists hold anti-death penalty views. In fact, the American Society of Criminology (ASC)—the flagship association for criminologists worldwide—adopted the following official policy position on the death penalty:

> Be it resolved that because social science research has demonstrated the death penalty to be racist in application and social science research has found no consistent evidence of crime deterrence through execution, The American Society of Criminology publicly condemns this form of punishment, and urges its members to use their professional skills in legislatures and courts to seek a speedy abolition of this form of punishment.[32]

This official policy position was written in 1989 and yet criminologists have been unable to use their research to persuade the Court that the death penalty should be abolished for adults. Recently, however, the death penalty has been ruled unconstitutional for juveniles.

The ultimate decision to abolish the death penalty for minors was heavily driven by empirical research. It would seem reasonable to assume that much of this research was drawn from the criminological literature, especially in light of ASC's stand on the death penalty; however, that would be an erroneous conclusion. Instead the overwhelming amount of research that ultimately led to the abolishment of the death penalty for minors came from neuroscience research showing that there are structural and functional differences between the brains of adolescents and the brains of adults. The decision to eliminate the death penalty for adolescents was thus grounded in biological research, not in sociological criminology research. So much for assuming that biological research can only lead to oppressive policies.

The Court's decision to abolish the juvenile death penalty also provides further evidence of the marginalization of criminological research when it comes to shaping public policy. A team of eight professional societies and associations submitted an *Amici Curiae* in support of abolishing the death penalty for minors. Out of the eight associations that submitted this brief, guess how many were criminological associations? None, zero, zilch. The associations who filed the *Amici Curiae* were comprised of psychiatrists, medical doctors, and social workers. This is a sad state of affairs, especially given ASC's official policy position on the death penalty. Taken together, the assumption that sociological research leads to progressive public policies, while biological research results in oppressive and dangerous public policies, is simply wrong. In fact, in one of the most important decisions affecting the criminal justice system—that is, the abolishment of the juvenile death penalty—it was the research from the biological sciences that swayed the Court's opinion. Sociological criminologists watched from the sidelines.

Common Misconceptions about Biological Explanations to Criminal Behavior

There is some reason to believe that biological explanations to criminal behavior are becoming more and more accepted among the youngest generation of criminologists. Even so, many concerns over the biology-behavior nexus remain evident even among the newest cohorts of criminologists. These concerns are mostly unfounded and stem in part from the fact that there are numerous misconceptions (most of which were passed on by their sociologically trained professors) about how, and in what ways, biological factors ultimately lead to criminal involvement.[33] Below the most common misconceptions about biological explanations to criminal behaviors are discussed.

1. Criminal behavior is defined by laws that are socially constructed and that vary from time to time and from country to country. How could biology matter to the explanation of crime if laws are ever-changing?

The problem with this concern is the confusion between criminal behavior and criminality. Criminal behaviors are defined by socially enacted contracts prescribing appropriate and inappropriate behaviors. Criminality, in contrast, refers to the underlying traits that are ultimately responsible for bringing about criminal conduct. Previously we discussed Gottfredson and Hirschi's theory which maintains that low levels of self-control are the cause of crime. In this case, low self-control is a personality trait and thus biosocial criminologists are more concerned with identifying the biosocial influences on self-control than they are with identifying the biosocial influences on criminal behavior per se. Biological factors do not directly cause behaviors, but they can make some behaviors more or less likely due to their influence on personality traits. Why?—because personality traits are shaped by a range of biosocial factors and it is these personality traits (in conjunction with other factors) that ultimately lead a person to commit a crime.

It is true that researchers sometimes examine biological influences on criminal and delinquent behaviors. We may hear, for instance, that 50 percent of criminal behavior was found to be due to genetic factors. Such a statement does not really mean that genes are directly responsible for creating the behavior. Rather, this methodological approach is a way of simultaneously capturing all of the genetically influenced traits (i.e., criminality) that cause criminal behavior. When biosocial researchers talk about biological influences on crime, they are really talking about how biology shapes criminality. It is criminality, in turn, that is responsible for criminal behaviors; thus biology works indirectly, not directly, on behaviors.

2. Crime rates vary across time and space, and criminal involvement varies significantly over different sections of the life course; but biology remains unchanging. Once again, how could biology matter?

The assumption in this statement is that biological effects are constant across time, space, and human development. There is not a shred of evidence to support this view and instead research has revealed that biology has varying effects on behaviors depending on environmental conditions and depending on the stage of the life course. Genetic effects, for instance, tend to have their strongest effects on antisocial behaviors when paired with a criminogenic environment.[34] Similarly, environmental effects tend to be strongest during childhood, while genetic effects become stronger during adolescence and even more powerful during adulthood.[35] The reasons underlying why genetic effects vary, and how genetic influences are affected by the environment, will be examined more closely in Chapter 3.

3. If genes are found to be related to crime, wouldn't that remove the burden of responsibility from the individual and place it in their genes?

Concerns about individual culpability always seem to creep into conversations about biosocial criminology. For some reason, the tacit understanding is that if biology is related to crime, then criminals are not responsible for their behaviors. Two points should be made. First, biosocial criminologists attempt to explain, study, and understand behavior; they are not in the business of removing blame or justifying behaviors. Just because a particular biological factor is found to relate to crime does not mean that crime was the inevitable outcome; it simply means that this particular biological factor was found to be associated with subsequent criminal behavior. Second, this attack could easily be levied against sociological criminologists who attempt to explain crime through environmental factors. Here we could argue that it is not the criminal's fault that they murdered five people, it was their parents fault for not showing them enough affection; it was not the criminal's fault for sexually assaulting a teenage girl, it was because they were molested as a child; it was not the criminal's fault for robbing the bank, it was because they grew up in poverty; it was not the terrorist's fault for bombing an embassy, it was their love for a particular God. Every single theory of human behavior, not just ones that focus on biology, can be used as a way of trying to deflect personal responsibility to other factors. So if we are going to condemn biosocial theories on the grounds that they exculpate personal responsibility, then we should condemn sociological theories as well.

4. Biosocial explanations are deterministic and evil, while environmental explanations are humane.

Biosocial criminologists are often viewed as mad scientists conspiring to bring about a society that is reminiscent of Aldous Huxley's *Brave New World*.[36] If biology matters, according to biosocial opponents, then we could examine each person's biology at birth; if they are destined to become a criminal, then we could warehouse them in a prison, sterilize them, and crime should cease to exist. This line of reasoning is absurd and is based in part on the erroneous thinking that biology determines with 100 percent accuracy who will and who will not become a criminal. All criminologists who examine the biological underpinnings to human behavior take a biosocial approach where environmental conditions and biological factors are examined in unison. Moreover, biological risk factors work in a probabilistic not deterministic fashion, where the presence of a biological risk factor increases the risk of criminal behaviors, but does not make such an outcome inevitable.

To argue that biology is unimportant to human behavior, and that only the environment matters, as most criminologists believe, is far more dangerous than recognizing that biology and the environment both matter. Take, for example, the now-famous quote spoken by John Watson, the founder of behaviorism:

> Give me a dozen healthy infants, well-formed, and my own specified world to bring them up in and I'll guarantee to take any one at random and train him to become any type of specialist I might select—doctor, lawyer, artist, merchant-chief and, yes, even beggar-man and thief, regardless of his talents, penchants, tendencies, abilities, vocations, and race of his ancestors.[37]

Watson clearly believed that human behaviors were solely determined by the environment, a view that still dominates criminology. But think about what this really means: any evil-minded person could sculpt their children (or other children) into automatons that would murder, rape, and rob. But biosocial research shows us that children do not simply follow in their parents' footsteps and not all children can be socialized by their parents to behave in one way or another. It is the interactions that occur between biology and the environment that produce behaviors, and accusations that biology is deterministic are completely misguided.

It is also simply not true that environmental explanations are more humane than biosocial explanations. Autism research will make this point clear. In the 1950s, most autism researchers believed that mothers who were cold, withdrawn, and unattached to their children caused autism. Known as "refrigerator mothers", these mothers were saddled with the guilt of thinking that it was their actions that resulted in their child becoming autistic. Today, such a view is not taken seriously and instead it is becoming increasingly clear that autism is largely a biological disorder, and is not caused in any way, shape, or form by parents. It is likely that a similar situation is at work today, where parents are often blamed for their child's delinquent actions when, in fact, a large component to delinquency is biological in origin.

More evidence showing that environmental research is not necessarily more humane than biosocial research comes from the public's view towards homosexuals. The renowned legal scholar Richard Posner argues that the public has become more tolerant and more accepting of homosexuals because there is now good evidence to suspect that sexual orientation is guided by biology, and is not necessarily a personal choice.[38] Environmental explanations to sexuality appear to have opened the door for discrimination against homosexuals, while biological research on sexuality has, in part, promoted the equal and fair treatment of this historically oppressed group.

Sociological criminologists can no longer argue that environmental explanations are more humane, or result in the more humane treatment of disadvantaged groups, than are biosocial explanations. Biosocial perspectives, in fact, have been shown to increase the acceptability of some groups, pointing toward the possibility that the public's view towards criminals and ex-offenders would increase if only sociological criminologists abandoned their alliance with sociology.

5. Biology is immutable, so if biological factors are associated with crime, then prevention of crime and treatment of offenders is not possible.

Chapter 6 will discuss the treatment and prevention options that flow directly from biosocial research, but most criminologists assume that if crime is the result of biological factors, then there is nothing that can be done about the crime problem. After all, biology is immutable, right? Wrong. Environmental interventions can be used to alter biological predispositions, something that happens all of the time. Let's use the example of vision. All of us have different vision; some of us might be lucky enough to have been born with 20/20 vision, while others might be near-sighted or far-sighted. What is important is that eyesight is largely scripted by genetic factors. Yet if we discover that we are not seeing things well, or if we notice that our child is having difficulty viewing objects, do we throw our hands up on the air and proclaim that we are stuck with poor vision? Of course not, instead we seek out an optometrist who will ultimately prescribe corrective lenses to improve our vision. How could this be? After all, eyesight is largely determined by genetic factors, and as some criminologists argue, genetic effects are immutable. Obviously criminologists have a misperception when it comes to the changeability of biological factors; environmental patches can be used to overcome biological liabilities.

Summary
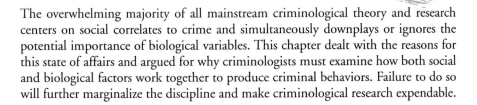

The overwhelming majority of all mainstream criminological theory and research centers on social correlates to crime and simultaneously downplays or ignores the potential importance of biological variables. This chapter dealt with the reasons for this state of affairs and argued for why criminologists must examine how both social and biological factors work together to produce criminal behaviors. Failure to do so will further marginalize the discipline and make criminological research expendable.

Key Points

- The field of criminology has been dominated by social explanations to crime and has ignored the possibility that biology is implicated in the etiology of criminal behaviors.

- The scientific method is an objective way of testing hypotheses about the causes and correlates to crime.

- Standard social science methodologies (SSSMs) are the dominant research design used by criminologists.

- SSSMs cannot take into account the effects of genetic factors thus leaving open the possibility that the relationship between social factors and crime outcomes is spurious.

- All research that uses SSSMs assumes that genetic factors are unimportant to the etiology of criminal behaviors.

- Many social factors, such as delinquent peers, are partially if not largely influenced by genetic factors.

- Research flowing from the hard sciences was more influential in abolishing the juvenile death penalty than was research flowing from mainstream criminological research.
- Biology influences criminality, not criminal behavior per se, and criminality ultimately is responsible for bringing about criminal behaviors.
- Biological risk factors to human behavior work in a probabilistic, not deterministic, fashion.
- Some biological factors can be altered through environmental interventions.

Name _____ Date _____

MINI Quiz

1. Most criminologists were trained as _____.

   a) biologists   b) sociologists   c) chemists   d) psychologists

2. Most criminologists _____ biological explanations to human behavior.

   a) study   c) do not study
   b) like   d) none of the above

3. The scientific method is a(n) _____ process used to acquire knowledge about a particular phenomenon.

   a) subjective   b) impossible   c) easy   d) objective

4. The best way to determine whether two variables are related is by _____.

   a) relying on our intuitions   c) guessing
   b) employing the scientific method   d) all of the above

5. Standard social science methodologies (SSSMs) are _____used in criminological research.

   a) almost always   b) rarely   c) never   d) sometimes

6. Spurious relationships exist when there is a relationship between two variables and that relationship _____ when taking into account the effects of another variable.

   a) remains the same   c) disappears
   b) becomes stronger   d) none of the above

7. SSSMs are extremely limited because they cannot take into account
_____.

  a) social factors   c) genetic factors
  b) ecological factors   d) all of the above

8. Research has revealed that many social variables are _____.

  a) influenced by genetic factors   c) influenced only by social factors
  b) not affected by genetic factors   d) none of the above

9. Hard science research appears to be _____ influential when
compared to criminological research.

  a) more   c) equally
  b) less   d) none of the above

10. Biological factors can _____ be changed.

  a) never   c) sometimes
  b) always   d) none of the above

1. Discuss the major problem with standard social science methodologies (SSSMs). How does this problem affect existing criminological research that examines the relationship between family-level variables and crime outcomes?

2. Criminologists often argue that biological explanations of human behavior should be left to researchers from other disciplines. Provide at least two reasons for why this type of thinking is misguided.

3. Opponents to biosocial research argue that biological explanations are evil and dangerous while sociological explanations are humane. Discuss the merit of this claim.

4. What type of research was used in the decision to abolish the juvenile death penalty?

5. Describe two main reasons why sociological explanations to criminal behavior have dominated the field of criminology.

Further Reading

Anderson, G. S. (2007). *Biological influences on criminal behavior.* Boca Raton, FL: CRC Press.

Denno, D. W. (1990). *Biology and violence: From birth to adulthood.* New York: Cambridge University Press.

Fishbein, D. (2001). *Biobehavioral perspectives on criminology.* Belmont, CA: Wadsworth.

Harris, J. R. (1998). *The nurture assumption: Why children turn out the way they do.* New York: Touchstone.

Nelson, R. J. (2006). *Biology of aggression.* New York: Oxford University Press.

Pinker, S. (2002). *The blank slate: The modern denial of human nature.* New York: Viking

Raine, A. (1993). *The psychopathology of crime: Criminal behavior as a clinical disorder.* San Diego, CA: Academic Press.

Rowe, D. C. (2002). *Biology and crime.* Los Angeles, CA: Roxbury.

Walsh, A. (2002). *Biosocial criminology: Introduction and integration.* Cincinnati, OH: Anderson.

Walsh, A., & Beaver, K. M. (2009). *Biosocial criminology: New directions in theory and research.* New York: Routledge.

End Notes

1. Wright, J. P., & Beaver, K. M. (2008). The behavioral genetics of predatory criminal behavior. In M. Delisi, & Conis, P. (Eds.), *Violent offenders: Theory, research, public policy, and practice*. Sudbury, MA: Jones and Bartlett.

2. The mean number of sociology courses completed by criminologists during their undergraduate studies was 6.23 and during their graduate studies was 9.10. In contrast, criminologists, on average, completed 1.69 undergraduate biology and .028 graduate biology courses. For more information about the training of criminologists and how this is linked with their views about the causes of crime see: Walsh, A., & Ellis, L. (2004). Ideology: Criminology's Achilles' heel? *Quarterly Journal of Ideology, 27*, 1–25.

3. Ellis, L., & Walsh, A. (1999). Criminologists' opinion about causes and theories of crime. *The Criminologist, 24*, 1–6.

4. van den Berghe, P. L. (1990). Why most sociologists don't (and won't) think evolutionarily. *Sociological Forum, 5*, 173–185.

5. Wright, R. A., & Miller, J. M. (1998). Taboo until today? The coverage of biological arguments in criminology textbooks, 1961 to 1970 and 1987 to 1996. *Journal of Criminal Justice, 26*, 1–19.

6. Robinson, M. B. (2004). *Why crime? An integrated systems theory of antisocial behavior*. Upper Saddle River, NJ: Prentice Hall, pp. ix–x.

7. van den Berghe, P. L. (1975). *Man in society: A biosocial view*. New York: Elsevier.

8. This does not mean that quantitative methodologies are superior to qualitative methodologies. Within criminology, however, quantitative methods are used more frequently than are qualitative methods. In addition, the only way of testing for genetic effects is by employing some type of statistical technique. As a result, this book will focus almost exclusively on quantitative methods.

9. Ellis, L. (1996). A discipline in peril: Sociology's future hinges on curing its biophobia. *The American Sociologist, 27*, 21–41.

10. The problems with SSSMs primarily apply to family-level studies because it is within the family where socialization effects are confounded with the effects of genetic factors. However, SSSMs are also limited in their ability to distinguish the effects of the shared environment from the effects of the nonshared environment, limitation that applies to all studies examining the effects of all environments. This issue will be discussed in Chapters 2 and 4. For more information see: Beaver, K. M. (2008). Nonshared environmental influences on

adolescent delinquent involvement and adult criminal behavior. *Criminology, 46*, 501–530.

11. Harris, J. R. (1995). Where is the child's environment? A group socialization theory of development. *Psychological Review, 102*, 458–489; Harris, J. R. (1998). *The nurture assumption: Why children turn out the way they do.* New York: Touchstone; Rowe, D. C. (1994). *The limits of family influence: Genes, experience, and behavior.* New York: Guilford; Udry, J. R. (1995). Sociology and biology: What biology do sociologists need to know? *Social Forces, 73*, 1267–1278.

12. Gottfredson, M. R., & Hirschi, T. (1990). *A general theory of crime.* Stanford, CA: Stanford University Press.

13. Pratt, T. P., & Cullen, F. T. (2000). The empirical status of Gottfredson and Hirschi's general theory of crime: *Criminology, 38*, 931–964.

14. Cullen, F. T., Unnever, J. D., Wright, J. P., & Beaver, K. M. (2008). Parenting and self-control. In E. Goode (Ed.), *Out of control: Assessing the general theory of crime.* Stanford, CA: Stanford University Press; Hay, C. (2001). Parenting, self-control, and delinquency: A test of self-control theory. *Criminology, 39*, 707–736.

15. Wright, J. P., & Beaver, K. M. (2005). Do parents matter in creating self-control in their children? A genetically informed test of Gottfredson and Hirschi's theory of low self-control. *Criminology, 43*, 1169–1202.

16. Harden, K. P., Turkheimer, E., Emery, R. E., Slutske, W. S., D'Onofrio, B. M., Heath, A. C., & Martin, N. G. (2007). Marital conflict and conduct problems in children of twins. *Child Development, 78*, 1–18.

17. Plomin, R., & Bergeman, C. S. (1991). The nature of nurture: Genetic influences on "environmental" measures. *Behavioral and Brain Sciences, 14*, 373–427.

18. To be fair, some criminologists, such as Gottfredson and Hirschi (1990), would argue that contact with delinquent peers is not necessarily a social process, but one that is guided by personality traits, such as low self-control. A more detailed discussion of the different issues surrounding the delinquent peers-delinquency connection will be provided in Chapter 3.

19. Warr, M. (2002). *Companions in crime: The social aspects of criminal conduct.* New York: Cambridge University Press.

20. Cleveland, H. H., Wiebe, R. P., & Rowe, D. C. (2005). Sources of exposure to smoking and drinking friends among adolescents: A behavioral-genetic evaluation. *The Journal of Genetic Psychology, 166*, 153–169.

21. Plomin, R. (1994). *Genetics and experience: The developmental interplay between nature and nurture.* Newbury Park, CA: Sage.

22. It is true that criminologists are interviewed about different topics related to crime, but many of these interviews have nothing to do with the *etiology* of criminal conduct. Instead, they often center on the public's fear of crime, criminal statistics, or other issues related to the day-to-day operations of the criminal justice system. Moreover, criminological research is rarely *featured* in highly-visible media outlets, such as *Time* or *Newsweek*.

23. Wilson, J. Q. (1975). *Thinking about crime.* New York: Vintage Books.

24. Bureau of Justice Statistics (2001). *Sourcebook of criminal justice statistics, 2000.* Washington, DC: U.S. Government Printing Office; Warr, M. (1995). Public opinion on crime and punishment. *The Public Opinion Quarterly, 59,* 296–310.

25. Actually, the gene only had an effect on antisocial behavior for males who were maltreated. This study will be covered in much greater detail throughout the rest of this book. The complete set of findings can be found in: Caspi, A., McClay, J., Moffitt, T. E., Mill, J., Martin, J., Craig, I. W., Taylor, A., & Poulton, R. (2002). Role of genotype in the cycle of violence in maltreated children. *Science, 297,* 851–854.

26. All of the information pertaining to impact factors was drawn from ISI's Web of Knowledge.

27. Cohn, E. G., Farrington, D. P. (2008). Scholarly influence in criminology and criminal justice journals in 1990–2000. *Journal of Criminal Justice, 36,* 11–21; Steiner, B., & Schwartz, J. (2006). The scholarly productivity of institutions and their faculty in leading criminology and criminal justice journals. *Journal of Criminal Justice, 34,* 393–400.

28. The one exception to this general rule is a recent study that included all studies, regardless of where they were published, in the ranking system. For more details see: Kleck, G. Wang., S.-Y. K., & Tark, J. (2007). Article productivity among the faculty of criminology and criminal justice doctoral programs. *Journal of Criminal Justice Education, 18,* 385–405.

29. *Science* has an impact factor greater than 30.

30. I thank Anthony Walsh for bringing this issue to my attention.

31. Ridley, M. (1998). *The origins of virtue: Human instincts and the evolution of cooperation.* New York: Viking.

32. American Society of Criminology (ASC). *Policy positions* [www document]. Retrieved online at: http://www.asc41.com/policyPositions.html.

33. Some of these misconceptions were drawn from: Walsh, A. (2002). *Biosocial criminology: Introduction and integration.* Cincinnati, OH: Anderson.

34. Criminogenic environments are environments that have been found to increase the odds of delinquent and criminal involvement. Abusive homes, for instance, are considered criminogenic environments because abusive homes

have been found to increase the odds of later life criminal and delinquent behaviors.

35. Reiss, D., Neiderhiser, J. M., Hetherington, E. M., & Plomin, R. (2000). *The relationship code: Deciphering genetic and social influences on adolescent development*. Cambridge, MA: Harvard University Press.

36. Huxley, A. (1998). *Brave new world*. New York: Perennial Classics.

37. Watson, J. B. (1930). *Behaviorism* (revised edition). Chicago: University of Chicago Press, p. 82.

38. Posner, R. A. (1992). *Sex and reason*. Cambridge, MA: Harvard University Press.

The
Genetic Origins of
Human Behavior

Introduction

As the previous chapter discussed, most sociological criminologists maintain that only the environment is implicated in the development of criminal behaviors and that biological factors are unimportant. Biosocial criminologists, in contrast, draw attention to the complexity of human behavior and maintain that crime and delinquency are the result of both environmental and biological factors. The question thus becomes: Which perspective is supported by the empirical research? To answer this question it is necessary to consult research findings drawn from disciplines other than criminology. Remember that criminologists do not generally examine the association between biological factors and crime and so it would be unreasonable to look to the criminological research for an answer to this question. It is possible, however, to examine studies from the fields of behavioral genetics, molecular genetics, and psychology to arrive at an answer to this question.

Before proceeding to a discussion of how genetic factors relate to human behavior, we need to clearly delineate the difference between what we mean when we speak of environmental factors and what we mean when we speak of biological factors. When biosocial criminologists speak of biological factors, they are generally referring to genetics, principles of human evolution, and brain structure and functioning as well as other physiological processes that occur within the human body and brain. When biosocial criminologists speak of environmental factors they are generally referring to socialization processes that are the result of factors external to the human body and brain. Most of the time the distinction between biology and the environment is obvious, but sometimes the boundaries become clouded. Take, for example, a woman who smokes while pregnant. The act of smoking is clearly a social behavior but the effect that nicotine has on the developing fetus is biological in origin. Just keep in mind that the environment mainly refers to socialization processes, while biology typically captures genetic factors as well as other processes that occur inside the human body and brain.

This chapter focuses on the genetic underpinnings to human behavior. Genetics, in its broadest sense, refers to everything that is coded into the human genome, where the human genome captures all of the information found in DNA. Since most criminologists have virtually no background in genetics, much of the genetic literature is not readily accessible to them. So the purpose of this chapter is twofold. First, it will provide an overview and thorough discussion of the main genetic concepts and terms needed to understand the genetic literature. Second, the empirical literature examining the association between genetic factors and criminal conduct will be presented. Toward this end, we will first explore the field of behavioral genetics and then move into a discussion of the exciting new findings being generated from molecular genetic studies.

Behavioral Genetics

Behavioral genetics is a field of study interested in examining both the environmental and genetic influences on a phenotype.[1] Phenotypes are measurable characteristics, such as IQ, height, and weight, but for the purposes of this book, the term phenotype should be equated with behaviors or personality traits. To understand the methods employed by behavioral geneticists, and how they estimate genetic and environmental influences, we first must define variance. Variance is a statistic that captures the degree of heterogeneity among people on a particular phenotypic measure. For example, suppose we were interested in measuring the height of one hundred people. Of those one hundred people, some would be very tall, some would be very short, and others would be of average height. Height, in other words, varies from person-to-person, and variance is a statistic that can be calculated to estimate these differences in height that exist across people. Variance can also be estimated for issues related to criminology. We could, for instance, measure the amount of criminal offenses committed by each person in a sample of one hundred adolescents. Some of the youths in the sample may have committed a lot of crimes in the past year, some may have committed an average number of crimes, and some may not have committed any crimes. Variance could then be calculated as a way of indexing the person-to-person differences in criminal involvement.

In both examples, variance is used as a way of gauging variability, but perhaps the more interesting question that comes into focus is what factors account for differences (i.e., variance) across people. Why are some people tall and others short? Why are some adolescents highly criminal and others not? Behavioral geneticists tackle these questions by estimating the environmental *and* genetic contributors to phenotypic variance. This represents a major departure from criminological research that only examines the environment and assumes genetic factors to be nonexistent. Remember that criminologists typically use standard social science methodologies (SSSMs) which are unable to test for genetic effects. Behavioral geneticists, in contrast, use research designs that typically include at least two siblings from each household. As will be discussed in greater detail later in this chapter, including two siblings from the same family allows behavioral geneticists to estimate the genetic and environmental bases to phenotypic variance.

Behavioral genetic research divides the proportion of phenotypic variance into three different components. The first component, which is referred to as heritability and symbolized as h^2, measures the proportion of phenotypic variance accounted for by genetic variance. Put simply, heritability captures the degree to which genetic factors are implicated in explaining phenotypic variance. Heritability is expressed as a proportion and, as a result, heritability estimates can range from .00 to 1.0.

A heritability estimate of .00 would mean that none of the phenotypic variance is accounted for by genetic factors. A heritability estimate of .50 would mean that one-half of the phenotypic variance is accounted for by genetic factors. A heritability estimate of 1.00 would mean that all of the phenotypic variance is accounted for by genetic factors. For ease of interpretation, heritability estimates can be converted to percentages, which essentially indicate the percentage of variance (out of a total of 100 percent) in the phenotype accounted for by genetic factors.

Discussions of heritability often produce confusion over what heritability estimates mean and what heritability estimates can reveal. So let us explore heritability in a little more detail. Heritability estimates cannot be extrapolated to the individual—that is, heritability can only be applied to group-level variance. What this means is that just because 50 percent of the variance in a particular phenotype is due to heritability does not necessarily mean that we can say that 50 percent of an individual person's phenotype is due to genetic factors. Heritability simply explains variance at the group level and it does not provide any information about the role that genetic factors play for each individual person. In addition, heritability estimates should also not be equated with some fixed, constant value. Genetic influences wax and wane in response to different environments, and genetic effects can change at different periods of human development. These issues will be discussed at length later in this chapter as well as in Chapter 3.

It is also noteworthy to point out that there are two different "types" of heritability: broad heritability and narrow heritability. To understand the difference between these two types of heritability we first must discuss three different sources of genetic variance—additive, dominance, and epistasis—and how they relate to heritability. Additive genetic variance is simply the sum of each gene's contribution to phenotypic variance. The assumption is that each gene's effect on the phenotype is independent of all the other genes' effects. Dominance is a nonadditive source of genetic variance, and dominance effects capture the interaction between the alleles (alleles are alternative copies of a gene; alleles will be explained in greater detail later in this chapter) of one gene. Epistasis is also a nonadditive source of genetic variance, but instead of capturing the interaction between the alleles of a single gene, epistasis refers to the interaction between alleles of two (or more) different genes. Now that we have defined additive, dominance, and epistasis we are in position to differentiate broad heritability from narrow heritability. Broad heritability captures the effects that all sources of genetic variance (additive, dominance, and epistasis) have on phenotypic variance. Narrow heritability captures only the effects of additive genetic variance on phenotypic variance. Dominance and epistasis are thought to have relatively small effects on most human phenotypes. As a result, behavioral geneticists often overlook sources of genetic variance that arise from dominance and epistasis.[2]

Genetic factors that are captured by heritability estimates can make siblings similar to each other (on a phenotype) and they can also make siblings different from each other (on a phenotype). To see how this is the case, consider that full siblings share, on average, 50 percent of their genes and consequently do not share the other 50 percent of their genes. What this means is that part of the reason that siblings may be similar to each other is because they share one-half of their genetic material. What this also means is that part of the reason that siblings may be dissimilar from each other is because half of their genetic material is different.

In behavioral genetic research, the phenotypic variance that is not explained by heritability (genetic factors) is partitioned to the environment. Behavioral geneticists make the distinction between two very different types of environments. The first type of environment is referred to as the shared environment and is symbolized as c^2. Shared environments include any environments that are the same between siblings from the same household. Shared environments are often equated with environments that are found within the family, such as parental socialization techniques, the economic well-being of the family, and family abuse or neglect, among others. The assumption here is that the environments that one sibling experiences are the same environments that their sibling also experiences. There are shared environments that are found outside the family as well, such as neighborhood-level factors and even some school-level characteristics.

Shared environmental effects work to make siblings similar to each other in respect to phenotypes. The logic underlying this assumption is relatively straightforward: if a particular environment is influential, and if it is experienced by both siblings, then the environmental effect should impact both siblings thereby making them more similar to each other. Take, for instance, the effect that living in an abusive home has on the development of problem behaviors. If abuse is positively correlated with problem behaviors, and if both siblings are abused, then both siblings should display behavioral problems.

Nonshared environments are the second type of environments studied by behavioral geneticists and they are symbolized as e^2. Any environment that is different between siblings is considered a nonshared environment. Some of the more common examples of nonshared environments are different peer groups, different schools, and even different prenatal environments. The distinction between shared and nonshared environments is not always clear cut and some environments may be considered shared environments in one situation, but nonshared environments in another situation. The school environment, for example, would be considered a shared environment for two siblings who attend the same school, but it would be considered a nonshared environment for two siblings who are enrolled at two different schools.

Even though nonshared environments are often equated with environments that are experienced outside the family this does not necessarily have to be the case; nonshared environments can also be found inside the family. Research has shown, for instance, that parents often treat their children very differently.[3] They may be loving and affectionate to one and cold and withdrawn to the other. Even experiences that are found within the family and appear, at first glance, to be shared environments may actually be nonshared environments. Divorce, for example, is experienced by all siblings in the household and would typically be viewed as a shared environment. Divorce, however, may be interpreted differently by siblings due to a variety of individual-level characteristics, such as age. One sibling may be a teenager at the time of the divorce, while their sibling may be a young adult who no longer resides in the home. These age differences would likely result in divergences in the way that the two siblings experience and interpret the divorce. In this case, the environment (divorce) is a nonshared environment. Nonshared environments, more broadly defined, would encompass any environment that is experienced or interpreted differentially between two siblings.

Where shared environments work to make siblings similar to each other, nonshared environments work to make siblings dissimilar to each other. Again, logically this makes sense because if a particular environment is influential in shaping a phenotype and if that environment is experienced by one sibling but not the other, then differences in exposure to the environment should cause differences in the phenotype. Suppose that one sibling is exposed to delinquent peers on a daily basis, but their sibling is not. It is likely that the sibling who affiliates with delinquent peers will become more delinquent than their sibling who does not associate with antisocial friends.

At this point it is important to note that most criminologists never make the distinction between the shared environment and the nonshared environment.[4] In fact, you would be hard-pressed to find a discussion of shared environments and nonshared environments in any criminological study or in any criminological textbook. This is somewhat ironic given that criminologists have spent so much time defending the importance of the environment, yet it was behavioral geneticists, not criminologists, who demarcated these two types of environments. As we will discuss later, it is impossible to test the relative effects of the shared environment and the nonshared environment using SSSMs.

So behavioral geneticists calculate the variance for a particular phenotype and then divide that variance into three components: a heritability component, a shared environmental component, and a nonshared environmental component. To see how this works let us take a look at Figure 2.1. Figure 2.1 portrays the results of

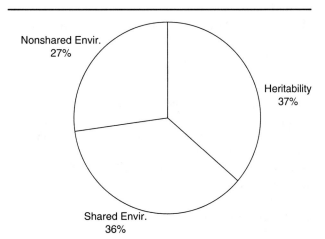

Nonshared Envir.
27%

Heritability
37%

Shared Envir.
36%

Figure 2.1
A behavioral genetic analysis revealing the effects of heritability, the shared environment, and the nonshared environment, on illicit drug dependence.

a study that employed behavioral genetic methods to examine the genetic and environmental influences on illicit drug dependence.[5] As can be seen, heritability accounted for 37 percent of the variance, the shared environment accounted for 36 percent of the variance, and the nonshared environment accounted for 27 percent of the variance. This behavioral genetic approach of apportioning phenotypic variance has been applied to virtually every imaginable phenotype.

We know that SSSMs cannot be used in analyses that are interested in determining the relative effects of genetic factors and environmental factors on a phenotype. So, what types of research designs can be used to estimate heritability, shared environmental effects, and nonshared environmental effects? And, what do the results of the studies reveal about the effects of the environment and genetic factors on antisocial phenotypes? These two questions will be answered in detail below. Before moving forward, however, it is important to remember that with SSSMs only one child per household is included in the sample. In almost all behavioral genetic research, at least two siblings per household are included in the sample. To see why this is the case, let us begin by exploring twin-based research, which is the most commonly analyzed type of kinship pair in behavioral genetic research.

Twin-based research. Twins can be thought of as a naturally-occurring experiment that behavioral geneticists exploit in attempt to tease apart the effects of genes from the effects of the environment. To understand how this is possible, let us explore the process of twinning in a little more detail. There are two types of twins: dizygotic (DZ) twins and monozygotic (MZ) twins. DZ twins, sometimes referred to as fraternal twins, occur in approximately 1 out of every 125 births and they are the result of two separate eggs being fertilized by two separate sperms but implantation occurs during the same pregnancy. On average, DZ twins share about 50 percent of their genetic material which makes them no more alike than "regular" siblings. MZ twins, in contrast, are sometimes referred to as identical twins, and MZ twins occur in approximately 1 out of every 250 births. The MZ twinning process begins like non-twin pregnancies, where one sperm fertilizes one egg, but then, for reasons that are unknown, the fertilized egg splits to form two identical embryos. These two embryos eventually develop into two genetically-identical siblings (i.e., MZ twins) who share 100 percent of their genetic material.

Behavioral geneticists analyze samples that include MZ twins and DZ twins to estimate heritability, shared environmental effects, and nonshared environmental effects on a phenotype. They do so by examining the similarity between twins from the same twin pair. Pretend that a team of researchers was interested in using a behavioral genetic approach to study the frequency of marijuana use among adolescents. Perhaps the sample contained 100 MZ twin pairs and 200 DZ twin pairs. Researchers could first interview each twin (a total of 200 MZ twins and a total of 400 DZ twins) about the frequency with which they use marijuana. They would then match each twin with their co-twin (i.e., the other half of their twin pair) and examine how similar the two twins were. For example, maybe one twin, Bob, reported smoking marijuana ten times, while his co-twin, Rob, reported smoking marijuana eleven times. Clearly Bob and Rob (twin brothers) are similar in terms of their marijuana use. Behavioral geneticists then perform the same process for all twin pairs, where they match the two twins together and examine how similar they are on that particular measure.

One way of measuring the similarity between twins from the same twin pair is by calculating a cross-twin correlation. Cross-twin correlations are very similar to the correlation coefficient that was discussed in Chapter 1. Remember that a correlation coefficient measures the direction and magnitude of the relationship between two measures, where values close to +1 indicate strong positive relationships. Cross-twin correlations measure the strength of the relationship between one twin's score on a phenotypic measure and their co-twin's (i.e., their sibling) score on that same measure. A cross-twin correlation of +1 would mean that the two twins were virtually identical on the phenotype, while a cross-twin correlation of 0.00 would mean that there was no similarity between twins on that phenotype. If we return back to the previous example examining marijuana use, we could estimate the correlation between how many times one twin (e.g., Bob) uses marijuana with how many times their co-twin (e.g., Rob) uses marijuana. In behavioral genetic research, cross-twin correlations are calculated separately for MZ twins and DZ twins.

The MZ cross-twin correlation can then be compared to the DZ cross-twin correlation to gain estimates of heritability, shared environmental effects, and nonshared environmental effects. To understand the logic underlying twin-based research realize that most twins from the same MZ twin pair share the same parents, they live in the same neighborhoods, they attend the same schools, and they experience all historical events at the same age. The same is true for DZ twins from the same twin pair. As a result, if the environment was the only factor that shaped phenotypic variance, then MZ twins from the same MZ twin pair should be just as similar to each other (on a phenotype) as DZ twins from the same DZ twin pair. However, what if MZ twins were found to be more similar to each other (on a phenotype) than were DZ twins? Obviously, the environment could not explain differences in phenotypic similarity because the environments between DZ twins and MZ twins should be relatively similar. What, then, could explain the greater similarity of MZ twins? If you answered genetic factors then you would be correct. The only reason that MZ twins should be more similar to each other than DZ twins is because MZ twins share twice as much genetic material as do DZ twins.

We can now use this logic as a springboard to present a few mathematical equations that are used to gain estimates of heritability (h^2), shared environmental effects (c^2), and nonshared environmental effects (e^2). Let us begin with the equation for h^2, which takes the following form:

$$h^2 = 2(\text{rMZ} - \text{rDZ}) \tag{2.1}$$

In this equation, rMZ represents the cross-twin correlation for MZ twins and rDZ represents the cross-twin correlation for DZ twins.[6] As can be seen, the cross-twin correlation for DZ twins is subtracted from the cross-twin correlation for MZ twins. Subtracting rDZ from rMZ removes all of the variance in the phenotype that is due to shared environmental factors and *half of the variance due to genes*. In order to take into account that MZ twins share twice as much genetic material as DZ twins the absolute difference needs to be doubled. After the difference in the cross-twin correlations has been doubled, the resulting value indexes the proportion of variance accounted for by genetic factors.

Let us work through an example to show how easy it is to calculate heritability. Suppose that we were interested in examining the heritability of impulsivity and we were told that rMZ = .84 and that rDZ = .54. We could substitute these values into equation 2.1 and we would arrive at the following:

$$h^2 = 2(.84 - .54)$$
$$h^2 = 2(.30)$$
$$h^2 = .60$$

Based on the values we were presented with, we would conclude that 60 percent of the variance in impulsivity is due to heritability (i.e., genetic factors).

We can also use rMZ and rDZ to estimate the variance accounted for by shared environmental effects. To do so, the following equation is used:

$$c^2 = 2rDZ - rMZ \tag{2.2}$$

One of the most obvious features in equation 2.2 is that rDZ is doubled prior to subtraction. rDZ is doubled as a way of standardizing for the fact that MZ twins share twice as much genetic material as DZ twins. Doubling rDZ essentially makes the proportion of variance accounted for by genetic factors equal for DZ and MZ twins. After doubling rDZ, we can subtract rMZ from it, and we are left with an estimate of shared environmental effects.

If we return to our previous example, we can use the estimates of rDZ (.54) and rMZ (.84) to calculate c^2. In so doing, we would arrive at:

$$c^2 = (2)(.54) - .84$$
$$c^2 = 1.08 - .84$$
$$c^2 = .24$$

In our example, we found that $c^2 = .24$ and we would then conclude that 24 percent of the variance in impulsivity is attributable to the effects of the shared environment.

The last piece of the puzzle that we would need to calculate would be the proportion of variance accounted for by the nonshared environment. The equation for estimating the effects of the nonshared environment takes the following form:

$$e^2 = 1 - (h^2 + c^2) \tag{2.3}$$

The equation to estimate e^2 is relatively straightforward: any effects that are not accounted for by heritability or by the shared environment are apportioned to the nonshared environment. It is also important to note that the effects of measurement error are captured in e^2.

We can use equation 2.3 to finish our example with impulsivity. Previously we had found that $h^2 = .60$ and that $c^2 = .24$. If we enter those estimates into equation 2.3, we have the following:

$$e^2 = 1 - (.60 + .24)$$
$$e^2 = 1 - .84$$
$$e^2 = .16$$

Since we found that $e^2 = .16$, we would be justified in concluding that 16 percent of the variance in impulsivity is explained by nonshared environmental factors, which, as pointed out above, also includes the effects of measurement error.

A few more issues about equations 2.1 through 2.3 warrant further comment. First, the estimates of h^2, c^2, and e^2 will always equal 1.0 (or 100 percent if h^2, c^2, and e^2 are transformed into percentages).[7] Let's take a look a look at our current example, where we found that $h^2 = .60$, $c^2 = .24$, and $e^2 = .16$. If we add these values together $(.60 + .24 + .16)$, we arrive at a value of 1.00. Second, these equations are relatively versatile and can be used with different types of kinship pairs besides just twins. The math becomes a little more cumbersome, and the equations change accordingly, but the logic remains the same. More detail about how other types of kinship pairs are used in behavioral genetic research will be provided later in this chapter. Third, with the introduction of statistical software programs, the use of these equations is somewhat antiquated. There are now a number of computer programs that can be used by behavioral geneticists to provide more accurate estimates of h^2, c^2, and e^2 than are typically garnered from the equations presented above. Still, the logic that is used by these computer programs remains the same as the logic we used in equations 2.1 through 2.3. We will explore some of these statistical packages in Chapter 7.

Now that we have a general understanding of how twin-based research can be used to calculate h^2, c^2, and e^2 let us take a look at what twin-based research reveals about the genetic and environmental underpinnings to criminal, delinquent, and antisocial phenotypes. More than one hundred studies have employed behavioral genetic methodologies to examine a wide range of antisocial phenotypes[8] so it would not be possible to review all of the studies. Moreover, heritability estimates vary from study-to-study in part because of differences in sample characteristics (e.g., the age of the respondents) and differences in the measurement of antisocial behaviors. So even if all the studies were summarized, we would be left wondering which heritability estimate should be believed. Luckily, there have been three meta-analyses published that summarize the state of the research on this topic.[9]

A meta-analysis is a methodological tool that can be used to summarize all of the studies that have examined a particular topic. This is an especially valuable technique when there is a lot of research bearing on one issue. Why? Because as was pointed out above, it simply is not feasible to summarize what all of the studies reveal. Plus, in research we often find conflicting results, where one study shows one set of findings and another study shows a completely divergent set of findings. Even when there is consistency in findings, we are often left wondering how strong (or weak) the effect is. When it comes to the heritability of antisocial behaviors there are too many studies to summarize and even if we reviewed all of the studies, we would still probably be confused as to exactly what the findings show (should we believe study #1, study #2, study #100?). Meta-analyses provide a relatively objective and parsimonious way of summarizing what all of the research reveals. Figure 2.2 displays the heritability estimates reported in three meta-analyses that examine the heritability of antisocial behavior. As can be seen, the results show considerable convergence in heritability estimates, with all of the estimates hovering around .50. These heritability estimates are based on thousands of twins (and adoptees), more than eighty studies, and multiple measures of antisocial behavior. By all accounts, heritability appears to explain about 50 percent of the variance in antisocial phenotypes.

Genetic factors have also been found to explain a significant amount of variance in some of the strongest correlates to criminal and delinquent behavior. For example, behavioral genetic research has indicated that low self-control, antisocial personality disorder, impulsivity, attention deficit hyperactivity disorder (ADHD), and substance use are all influenced by genetic factors. Early-life behavioral problems, including conduct disorder (CD) and oppositional defiant disorder (ODD), have also been found to have strong genetic origins.[10] So almost all variables analyzed by criminologists and almost all variables that are of central importance to criminological theories are influenced by genetic factors.

There is also some evidence to indicate that heritability estimates fluctuate over the life course. Some studies have shown that heritability estimates of early childhood antisocial behaviors are very high, sometimes explaining more than 80 percent of the variance[11], which is typically higher than heritability estimates of adolescent or adulthood antisocial behavior. Findings from other studies have

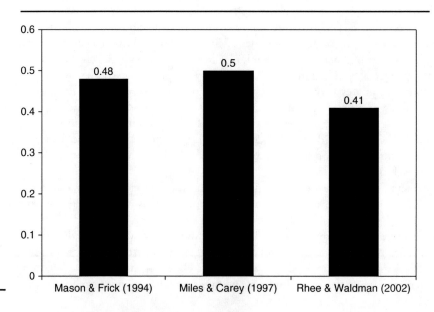

Figure 2.2

Heritability Estimates of Antisocial Behavior across Three Meta-Analyses.

revealed that heritability estimates are relatively low during adolescence ($h^2 \sim .10$), but become much stronger in adulthood ($h^2 \sim .40$).[12] By implication this means that the environment has relatively stronger effects during adolescence, but those effects erode by the time adulthood rolls around. One possible explanation for the changing heritability is that during adolescence, youths are subjected to the control of their parents. Parental control can act to curtail their adolescent's predispositions, predispositions that are genetically influenced. A youth, for example, might have a penchant for wild adventures, but their parents do not allow them to pursue such interests. During late adolescence and early adulthood—around the same time that some research shows genetic effects to strengthen—youths escape the surveillance of their parents and are able to pursue their interests thereby allowing for optimal genetic potential. Much more will be said about the interplay between genes and the environment in Chapter 3.

The findings garnered from behavioral genetic research provide some of the strongest evidence in support of the role of the environment, much stronger than is gathered from criminological research. Keep in mind that criminologists who use SSSMs leave open the possibility that their findings are spurious due to unmeasured genetic factors. That simply does not apply to behavioral genetic research because the effects of genetic factors are taken into account leaving only environmental factors (and measurement error) to explain the remaining variance. So, behavioral genetic studies are actually a criminologist's best friend. Why? Because their research shows that although genetic factors account for 50 percent of the phenotypic variance, environmental factors also account for 50 percent of the variance in antisocial phenotypes. This environmental variance could be attributable to the shared environment, the nonshared environment, or some combination of the two. According to Terrie Moffitt, the available behavioral genetic research suggests that shared environmental effects account for 15–20 percent of the variance and nonshared environmental effects account for 30–35 percent of the variance in antisocial phenotypes.[13] Figure 2.3 summarizes the estimates provided by Moffitt and shows that when the three sources of variance are compared the shared

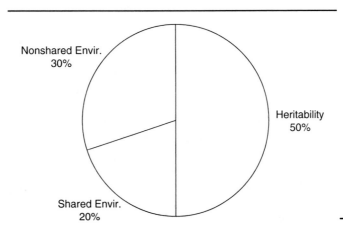

Figure 2.3
Estimates of heritability, shared environmental, and nonshared environmental effects on antisocial behaviors.

environment has the smallest effect and heritability has the largest effect. The nonshared environment explains a moderate-to-high percentage of phenotypic variance.

Which piece of the puzzle do criminologists study? The smallest one—shared environmental effects. Even more devastating than focusing on the shared environment is that researchers who use SSSMs simply cannot tease apart genetic effects, shared environmental effects, and nonshared environmental effects. Instead, all of these effects are pooled together and the researcher really has no idea what they are studying. For example, suppose a criminologist was interested in examining the relationship between parental warmth and adolescent delinquency. The measure of parental warmth is likely influenced by genetic factors as too is delinquency. Criminologists, however, treat the parental warmth variable as purely environmental and they also assume (because they are using SSSMs) that delinquency is not influenced by genetic factors, an assumption that is most likely wrong. Likewise, it is not possible to measure nonshared environmental effects with SSSMs; the nonshared environment captures phenotypic differences between siblings, but SSSMs only focus on one child per household making it impossible to examine sibling differences. These shortcomings with SSSMs are very severe and cast serious doubt on the believability of findings that flow from SSSM research.

Even with all of this rich empirical research showing the effects that genetic factors have on human phenotypes, and even with all of the pitfalls associated with SSSMs, many criminologists argue that all twin-based research is flawed and thus not convincing. Attacks against the twin-based research design tend to center on issues related to the equal-environment assumption (EEA). The EEA refers to the assumption that twins from the same MZ twin pair have environments that are no more similar than twins from the same DZ twin pair. Stated differently, the EEA assumes that the environments between MZ twins are just as similar as the environments between DZ twins. If the EEA is violated, then heritability estimates *may* be upwardly biased. This is exactly what many sociologists and some criminologists argue—that is, that MZ twins are more similar to each other than are DZ twins because MZ twins have more similar environments than DZ twins do.

Opponents of behavioral genetic research often make off-the-cuff remarks about how the EEA is not supported and consequently all of the heritability estimates are biased. This simply is not the case. Researchers have tested the EEA in a number of different ways and the results have revealed evidence upholding the EEA. Using an innovative approach, some researchers have examined twin pairs who had their zygosity incorrectly determined, where DZ twins thought they were MZ twins and MZ twins thought they were DZ twins.[14] These misclassifications often occur because the twins are not genotyped to determine their zygosity and instead physical similarities are used to classify the twins. Sometimes MZ twins do not look the same (because of prenatal environments where one may have absorbed more of the nutrients) and sometimes DZ twins look indistinguishable from each other. If the EEA is violated, then DZ twins (who were misclassified as MZ twins) should be more similar to each other than DZ twins who were correctly classified. Likewise, if the EEA is violated, then MZ twins (who were misclassified as DZ twins) should be less similar to each other than MZ twins who were correctly classified. This was not borne out; the twins' similarity was in line with genetic expectations and not in line with the misclassification. Researchers have also looked at situations where the EEA is known to be violated. The results of these studies have revealed that violation of the EEA has no affect on making MZ twins more similar to each other on behavioral phenotypes.[15]

Perhaps it is true, as some criminologists point out, that MZ twins are more likely to be dressed in the same clothes or that they resemble each other physically more so than DZ twins.[16] However, the only way that these violations of the EEA would bias heritability estimates is if they actually increased the similarity of MZ twins on the phenotype. And criminologists know that the way a person dresses or the physical appearance of a person are unrelated to crime; to argue otherwise, would be to argue in favor Cesare Lombroso's atavistic theory of the criminal man, a theory that is known to be invalid.

All twin-based research, not just twin-based research that examines antisocial phenotypes, has been attacked on the grounds that the EEA is violated. Perhaps the most vehement attacks have been leveled against twin-based research that examines IQ. Arthur Jensen responded to the EEA argument in the context of IQ research, but the same logic can be applied to twin-based research involving antisocial phenotypes. In the words of Jensen:

> If those who really believe that the IQ [antisocial behavior] correlation between MZ twins is better explained in terms of their physical similarity than in terms of their genetic correlation, they should go out and find unrelated people who look alike, such as movie stars and their doubles, and determine the correlation between their IQs [antisocial behaviors]. That would put this theory to the acid test...Of all the failed attempts I've ever heard to explain away the importance of genetics in individual differences in intelligence [antisocial behavior], the look-alike theory is the most absurd.[17]

Violation of the EEA may artificially increase heritability, but there are also at least three methodological problems with twin-based research that can artificially deflate heritability. First, there is some reason to believe that MZ twins may actually make a concerted effort to be different from their co-twin. Where one twin focuses on their musical talents, their co-twin may focus on their artistic talents; where one twin chooses to play football, the other may choose to play basketball; and where one twin chooses to affiliate with one set of friends, their co-twin may choose a different group of peers. In other words, MZ twins may place particular emphasis in staking out their own individuality and attempt to separate from their twin. If this process is at work, and there is some evidence to support that it is[18], then heritability will be artificially decreased.

Second, Adrian Raine points out that:

> Though MZ twins are genetically identical, identical twinning can result in biological differences that can accentuate human differences. For example, there is

a greater discrepancy in the birthweights of MZ twins relative to DZ twins, and birth complications have been linked to differences in behavior and cognition. This nongenetic, biological factor will result in an exaggeration of behavioral differences in MZ twins and a reduction in heritability estimates.[19]

If MZ twins are indeed more different biologically than DZ twins, then this too would artificially decrease heritability estimates.

Third, people do not tend to mate at random, and they tend to produce offspring with mates who are similar in terms of their behaviors and personality traits—a process referred to as assortative mating. People mate assortatively on an array of phenotypes, including antisocial phenotypes[20], and when assortative mating occurs the two mates share more genetic material than would be expected if mating occurred at random. The end result of assortative mating is that DZ twins, on average, share more than 50 percent of their genes. This necessarily makes the equations presented previously (equations 2.1–2.3) somewhat biased, and this bias works to reduce heritability. Taken together, if any of these three situations occur, then heritability estimates will be downwardly biased.

Even though twin-based studies have provided a great deal of information about the relative effects of genes and the environment on antisocial behaviors, many criminologists and sociologists remain skeptical. Fortunately, the traditional behavioral genetic method of comparing MZ twins to DZ twins is not the only way to examine genetic and environmental influences on human phenotypes. We next explore an alternative methodology, one that looks at the unique situation where MZ twins are separated from each other and reared apart.

Monozygotic twins reared apart (MZA). In rare instances, MZ twins are separated from each other at birth, reared in different homes by different parents and grow up without even knowing that they have a twin. Known as MZAs, these twins are genetically identical yet have been raised in completely different environments. As a result, the main attack against twin-based research—that is, violation of the EEA—does not apply to MZAs. MZAs thus provide the "gold standard" for separating genetic and environmental effects on phenotypic variance. If genes are unimportant, then MZAs should be no more similar to each other (on phenotypes) than two people chosen at random. Why? Because they share different environments just like two random people. If, however, genes are important, then MZAs should be at least somewhat similar to each other on a range of different phenotypes. Why? Because MZAs only share their genetic material; their environments are different.

Although MZAs are extremely rare, Thomas Bouchard and colleagues at the University of Minnesota founded the Minnesota Study of Identical Twins Reared Apart (MISTRA) in an attempt to identify, interview, and study MZAs. They began their study with just a few MZAs, but over the years the number of MZAs included has increased to more than 100 pairs. Bouchard and his researchers have been extremely methodologically careful and rigorous in their study. When an MZA is identified, they bring both twins to their laboratory to go through a week-long battery of tests that assesses almost every imaginable human phenotype from fingerprint ridges to IQ to virtually every personality dimension. The spouses of

MZAs are also interviewed whenever possible and asked detailed questions about the MZAs.

Some truly fabulous stories have been reported about the similar personalities, behaviors, and idiosyncrasies of MZAs. One set of MZAs—known as the Jim twins (named Jim Lewis and Jim Springer)—were the source of a considerable amount of media attention because of how eerily similar they were. Lawrence Wright explains:

> It was odd enough that both of the twins were named Jim, but it was utterly uncanny that each man had married and divorced a woman named Linda, then married a woman named Betty; the names of their firstborn children were James Alan Lewis and James Allen Springer; each had owned a dog named Toy...Both had worked part-time in law enforcement. They were each six feet tall and weighed 180 pounds...Each lived in the only house on his block, with a white bench around a tree in the backyard; each had elaborate workshops where they made miniature picnic tables (Lewis) or miniature rocking chairs (Springer); each followed stockcar racing and hated baseball. Their wives told the Minneapolis researchers that both Jims were romantics who left love notes around the house, but they were also anxious sleepers who ground their teeth at night and bit their nails to the quick during the day....The measurable features of their personalities, such as sociability, flexibility, tolerance, conformity, and self-control were all so similar that they could have been the same person, as were their mental ability scores.[21]

These types of accounts are truly captivating, but they are not really scientific. They provide interesting insight into the similarities between certain pairs of MZAs, but again, they do not provide any information about the relative effects of genetic factors and environmental factors.

The MISTRA team of researchers, however, moved beyond what was covered in the popular press and analyzed all of the data collected during the week-long interviews using sophisticated methodological and statistical techniques. These studies produced empirical evidence of the genetic and environmental sources of phenotypic variance.[22] Guess what they found? The results of these studies have revealed that almost every human phenotype is partially the result of genetic factors and some phenotypes are highly heritable. For example, measures of aggression, self-control, negative emotionality, and constraint—all of which are highly predictive of criminal involvement—were found to have heritability estimates of about .50 or greater.[23] These heritability estimates are strikingly similar to those garnered that use the more traditional twin-based research design. The convergence in findings lends credence to the twin method, and also provides reinforcement that the heritability of antisocial phenotypes is probably around .50.

One of the most interesting findings to flow from the MISTRA research is that *MZ twins who are reared together are no more similar to each other when compared with MZ twins who are reared apart.*[24] This bears repeating: MZAs are just as similar to each other as MZ twins who were raised together. This is truly an astonishing finding and one that flies in the face of purely environmental explanations to human behavior. Another finding that environmental research needs to reconcile is that the MZA studies have revealed time and again that the rearing environment (i.e., the shared environment) has absolutely no effect on adult personality traits. What the MZA research does indicate is that about 50 percent of the variance in all human phenotypes are due to the nonshared environment, not the shared environment. Again, criminological theory and research needs to be readjusted to take this finding into account.

The MZA research design is not without its critics, critics who argue that MZA research, just like traditional twin-based research, is fatally flawed. One of the main concerns raised is that the environments into which MZAs are adopted are similar. For instance, adoptive parents are likely to be from middle- or high-socioeconomic classes and they are not likely to live in impoverished, crime-ridden neighborhoods. If the environments between MZAs are similar, then it is possible that heritability estimates may be artificially inflated. Given that the heritability estimates from twin-based research and from MZA research are so similar it is unlikely that this potential problem biases heritability estimates drawn from MZA studies. For the skeptics who remain, there is still another type of research design that can be used to estimate genetic and environmental influences on behaviors—the adoption research design—to which we now turn.

Adoption-based research. Adoption-based research is an alternative to the twin method for estimating genetic and environmental effects on a phenotype. To understand how this works, realize that adopted children share 50 percent of their genes with their biological mother and 50 percent of their genes with their biological father. They do not, however, share the environment with their biological parents. Adopted children do share the environment with their adoptive parents, but they do not share any genes with them. Using this information, it is easy to see that if genes are influential for a particular phenotype, then the adopted child should resemble their biological parents on that phenotype. If the environment is important for a particular phenotype, then the adopted child should resemble their adoptive parents on that phenotype.

The adoption research design has been applied to the study of criminal behaviors. In what is perhaps the most famous of all adoption studies to examine criminal behavior, Sarnoff Mednick and his colleagues compared whether the adoptee had been convicted of a crime with whether their biological parents were criminals and with whether their adoptive parents were criminals.[25] Figure 2.4

Figure 2.4

Results of Mednick and colleagues' adoption-based research examining the genetic and environmental influences on criminal convictions.

		Are the biological parents criminal? (Genetic risk factor)	
		Yes	No
Are the adoptive parents criminal? (Environmental risk factor)	Yes	24.5%	14.7%
	No	20.0%	13.5%

displays the results of this study. Three findings are worthy of mention. First, adoptees who had a genetic risk factor (i.e., their biological parents were criminal) and who had an environmental risk factor (i.e., their adoptive parents were criminal) had the highest rate of being convicted of a crime—24.5 percent. This finding indicates that crime is the result of both genetic and environmental factors. Second, 20 percent of all adoptees who had a genetic risk factor, but not an environmental risk factor were convicted of a crime. This finding indicates that genetic factors in isolation are implicated criminal behaviors. Third, 14.7 percent of all adoptees who had an environmental, but not genetic, risk factor were convicted of a crime—a percentage not much greater than the 13.5 percent of all adoptees who were convicted of a crime but lacked both risk factors. This finding seems to indicate that environmental factors do not, in isolation, have much of an effect on criminal behaviors.

Additional studies using the adoption-based research design have also explored the genetic and environmental effects on different antisocial phenotypes. The results of these studies have revealed strong genetic influences on aggression ($h^2 = .70$) and delinquency ($h^2 = .39$)[26], but these significant genetic effects should be tempered by the fact that some adoption studies have failed to detect a significant genetic effects on serious violent crimes.[27] However, Adrian Raine's review of adoption studies provided strong and consistent evidence of a genetic basis to criminal behaviors.[28] Of the fifteen adoption studies included in his review, he found that fourteen of them revealed significant genetic influences on antisocial phenotypes. Overall, adoption-based research indicates a heritability of about .40[29], which is consistent with, albeit a little lower than, the heritability estimates garnered from twin-based research and MZA studies.

Family-based research. One criticism that is directed at twin-based studies and adoption-based studies is that twins and adoptees are different from non-twins or non-adoptees. What this means is that the findings that are garnered from twin/adoption studies are not generalizable to the larger population of non-twins/non-adoptees. There is not much evidence to support such a view[30] (with the main exception that twins tend to have delayed language development)[31], but still some skeptics view twin- and adoption-based research as somewhat limited in scope. Enter family-based studies. Family-based studies, like twin-based studies, analyze samples that include at least two siblings per household. Unlike twin-based studies, the two siblings do not have to be twins; they can be regular siblings, half-siblings, genetically unrelated siblings (e.g., stepsiblings), or any other type of kinship pair. The equations presented previously (equations 2.1–2.3) can then be altered to include different levels of genetic relatedness. For example, half siblings could be compared to full siblings on a phenotype. Again, if genetic effects are influential, then we would expect full siblings to be more similar to each other than half siblings. This same logic can be applied to all kinship pairs, where we compare phenotypic similarity among kinship pairs of different genetic relatedness. Oftentimes, all different types of kinship pairs, including twins, are contained in the same sample. This necessarily helps to eliminate concerns about the generalizability of behavioral genetic research findings to non-twins or non-adoptees. It should be noted that studies analyzing samples that include different types of siblings produce heritability estimates that are consonant with those garnered from twin- and adoption-based research designs.[32]

Summary of Behavioral Genetics

The methodologies of behavioral geneticists have provided a great deal of information about the relative effects of genetic factors and environmental factors in the etiology of antisocial phenotypes. However, no research design is perfect and behavioral genetic research designs are no exception. There are some shortcomings with twin-based research, but these shortcomings can be overcome by using adoption-based research designs. And the shortcomings with twin- and adoption-based research designs can be overcome by using family-based studies. This is exactly what behavioral geneticists have done; they have used multiple methodologies and still the results converge on the same conclusion: about one-half of the variance in antisocial phenotypes is accounted for by genetic factors. Even with this rich knowledge base at their disposal, criminologists continue to use SSSMs without second-thought and without criticism. Perhaps this is why Anthony Walsh concluded that:

> ...behavior geneticists are held to higher standards than strict environmentalists. Criticism, even virulent criticism, is good, for sentries fall asleep and troops grow fat and complacent when there is no enemy at the gates. Behavior genetics has become very muscular indeed from standing up to this scrutiny. It has become arguably as meticulous in its methods as any branch of science, and certainly more meticulous than any other branch of the social/behavioral sciences.[33]

Molecular Genetics

Behavioral genetic research represents a first step in determining the relative effects of genetic and environmental factors in the etiology of criminal and delinquent outcomes. The results from these studies, as discussed above, provide strong empirical evidence indicating that about one-half of the variance in antisocial phenotypes is due to genetic factors. The next logical question thus becomes: What specific genes are implicated in the etiology of antisocial phenotypes? The research designs reviewed above (e.g., twin- and adoption-based research designs) are unable to answer this question; all that they can reveal is the percentage of variance accounted for by genetic factors and the percentage of variance accounted for by environmental factors. Other research designs, collectively known as molecular genetic research designs, are needed to identify the precise genes that are tied to the development of antisocial phenotypes. Before moving into a discussion of molecular genetic studies, first a primer on molecular genetics will be presented.

Introduction to Genetics

Deoxyribonucleic acid (DNA) is a chemical code found in the nucleus of all cells except red blood cells and contains the genetic blueprint that allows humans and all other living organisms to form, develop, function, and live. The information transcribed into DNA determines many observable human characteristics, including hair color and eye color, but DNA also influences non-physical features as well, such as personality traits, disorders, and diseases. DNA is passed from parents-to-offspring, and all people inherit their own unique DNA sequence that is distinct from everyone else's (except MZ twins who have the same DNA). These differences in DNA are important because they are *partially* responsible for creating person-to-person differences in almost every imaginable human phenotype, including differences in antisocial phenotypes. To understand the connection between DNA and phenotypic variance, let us take a closer look at DNA.

Figure 2.5 shows the structure of DNA. As can be seen, DNA consists of two genetic fibers, each known as a polynucleotide, twisted around each other to form the well-known double helix. Each polynucleotide consists of a sugar phosphate backbone, and situated along each of the backbones is a sequence of nucleotides, also referred to bases. DNA consists of four nucleotides: adenine, thymine, guanine, and cytosine. Each of the four bases are typically referred to by a one letter abbreviation, where A → adenine, T → thymine, G → guanine, and C → cytosine. The two strands of DNA are then held together by the bonding of base pairs, where the nucleotides on one polynucleotide bond with the nucleotides on the other polynucleotide. The bonding of base pairs is not a random occurrence; A can only bond with T, T can only bond with A, G can only bond with C, and C can only bond with G. To see how this works, pretend that we are presented with the following hypothetical arrangement of nucleotides for *one* polynucleotide:

ACTGGAGCTGGCCAT

With the bonding processes described above, we could easily figure out the sequence of nucleotides for the complementary polynucleotide. For each "A", we need to substitute a "T"; for each "T", we need to substitute an "A"; for each "C" we need to substitute a "G"; and for each "G" we need to substitute a "C." If we follow these base-pair rules, then the sequence of nucleotides for the *other* polynu-cleotide would be:

TGACCTCGACCGGTA

Figure 2.5 illustrates the bonding of base pairs for a section of DNA and also reveals that the A-T and T-A bonds are held together by two hydrogen bonds, while the C-G and G-C bonds are held together with three hydrogen bonds. These examples are extremely simplified, but this is the same base-pairing procedure that is used for the approximately 3 billion base pairs present in human DNA.

At certain points on DNA, contiguous base pairs work together to perform specialized functions. These contiguous base pairs working in collaboration are

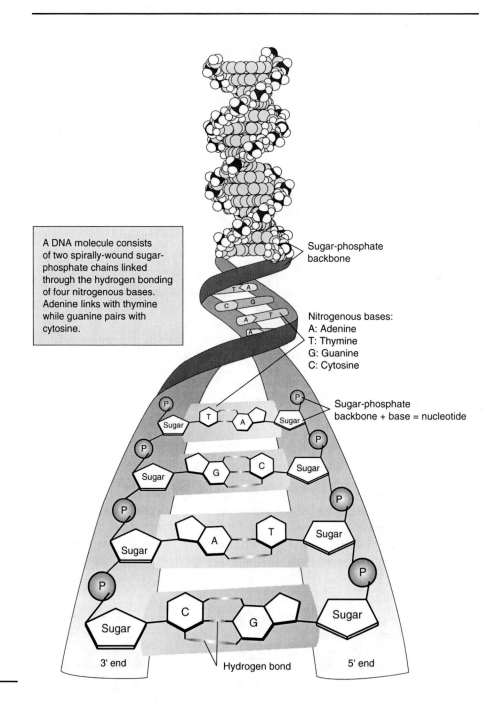

A DNA molecule consists of two spirally-wound sugar-phosphate chains linked through the hydrogen bonding of four nitrogenous bases. Adenine links with thymine while guanine pairs with cytosine.

Sugar-phosphate backbone

Nitrogenous bases:
A: Adenine
T: Thymine
G: Guanine
C: Cytosine

Sugar-phosphate backbone + base = nucleotide

3' end

Hydrogen bond

5' end

Figure 2.5
The structure of
DNA.

called genes. Pretend, for example, that the following series of base pairs were found on a section of DNA:

AACCTT**AAGGGCCTA**TATCGT
TTGGAA**TTCCCGGAT**ATAGCA

If the string of bold-typed base pairs worked in unison to carry out a particular function then they would be considered a gene. This example is overly-simplified and in reality the 20,000–25,000 genes that are found in the human genome are usually comprised of 1,000 or more base pairs.

At this point it is important to become familiar with the more conventional way of presenting base pairs. In the above example, the nucleotides from each polynucleotide (i.e., the top polynucleotide and the bottom polynucleotide) were presented; however, it is redundant to present the nucleotides of each polynucleotide. Why? Because we know that A only pairs with T (and vice versa) and that C only pairs with G (and vice versa). Thus if we know the nucleotide sequence of one polynucleotide we also know the nucleotide sequence of the complementary polynucleotide. As a result, by convention only the base pairs from one polynucleotide are presented. The above example would thus become:

AACCTT**AAGGGCCTA**TATCGT

This is the notation that will be used throughout the rest of this book. Just remember that the complementary strand of base pairs is always present, but is not shown.

There is much confusion among social scientists over what genes do, and there is often a misguided assumption that genes code directly for certain behaviors. Genes do not directly cause human phenotypes; instead the function of genes is to code for the production of proteins. Proteins are complex organic compounds that are essential to human life and they are implicated in many different processes in the human body and brain. Enzymes are one type of protein. Other proteins have structural properties, such as providing the shape to cells, or functional properties, such as aiding in metabolism. Proteins are produced by linked chains of amino acids. Amino acids are the building blocks of proteins and they are coded for by sequences of three contiguous base pairs known as codons. The codon, CCA, for instance, codes for the production of the amino acid, proline. There are a total of 20 different amino acids, each synthesized by a different codon.

Figure 2.6 presents a codon table which specifies the unique amino acid synthesized by each codon. Codon tables are relatively easy to use; the first column corresponds to the first base (nucleotide) in the codon, the column running across the top of the table corresponds to the second base in the codon, and the far right column contains the third base in the codon. Suppose, for example, that we were presented with the codon CCA and asked which amino acid corresponds to this codon. To find out, put your finger on row "C" for the first base. This is the row that we will be working with. Second, put your finger on column "C" for the second base. Now move down this column until you find where it intersects with row "C" from the first base. Within these cells, we see that there are four different options: CCU, CCC, CCA, and CCG. We know that the third base is A so the amino acid that corresponds to the codon CCA is proline.

Second Base

	U	C	A	G	
U	UUU phenylalanine	UCU serine	UAU tyrosine	UGU cysteine	**U**
	UUC phenylalanine	UCC serine	UAC tyrosine	UGC cysteine	**C**
	UUA leucine	UCA serine	UAA stop	UGA stop	**A**
	UUG leucine	UCG serine	UAG stop	UGG tryptophan	**G**
C	CUU leucine	CCU proline	CAU histidine	CGU arginine	**U**
	CUC leucine	CCC proline	CAC histidine	CGC arginine	**C**
	CUA leucine	CCA proline	CAA glutamine	CGA arginine	**A**
	CUG leucine	CCG proline	CAG glutamine	CGG arginine	**G**
A	AUU isoleucine	ACU threonine	AAU asparagine	AGU serine	**U**
	AUC isoleucine	ACC threonine	AAC asparagine	AGC serine	**C**
	AUA isoleucine	ACA threonine	AAA lysine	AGA arginine	**A**
	AUG(start) methionine	ACG threonine	AAG lysine	AGG arginine	**G**
G	GUU valine	GCU alanine	GAU aspartate	GGU glycine	**U**
	GUC valine	GCC alanine	GAC aspartate	GGC glycine	**C**
	GUA valine	GCA alanine	GAA glutamate	GGA glycine	**A**
	GUG valine	GCG alanine	GAG glutamate	GGG glycine	**G**

First Base *(left axis)*   Third Base *(right axis)*

Figure 2.6
A codon table.

Note that the letter "U" is included in the codon table. For now, we can ignore "U" but below we will talk about how "U" is the letter in a different genetic alphabet.

The main function of genes is to code for the production of proteins; interestingly, however, about 90 percent of the human genome is non-coding, meaning that only about 10 percent of the human genome actually codes for the production of proteins. The parts of a gene that code for protein production are known as exons and the parts of a gene that are non-coding are called introns. Exons and introns are interspersed throughout the human genome, and although the average gene is approximately 3,000 base pairs long, only about 1,200 of them actually code for protein production.

Keep in mind that the main function of genes is to code for the production of proteins. Genes do not, however, directly manufacture proteins; they only contain the *instructions* needed for a specific protein to be produced. The process by which genetic information (i.e., DNA) is ultimately converted into proteins has become known as the central dogma of molecular biology. Two steps make up the central dogma: transcription and translation. Figure 2.7 depicts both of these steps. Transcription refers to the process whereby a gene duplicates itself onto a new molecule called ribonucleic acid (RNA). The nucleotides on RNA contain all of the information needed to manufacture the amino acids that will ultimately result in the production of proteins. After the genetic information has been copied onto RNA, RNA leaves the cell nucleus and enters the cytoplasm.

DNA differs from RNA in at least three ways. First, after the gene is duplicated, the introns (the non-coding regions of the gene) are removed in a process referred to as splicing. Consequentially, only the exons, or the regions of the gene that code for protein production, are retained in RNA. Splicing transforms RNA into messenger RNA (mRNA). Second, and as Figure 2.8 shows, RNA is single stranded, while DNA is double stranded. Third, DNA and RNA use somewhat different genetic alphabets. Recall that DNA uses the four letter genetic alphabet that consists of A, C, T, and G. Like DNA, the RNA genetic alphabet also consists of A C, and G, but RNA includes the nucleotide uracil (U) instead of thymine (T). During the process of transcription, the DNA code (A, C, T, and G) is converted into the new RNA code (A, C, U, and G). After DNA has been duplicated and transcribed onto mRNA, mRNA leaves the cell nucleus and travels into the cytoplasm.

The top panel of Figure 2.7 depicts the second step in the central dogma of molecular biology: translation. During translation, mRNA meets up with and attaches itself to a ribosome, which are protein manufacturing machines found in the cytoplasm. The ribosome then reads the genetic information carried by mRNA and works in conjunction with another type of RNA—transfer RNA (tRNA)—to produce the appropriate amino acid. After the amino acid is produced it is added to a growing protein chain, known as a polypeptide chain. The polypeptide chain includes other amino acids that have already been produced and linked together. A protein is completed after all of the necessary amino acids have been manufactured and strung together in the polypeptide chain. On average, about 1,200 base pairs, equating to about 400 amino acids, are needed to produce one protein.[34] Once the protein is formed, it migrates away from the ribosome and performs its specialized function for the cell.

To recap, DNA is the genetic blueprint that is the foundation of life and each person has their own unique DNA sequence. DNA consists of a four-letter genetic alphabet (A, C, T, and G) and genes are sections of DNA that work together. The main function of a gene is to code for the production of proteins. The central

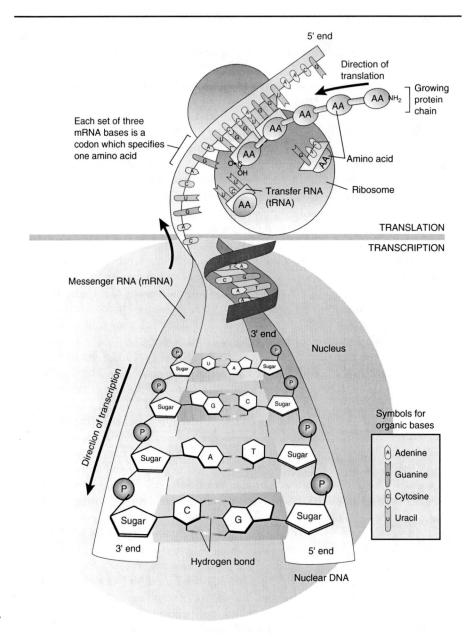

5' end

Direction of
translation

Growing
protein
chain

Each set of three
mRNA bases is a
codon which specifies
one amino acid

AA NH₂

AA

AA

Amino acid

Transfer RNA
(tRNA)

Ribosome

TRANSLATION

TRANSCRIPTION

Messenger RNA (mRNA)

3' end

Nucleus

Direction of transcription

Symbols for
organic bases

A	Adenine
G	Guanine
C	Cytosine
U	Uracil

3' end

Hydrogen bond

5' end

Nuclear DNA

Figure 2.7
The central dogma of
molecular biology.

dogma of molecular biology describes the two main processes—transcription and translation—that lead from a gene to the production of a protein. During transcription, a gene is copied from DNA to RNA. During translation, RNA works in conjunction with ribosomes to produce a protein. The protein is what is ultimately responsible for bringing about phenotypes.

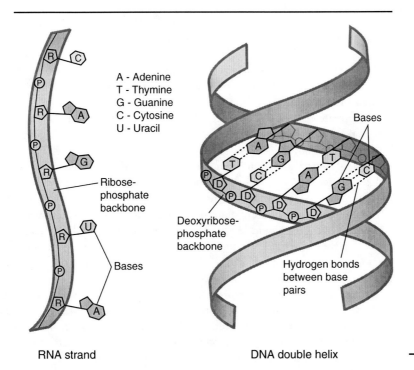

A - Adenine
T - Thymine
G - Guanine
C - Cytosine
U - Uracil

Ribose-
phosphate
backbone

Deoxyribose-
phosphate
backbone

Bases

Bases

Hydrogen bonds
between base
pairs

RNA strand   DNA double helix

Figure 2.8
Differences between
RNA and DNA.

Human Genetic Variation. Differences in DNA sequences (i.e., genotypic variance) can result in differences in phenotypes (i.e., phenotypic variance), including differences in antisocial phenotypes. Another way of saying this is that genotypic variance has the potential to explain phenotypic variance. Of particular interest, then, is how and why DNA varies from person-to-person. To understand the sources of genotypic variance, it is first necessary to understand that genes are inherited on threadlike structures called chromosomes. Barring any chromosomal abnormalities, all healthy humans inherit twenty-three pairs of chromosomes, where one pair is inherited maternally and the other pair is inherited paternally. One of the pairs of chromosomes is referred to as the sex chromosomes because they determine the sex of the offspring. Females inherit two X sex chromosomes, while males inherit one X sex chromosome and one Y sex chromosome. The remaining twenty-two pairs of chromosomes are called autosomes and each autosome is referred to by a distinct number (i.e., chromosome #1–#22). Each gene is found on a specific location on a specific chromosome. The location where a gene is found is called a genetic locus. A gene involved in the transmission of dopamine (DRD4), for example, is found on chromosome #11.

Genes that are located on the autosomes are made up of two different copies. One of the copies is inherited on the maternal chromosome and one of the copies is inherited on the corresponding paternal chromosome. The same is not necessarily true for genes located on the sex chromosomes. Females inherit two X chromosomes—one maternally and one paternally—and thus they have two copies of each gene that is located on the X chromosome. Females, however, do not have a Y chromosome and so they do not inherit any genes that are located on the Y chromosome. Males, in contrast, inherit one X chromosome and one Y chromosome. As a result, they have only one copy of each gene that is located on the X chromosome and they have only one copy of each gene located on the Y chromosome.

The maternal copy of the gene and the paternal copy of the gene are usually identical because for most genes there is only one version of the gene that can be inherited. For example, let us pretend that hair color was completely determined by one gene. Let us also pretend that there was only one copy of the hypothetical hair gene: a brown copy that results in the same shade of brown hair. There would be no differences in hair color (i.e., no phenotypic variance) because everyone would have inherited a brown copy maternally and a brown copy paternally. Even before a person is born, we would know that they will have brown hair because we would know that they inherited two "brown" copies of the hair color gene. This is precisely what occurs with most genes in the population: there is only one copy of the gene and thus these genes do not vary from person-to-person.

There are, however, a small percentage of genes, somewhere between 1 to 10 percent, where there are two or more copies of a gene available in the population.[35] Alternative copies of a gene are referred to as alleles and genes that consist of two or more alleles are called genetic polymorphisms.[36] If we return to our previous hypothetical example with hair color, let us now pretend that some people have brown hair and some people have red hair. Again, suppose that hair color is determined by one gene but this time pretend that there are two copies (i.e., alleles) of the gene: a brown copy and a red copy. Now it is easy to see that the reason that hair color varies (phenotypic variance) is because the hair color gene varies (genetic variance). Genetic variance is simply due to allelic differences and oftentimes allelic differences are inconsequential and do not result in phenotypic differences. Sometimes, however, allelic differences can result in functional differences (e.g., the production of different proteins), which may ultimately produce phenotypic variance.

Let us turn to another example in order to explain the inheritance of alleles in a little greater detail. For simplicity's sake, suppose that a hypothetical gene partially determines each person's level of self-control, where levels of self-control range between 0–10, with higher scores corresponding to more self-control. Suppose further that there are two alleles that comprise this hypothetical "low self-control gene", where A = increases self-control by 2 points and a = decreases self-control by 1 point. Let us also pretend that the mother has Aa for the low self-control gene and the father has AA for the low self-control gene. At this point, let us introduce the term genotype. Genotype refers to the specific combination of alleles for a particular polymorphism (or sometimes the specific combination of alleles for all of the polymorphisms). For example, the mother would have an Aa genotype, while the father would have an AA genotype. Their offspring could inherit one of two different genotypes: an AA genotype (i.e., they inherited an A maternally and an A paternally) or an aA genotype (i.e., they inherited an a maternally and an A paternally). (Note that the ordering of alleles is unimportant so, for instance, **aA** would be the same as **Aa**.) The **AA** genotype would increase self-control by 4 points, while the **aA** genotype would increase self-control by 1 point. In this case, genotypic variance (different combinations of the **a** and **A** alleles) could explain phenotypic variance (differences in levels of self-control). Of course, this is an extremely simplified example and in reality there may be a hundred or more genes that influence a particular phenotype (e.g., levels of self-control).[37]

Polymorphic genes that consist of two identical alleles are said to be homozygous. In the above example, the **AA** genotype would be considered homozygous because the two alleles are the same (i.e., they both are **A**). Polymorphic genes that consist of two different alleles are said to be heterozygous. In the above example, the **aA** genotype would be considered heterozygous because the two alleles are different (i.e., one is **a** and one is **A**).

We now have all the necessary background information needed to move into a discussion of the three different types of genetic polymorphisms. The first type of genetic polymorphism is called a single nucleotide polymorphism (SNP; pronounced "snip"). SNPs are the most commonly occurring genetic polymorphism and they emerge once in about every 100 to 300 base pairs. About 90 percent of all genetic polymorphisms are SNPs.

SNPs are due to a difference in a single nucleotide base, where two alleles are indistinguishable except for a one-letter difference. For example, pretend that the following was a section of a gene for Person #1:

AATCTT<u>A</u>TGTACGGA

Contrast the DNA sequence of Person #1 with the following DNA sequence for Person #2:

AATCTT<u>G</u>TGTACGGA

The two alleles between Person #1 and Person #2 are almost identical: of the fifteen nucleotides, fourteen of them are the same. The only difference is found in the seventh nucleotide, where Person #1 has an A and Person #2 has a G. While this difference might seem minute, it is important to point out that this slight change translates into different amino acids being produced. In Person #1, the tri-nucleotide sequence ATG corresponds to the amino acid, methionine and in Person #2 the tri-nucleotide sequence GTG corresponds to the amino acid, valine (e.g., in the catechol-O-methyltransferase gene). SNPs that result in the production of different amino acids are known as nonsynonomous, while SNPs that do not result in the production of different amino acids are known as synonymous. Nonsynonomous SNPs are likely to be functional polymorphisms because the proteins that are ultimately produced by the different alleles are comprised of different amino acids. Moreover, the fact that SNPs result from such a small change does not mean that the effects of SNPs are also small. Consider this: approximately 85 percent of all genetic disorders, including terminal diseases, can be traced to SNPs.[38]

The second type of genetic polymorphism is known as a microsatellite. Microsatellites are the result of allelic differences that vary in their end-to-end length, where one allele is longer than another allele. At certain places on a section of DNA, a small number of contiguous base pairs (the arbitrary cutoff is around six base pairs) can be repeated a varying number of times. Alleles with more repeat sequences are longer than alleles with shorter repeat sequences. For example, the tetra-nucleotide sequence, GATAn, could be repeated n number of times, where an allele with $n = 7$ repeats would be shorter than an allele with $n = 9$ repeats. The length of alleles varies because of the number of times a section of DNA is repeated. The number of times that the sequence of DNA can be repeated varies in microsatellites, with some base pairs sequences being repeated a thousand or more times. Another example will help clarify microsatellites. Take a look at the repeat sequence for the tri-nucleotide sequence, AGA, in the following two hypothetical alleles:

TAGGGT**AGA**AG**A**AG**A**AG**A**AG**A**AGA
TAGGGT**AGA**AG**A**AGA

In the first allele AGA was repeated six times and in the second allele AGA was repeated three times. Microsatellites, in summary, surface because of differences in the number of times that a short section of base pairs is repeated.

Minisatellites are the third type of genetic polymorphism and they are very similar to microsatellites. The main difference between the two is that where microsatellites refer to repeat sequences in a small number of base pairs, minisatellites refer to repeat sequences that occur in much larger blocks of base pairs (the aribitrary cutoff is around 10 or more base pairs). The dopamine transporter gene (DAT1), for example, has a section of 40 base pairs that can be repeated more than 10 times. A common type of minisatellite is referred to as a VNTR, which is the acronym for variable number of tandem repeats. Keep in mind that the key difference between microsatellites and minisatellites is the number of base pairs that is included in the repeat sequence.

How Genotypic Variance Can Produce Phenotypic Variance

There are at least three ways that genotypic variance can produce phenotypic variance.[39] The first way is known as a monogenic effect, where one gene is the cause of one particular phenotype. More than a thousand diseases and disorders, such as sickle-cell anemia and Huntington's disease, are the result of monogenic effects. In these cases, genes determine (with 100 percent accuracy in some disorders) who will and who will not develop the disorder. Monogenic effects can be due to recessive or dominant patterns of inheritance.

Many criminologists erroneously think that monogenic effects can be applied to the study of antisocial phenotypes; nothing could be farther from the truth. Human behavioral phenotypes, including antisocial phenotypes, are simply too complex to be determined by a single gene and instead are partially the result of multiple genes, something known as a polygenic effect. Polygenic effects are the second way that genotypic variance can produce phenotypic variance. To understand polygenic effects, it is important to realize that genes work in a probabilistic fashion, where the possession of certain alleles can increase or decrease the odds of developing a particular phenotype.

This is the way in which genetic variance can produce antisocial phenotypic variance. There are hundreds or even thousands of genes that are associated with criminality. Depending on what alleles a person possesses for each of these genes, their odds of becoming a criminal may increase or decrease. The important point is that the effects of each allele on criminality tend to be very small. Pretend that we are looking at ten genes that are thought to be associated with criminality. There are two alleles for each of the ten genes: one version increases the odds of offending by 1 percent and the other allele has no effect on the odds of offending. Let us pretend that a person inherited twenty alleles, all of which increased the odds of offending by 1 percent. In this case, the person would have a 20 percent greater chance of engaging in crime compared to someone who did not receive any of these alleles. Pay particular attention to the fact that possessing a particular allelic combination will not determine whether someone will or will not become a criminal, but it may increase or decrease the chances that a person acts in a particular way. Genes, in other words, are risk factors, just like any other correlate to criminal involvement. It is also worth mentioning that the environment has effects on offending behaviors and environmental factors can also interact with genetic factors to produce phenotypic variance. This topic will be discussed in detail in Chapter 3. For now just realize that there is nothing deterministic about the road from genotypic variance to phenotypic variance.

Pleiotropy is the third way that genotypic variance can produce phenotypic variance. Pleiotropy captures the effects that a single gene has on various different phenotypes. The allele that causes the disorder phenylketonuria (PKU), for instance, causes hair to lighten, but it also reduces tyronise and increases phenylalanine, and is responsible for a number of other phenotypic changes. Pleiotropic effects have also been detected in biosocial criminological research, too. A long line of literature has shown, for example, that there is a strong relationship between number of sex partners and criminal involvement, where criminals tend to have more sex partners than non-criminals.[40] What accounts for this association is not well understood, but there is some research indicating that an allele of the dopamine transporter gene (DAT1) is associated with increases in criminal involvement as well as increases in number of sex partners.[41] There is also some evidence showing that the same genetic factors that cause variation in levels of self-control also cause variation in exposure to delinquent peers and involvement in delinquency.[42] The importance of pleiotropic effects to criminology should not be casually overlooked; it is likely that part of the covariation between delinquency and many crime correlates (e.g., low self-control) are the result of pleiotropic effects. At this time, however, we simply do not have enough empirical research to provide any definitive answers about the role that pleiotropic effects play in the genesis of antisocial phenotypes.

Genetic Polymorphisms and Antisocial Phenotypes

We are now almost in a position where we can discuss the research that has examined the relationship between some genetic polymorphisms and myriad antisocial phenotypes. Most of the genes that have been identified as candidate genes[43] for antisocial phenotypes are involved in neurotransmission. As a result, in order to understand how these candidate genes may ultimately exert their effects on antisocial phenotypes, let us begin by providing an overview of neurotransmission, after which we will move into a discussion of the genetic polymorphisms that have been found to be associated with antisocial phenotypes.

The human brain is comprised of billions of nerve cells called neurons. As Figure 2.9 shows, neurons consist of a cell body (which contains the cell nucleus), an axon, and numerous dendrites. Each neuron is interconnected with other neurons and when two neurons need to communicate, an electrical impulse (i.e., an action potential) is passed from the cell nucleus down the axon until it reaches the synaptic terminal (also known as the axon terminal), where it will be transmitted to the dendrite of an adjacent neuron. The axon terminal of one neuron and the dendrite of a different neuron, however, are separated by a small gap known as a synapse. The synapse must somehow be bridged in order for the axon terminal and the dendrite to exchange information. Enter neurotransmitters. Neurotransmitters are chemical messengers that relay information across the synapse. When an electrical impulse reaches the synapse, the axon terminal of the transmitting neuron (also known as the presynaptic neuron) releases neurotransmitters which move across the synapse and lock into receptors on the dendrites of the receiving neuron (also known as the postsynaptic neuron). After a sufficient number of neurotransmitters have binded to the post-synaptic neuron, the electrical impulse will initiate an action potential in the postsynaptic cell and the impulse will travel down the axon where this process can then be repeated.[44]

After neurotransmitters have locked into the receptors on the postsynaptic neuron, they detach from the receptors, and float back into the synapse. As a result, they need to be eliminated from the synaptic gap to keep neurotransmission working effectively. There are a number of different mechanisms by which neurotransmitters can be discarded from the synapse, but we will focus on two. First, the presynaptic neuron can produce a transporter protein that enters the synapse, captures the neurotransmitters, and returns them to the axon terminal of the presynaptic neuron. This first way of "mopping up" neurotransmitters is known as reuptake and the process of reuptake is governed by specific genes. Genes, for example, code for the production of transporter proteins that aid in the reuptake of neurotransmitters, such as dopamine and serotonin. Reuptake is critically important in maintaining normal levels of neurotransmitters in the synapse and different genetic variants (i.e., alleles) have been found to correspond with differential efficiency in the reuptake process.

The second way that neurotransmitters are eliminated from the synapse is by the production of enzymes. Enzymes are proteins that are involved in a host of

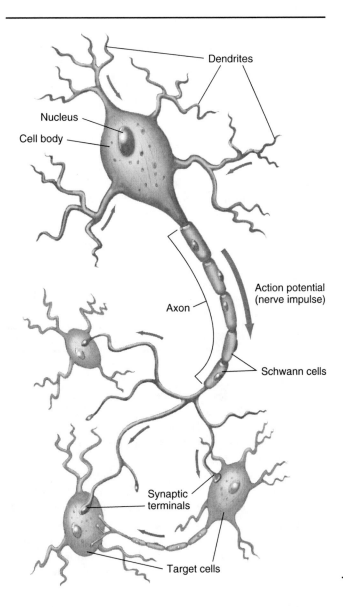

Dendrites

Nucleus

Cell body

Action potential
(nerve impulse)

Axon

Schwann cells

Synaptic
terminals

Target cells

Figure 2.9
A neuron.

different functions, but one of their responsibilities is to breakdown neurotransmitters into inactive particles. After the neurotransmitter has detached from the postsynaptic receptor, enzymes will locate and metabolize neurotransmitters, effectively terminating their functionality. Since enzymes are proteins, they are coded for by genes and some of these genes are polymorphic. What this means is that different alleles of these polymorphic genes may actually produce enzymes that vary in their efficiency; some alleles may code for the production of enzymes that are efficient at breaking down neurotransmitters,

Table 2.1   Candidate genes associated with antisocial phenotypes

Gene	Abbreviation(s)	Functionality
Dopaminergic genes		
Dopamine transporter gene	DAT1	Codes for the production of the dopamine transporter protein; implicated in the reuptake of dopamine
Dopamine receptor genes	DRD2, DRD3, DRD4, DRD5	Involved in the detection of dopamine at the postsynaptic neuron
Serotonergic genes		
Serotonin transporter gene	5-HTTLPR	Codes for the production of the serotonin transporter protein; implicated in the reuptake of serotonin
Serotonin receptor genes	5HTR2A, 5HTR1B, 5HTR2C	Involved in the detection of serotonin at the postsynaptic neuron
Tryptophan hydroxylase gene	TPH	An enzyme that facilitates the conversion of the amino acid tryptophan into serotonin
Enzymatic breakdown genes		
Catechol-O-methyltransferase gene	COMT	Codes for the enzyme, COMT, which metabolizes neurotransmitters, including dopamine, epinephrine, and norepinephrine
Monoamine oxidase A	MAOA	Codes for the enzyme, MAOA, which metabolizes neurotransmitters, including dopamine and serotonin

whereas other alleles may code for the production of enzymes that are not as efficient at breaking down enzymes. This will become important as we move into the discussion of candidate genes for antisocial phenotypes. For now, just keep in mind that enzymes and transporter proteins (that are involved in the process of reuptake) are both vitally important in maintaining normal levels of neurotransmitters in the synapse. And, the production of enzymes and transporter proteins is determined by genes, some of which are polymorphic.

We now have all of the necessary information needed to explore the genetic polymorphisms that may be associated with antisocial phenotypes. Numerous candidate genes have been identified[45], and more and more are being discovered each year, making it nearly impossible to examine all of these genes. Consequently, we will focus our attention on three broad systems of genes: genes from the dopaminergic system, genes from the serotonergic system, and genes implicated in the production of enzymes that metabolize neurotransmitters.[46] Table 2.1 provides a list of some of these genes, as well as their functions. Let us begin by exploring some of the dopaminergic genes.

Dopaminergic polymorphisms. Dopamine is an excitatory neurotransmitter that activates postsynaptic dopamine receptors, making an action potential more likely to occur in the postsynaptic neuron. Dopamine is part of the reward system of the human body and the release of dopamine is accompanied by feelings of euphoria. These euphoric feelings act as the body's natural reward system and any action that stimulates the release of dopamine is likely to be repeated time and again. Sleeping, eating, and sexual intercourse are all relatively pleasurable and are typically repeated because they all stimulate the release of dopamine. Likewise, the reason that some drugs, like cocaine and amphetamines, are highly addictive is because they hijack the dopaminergic system and artificially increase the amount of available dopamine in the synapse.

Baseline levels of dopamine vary from person-to-person and they also vary in response to certain environmental stimuli (e.g., eating a good meal). Most of the time, these fluctuations in dopamine levels remain in the normal range of variation and do not necessarily represent a risk factor for any particular phenotype. Sometimes, however, levels of dopamine are very low or very high, and these variations have been linked to an array of different maladaptive outcomes, including schizophrenia, anorexia, bulimia, and depression, among others.[47] There is also some evidence tying dopamine levels to antisocial phenotypes. The working assumption is that high levels of dopamine should confer an increased risk to violent and impulsive behaviors. Studies have used both human and non-human subjects to test this hypothesis and the results have provided some support in favor of the dopamine-aggression relationship.[48] The association between high levels of dopamine and aggressive behaviors should be viewed with caution; there is much conflicting evidence and there is even some research revealing that low levels of dopamine are related to greater involvement in aggressive behaviors.[49] It is quite possible, therefore that the relationship between dopamine levels and antisocial phenotypes is curvilinear (i.e., U-shaped), where both low and high levels of dopamine correspond to increases in antisocial phenotypes. For now, keep in mind that differential levels of dopamine have been able to explain variance in some antisocial phenotypes.

So why do dopamine levels vary? This is a complicated question because a lot of different factors contribute to dopamine levels. As mentioned previously, the environment most certainly will cause dopamine levels to wax and wane. Eating a juicy steak, for example, will cause dopamine levels to increase, while finding out that a loved one has just died will result in a drop in dopamine levels. But levels of dopamine also vary because of genetic reasons. Many of the genes that control the production, transportation, and metabolism of dopamine are polymorphic and some of these polymorphic genes have functional differences. What this means it that dopamine levels vary, in part, because of the different alleles that are inherited for these polymorphic genes.

The dopamine transporter gene (DAT1) codes for the production of the dopamine transporter protein, which is implicated in the reuptake of dopamine. DAT1 is a polymorphic gene that has a minisatellite (i.e., a VNTR) where a section of DNA can be repeated between 3 and 11 times. In other words, people can inherit an allele with a section of base pairs repeated 3 times (i.e., the 3-repeat allele), four times (i.e., the 4-repeat allele), five times (i.e., the 5-repeat allele), all the way up to eleven times (i.e., the 11-repeat allele). Geneticists have found some evidence indicating that the transporter protein coded for by the 10-repeat (10R) allele may be abnormally efficient at removing dopamine from the synapse during the reuptake process.[50]

Researchers have investigated the effect that DAT1 has on a range of antisocial phenotypes and the results of these studies have provided some evidence indicating that the 10R allele confers an increased risk of displaying antisocial tendencies. For example, two studies analyzing data from the National Longitudinal Study of Adolescent Health (Add Health) found that carriers of the 10R allele self-reported greater involvement in acts of serious violence and delinquency.[51] Additional research, using different samples, has also reported a link between the 10R allele and involvement in criminal and delinquent outcomes.[52]

There are also a number of receptor genes of the dopaminergic system that have been found to be related to myriad maladaptive outcomes. The dopamine D2 receptor (DRD2) gene, for instance, has an SNP that results in two alleles: the A1 allele and the A2 allele. The A1 allele has been found to increase the risk of alcoholism[53], drug use[54], gambling[55], and adolescent victimization[56], among others. In addition, there is some evidence tying the A1 allele to criminal and delinquent involvement.[57] Other dopamine receptor genes, including DRD3, DRD4, and DRD5, have also been found to be associated with maladaptive phenotypes, such as ADHD, impulsivity, gambling, and conduct disorder as well as criminal and delinquent behaviors.[58] Collectively, the results flowing from these studies thus provide some evidence that dopaminergic genes are associated with some antisocial phenotypes, but much more research is needed before any firm conclusions can be drawn.

Serotonergic polymorphisms. Serotonin is a neurotransmitter with inhibitory properties and the release of serotonin is thought to reduce innate drives, regulate behaviors, and control impulses. Serotonin can be thought of as the body's natural brake system and, as a result, biosocial criminologists have hypothesized that low levels of serotonin should relate to greater involvement in antisocial phenotypes. Although there is evidence to the contrary, an impressive line of research has found support for this contention.[59] The most compelling evidence for the serotonin-aggression link comes from two meta-analyses. The first meta-analysis consisted of twenty-eight studies that had tested for an association between levels of serotonin and antisocial outcomes.[60] The results of this meta-analysis revealed that there was a significant relationship between low levels of serotonin and antisocial behaviors. Importantly, the results also indicated the effect of serotonin was stronger and more consistent than were the effects of dopamine and norepinephrine. The second meta-analysis included twenty studies that had examined the relationship between the serotonin metabolite, 5-hydroxindoleacetic acid (5-HIAA), and antisocial behaviors.[61] The results of this study indicated that there was a statistically significant association between low 5-HIAA and a range of different violent and non-violent behaviors. Together these two meta-analyses provide relatively strong evidence indicating that serotonin is associated, in some capacity, with antisocial phenotypes, where low serotonin levels correspond with greater involvement in criminal and aggressive behaviors.

Similar to dopamine, levels of serotonin vary from person-to-person because of environmental factors and because of certain genetic polymorphisms that are involved in the production, transportation, and degradation of serotonin. The serotonin transporter promoter polymorphism (5-HTTLPR), for example, is responsible for coding for the production of the serotonin transporter protein, which is responsible for the reuptake of serotonin. The 5-HTTLPR has a 44-base-pair insertion/deletion (i.e., a minisatellite) that results in two different alleles: a long (L) allele and a short (S) allele. There is some evidence to indicate that this is a functional polymorphism, where the S allele, in comparison with the L allele, codes for the production of a transporter protein that has reduced reuptake activity.[62] In other words, the transporter proteins coded for by the S allele may not be as efficient as transporter proteins coded for by the L allele in removing serotonin from the synapse.

A considerable amount of empirical research has been conducted to examine whether there is a connection between alleles of the 5-HTTLPR polymorphism and a variety of antisocial phenotypes. The results of these studies have revealed that the S allele is associated with ADHD[63], nicotine dependence[64], alcohol consumption[65], and childhood conduct disorder[66] as well as childhood aggression.[67] Geneticists have also examined the association between 5-HTTLPR and more direct measures of violent and aggressive behaviors. The S allele of the 5-HTTLPR polymorphism has also been found to be able to differentiate violent offenders from nonviolent offenders, where violent offenders carry the S allele at higher rates than nonviolent offenders.[68] While these studies, along with others[69], provide some promise that the 5-HTTLPR may be related to antisocial phenotypes, these findings should be interpreted with caution because there is also evidence failing to detect a link between 5-HTTLPR and antisocial outcomes.[70]

In addition to 5-HTTLPR, there are also a number of serotonin receptor genes that are particularly promising candidate genes for antisocial phenotypes. These receptor genes code for the production of protein receptors that facilitate the detection of serotonin at the postsynaptic neuron. There are a handful of studies that have reported an association between three of these receptor genes—5HTR2A, 5HTR1B, and 5HTR2C—and a number of different antisocial outcomes.[71] However, given the limited empirical evidence bearing on these genes, it would be too hasty to make any definitive conclusions about the relationship between serotonin receptor genes and antisocial phenotypes. Lastly, there is some evidence to indicate that the tryptophan hydroxylase (TPH) gene may be related to impulsive behaviors. TPH codes for the production of an enzyme that is partially responsible for converting the amino acid tryptophan into serotonin. Although the evidence is mixed[72], some studies have revealed that alleles of the TPH gene may confer a risk to impulsive aggression and other antisocial phenotypes.[73] Given the limited empirical evidence bearing on the association that these genes have with antisocial phenotypes, the results from these studies should be viewed with caution.

Enzymatic breakdown polymorphisms. The last two genes that we will discuss in this chapter are those that code for the production of enzymes that breakdown neurotransmitters. The first gene, the catechol-O-methyltransferase gene (COMT), codes for the production of the COMT enzyme, which metabolizes neurotransmitters, such as dopamine, epinephrine, and norepinephrine. The COMT gene has a SNP that results in two different alleles: one that contains the codon ATG and one that contains the codon GTG (note that this SNP arises from a change in the first base of the codon, where A→G). The allele with the ATG sequence produces the amino acid methionine (known as the Met allele) and the allele with the GTG sequence produces the amino acid valine (known as the Val allele). This polymorphism is functional where the Met allele, in contrast to the Val allele, corresponds with reduced COMT activity. Researchers have speculated that the Met allele should increase the odds of antisocial phenotypes because COMT breaks down catecholamine neurotransmitters, which are thought to be positively correlated with antisocial phenotypes.

The available evidence is generally supportive of this hypothesis, where the Met allele has been found to be related to increases in aggressive personality traits[74], as well as aggressive and violent behaviors.[75] However, most of the studies that have reported a link between the Met allele and antisocial phenotypes have been conducted on samples of schizophrenics, raising concerns about the generalizability of the findings.[76]

The second enzymatic breakdown gene is the monoamine oxidase A (MAOA) gene, which codes for the production of the enzyme, MAOA. MAOA is one of the main enzymes responsible for breaking down neurotransmitters and, more specifically MAOA is involved in the catabolism of monoamine neurotransmitters, such as dopamine and serotonin. The MAOA gene has a 30 base-pair VNTR (a minisatellite) that can be repeated between two and five times (i.e., one allele has two repeats, another allele has three repeats, and so on). Some of the alleles correspond to the production of MAOA that is low functioning and some of the alleles correspond to the production of MAOA that is high functioning. Researchers have hypothesized that since low MAOA activity is not as efficient at clearing neurotransmitters from the synapse, then the low activity alleles, in comparison with the high activity alleles, should increase antisocial phenotypes.

Overall, there is mixed evidence on whether the MAOA genotype has any *direct* main effects on antisocial phenotypes. However, the research does appear to indicate that MAOA has a consistent effect on antisocial phenotypes in certain environmental contexts[77], a topic that we will discuss in great detail in the next chapter. For now, realize that there is some reason to suspect that COMT and MAOA may be implicated in the development of antisocial behaviors, but much more research is needed to unpack the true nature of these relationships.

Summary

Although criminologists use research designs (i.e., SSSMs) that assume genes have no effect on antisocial phenotypes, the available behavioral genetic studies provide persuasive evidence that genetic factors explain about one-half of the variance in antisocial phenotypes. With the recent mapping of the human genome, researchers have turned away from simply estimating the percentage of phenotypic variance that is accounted for by genetic factors, and have begun to examine whether measured genetic polymorphisms can explain phenotypic variance. The results of these studies have shown that certain genes—especially those involved in neuro-transmission—are associated with certain antisocial phenotypes. By no means should these findings be interpreted to mean that the environment is unimportant. As we will see in the next chapter, genes and the environment are intimately inter-twined and the effects that genes have on a phenotype are often conditioned by the environment.

Key Points

- Behavioral genetics is a field of study interested in estimating genetic and environmental influences on phenotypes.
- Heritability captures the degree to which genetic factors explain phenotypic variance.
- Shared environments refer to environments that are the same between siblings.
- Nonshared environments refer to environments that are different between siblings
- The most common type of research design used by behavioral geneticists is the twin-based research design.
- Monozygotic (MZ) twins share 100 percent of their DNA, while dizygotic (DZ) twins share, on average, about 50 percent of their DNA.
- Behavioral genetic research has revealed that about one-half of the variance in antisocial phenotypes is due to genetic factors.
- Behavioral genetic research has also revealed that about 30 percent of the variance in antisocial phenotypes is due to the nonshared environment and the remaining 20 percent of variance is due to the shared environment.
- Monozygotic twins reared apart (MZAs) have also indicated that about 50 percent of the variance in phenotypes is due to genetic factors.
- MZA research has revealed that MZ twins who are reared together are no more similar to each other when compared with MZ twins who are reared apart.
- Researchers analyzing samples of adoptees have also reported strong genetic influences on antisocial phenotypes.
- Molecular genetic studies examine whether particular genetic polymorphisms are associated with antisocial phenotypes.
- Deoxyribonucleic acid (DNA) is the genetic blueprint that orchestrates the development and functioning of the human body.
- Adenine (A), thymine (T), guanine (G), and cytosine (C) are the four bases that make up DNA.

- Genes code for the production of proteins.
- The process by which genes ultimately create proteins is known as the central dogma of molecular biology.
- Alleles are alternative copies of a gene.
- A gene that consists of at least two alleles is known as a genetic polymorphism.
- Single nucleotide polymorphisms (SNPs), microsatellites, and minisatellites are three types of genetic polymorphisms.
- Polygenic effects are the main way in which genetic variance produces phenotypic variance.
- Genes work in a probabilistic fashion, where different alleles of a polymorphism can increase or decrease the odds of displaying a particular phenotype.
- Genes that are involved in neurotransmission are among the most promising candidate genes for antisocial phenotypes.
- Neurons are nerve cells found in the brain.
- Neurons are not physically wired together, but rather are separated from each other by small gaps, known as synapses.
- Neurotransmitters are chemical messengers that allow neurons to communicate with each other.
- Dopamine is an excitatory neurotransmitter
- Serotonin is a neurotransmitter with inhibitory properties.
- COMT and MAOA are enzymes that breakdown neurotransmitters and terminate their activity.

1. Behavioral genetic research has shown that _____ explain phenotypic variance.

   a) genetic factors
   b) shared environmental factors
   c) nonshared environmental factors
   d) all of the above

2. Phenotypic variance captures _____ on a phenotype.

   a) person-to-person similarities   c) genetic effects
   b) person-to-person differences   d) environmental effects

3. Nonshared environmental factors refer to environments that are _____ between siblings from the same household.

   a) the same   b) different   c) important   d) unimportant

4. The two types of heritability are _____ and _____ heritability.

   a) broad, broader   c) broad, narrow
   b) narrow, narrower   d) broader, narrower

5. Shared environmental factors make siblings _____ to each other on a phenotype.

   a) more similar   c) neither of the above
   b) more dissimilar   d) both of the above

6. Behavioral genetic research has indicated that about _____ of the variance in antisocial phenotypes is due to genetic factors.

   a) zero   b) twenty-five   c) fifty   d) ninety

7. If we knew that the cross-twin correlation for monozygotic twins was .50 (rMZ = .50) and we also knew that the cross-twin correlation for dizygotic twins was .30 (rDZ = .30), what would the heritability estimate be equal to?

   a) .10   b) .20   c) .30   d) .40

8. Monozygotic twins who were reared apart (MZAs) share _____, but do not share _____.

   a) all of their environments, their DNA
   b) all of their DNA, their environments
   c) some of their DNA, their environments
   d) none of the above

9. What is the base pair sequence that would bond with the following series of bases: TTATTCCGGAATTCA?

   a) AATAACGCCTTAAGT   c) AATAAGGCCTTAAGT
   b) AATAAGGCCTTATGT   d) AATAAGGGGTTAAGT

10. Single nucleotide polymorphisms are the result of alleles that differ because of _____.

   a) a short section of DNA repeated a number of different times
   b) a long section of DNA repeated a number of different times
   c) a change in one nucleotide
   d) none of the above

11. Neurons are _____.

   a) nerve cells found in the spinal cord
   b) nerve cells found in muscles
   c) nerve cells found in tendons
   d) nerve cells found in the brain

12. Neurotransmitters are removed through the synapse by
    _____ and _____.

    a) reuptake, reprocessing   c) reuptake, enzymes
    b) reprocessing, enzymes   d) none of the above

13. What do genes do?

    a) They are solely responsible for making people act in certain ways.
    b) They are solely responsible for making criminals.
    c) They code for the production of criminals.
    d) They code for the production of proteins.

14. Dopamine and serotonin are _____.

    a) amino acids   c) polypeptides
    b) enzymes   d) neurotransmitters

15. COMT and MAOA are _____.

    a) amino acids   c) polypeptides
    b) enzymes   d) neurotransmitters

1. Discuss what heritability estimates can and cannot reveal about genetic influences on antisocial phenotypes. At the same time, also discuss the difference between broad heritability and narrow heritability.

2. Discuss how behavioral genetic methodologies represent a major improvement over standard social science methodologies (SSSMs).

3. Explain the central dogma of molecular biology. (Hint: discuss transcription and translation.)

4. Explain how neurotransmitters are removed from the synapse. (Hint: discuss reuptake and enzymatic breakdown.)

5. Skeptics of behavioral genetic research often argue that all twin-based research is flawed because the equal environments assumption (EEA) is violated. Discuss whether the EEA is violated and whether it casts doubt on behavioral genetic research.

6. List the different ways that twin-based research may artificially deflate heritability estimates.

7. Describe how the monozygotic twins reared apart (MZA) research design can be used to estimate genetic influences on phenotypes.

8. Choose one type of genetic polymorphism and describe it.

9. Contrast monogenic effect, polygenic effects, and pleiotropic effects. Do these three different effects contribute equally to antisocial phenotypes?

10. What is the relationship between dopamine levels and antisocial phenotypes? Be sure to discuss some of the literature bearing on this association.

Further Reading

Carey, G. (2003). *Human genetics for the social sciences.* Thousand Oaks, CA: Sage.

Carson, R. A., & Rothstein, M. A. (1999). *Behavioral genetics: The clash of culture and biology.* Baltimore, MD: John Hopkins University Press.

Kendler, K. S., & Prescott, C. A. (2006). *Genes, environment, and psychopathology: Understanding the causes of psychiatric and substance use disorders.* New York: The Guilford Press.

Plomin, R. (1990). *Nature and nurture: An introduction to human behavioral genetics.* Pacific Grove, CA: Brooks/Cole.

Plomin, R., DeFries, J. C., McClearn, G. E., & McGuffin, P. (2008). *Behavioral Genetics,* 5th Edition. New York: Worth.

Reiss, D., Neiderhiser, J. M., Hetherington, E. M., & Plomin, R. (2000). *The relationship code: Deciphering genetic and social influences on adolescent development.* Cambridge, MA: Harvard University Press.

Segal, N. L. (1999). *Twins and what they tell us about human behavior.* New York: Dutton.

Wright, L. (1997). *Twins and what they tell us about who we are.* New York: John Wiley and Sons.

End Notes

1. Plomin, R., DeFries, J. C., McClearn, & McGuffin, P. (2008). *Behavioral genetics*. Fifth edition. New York: Worth Publishers.

2. Walsh, A. (2002). *Biosocial criminology: Introduction and integration*. Cincinnati, OH: Anderson.

3. Caspi, A., Moffitt, T. E., Morgan, J., Rutter, M., Taylor, A., Arseneault, L., Tully, L., Jacobs, C., Kim-Cohen, J., & Polo-Thomas, M. (2004). Maternal expressed emotion predicts children's antisocial behavior problems: Using monozygotic twin differences to identify environmental effects on behavioral development. *Developmental Psychology, 40*, 149–161; Harris, J. R. (1998). *The nurture assumption: Why children turn out the way they do*. New York: Free Press.

4. Beaver, K. M. (2008). Nonshared environmental influences on adolescent delinquent involvement and adult criminal behavior. *Criminology, 46*, 501–530.

5. Button, T. M. M., Rhee, S. H., Hewitt, J. K., Young, S. E., Corley, R. P., & Stallings, M. C. (2007). The role of conduct disorder in explaining the comorbidity between alcohol and illicit drug dependence in adolescence. *Drug and Alcohol Dependence, 87*, 46–53.

6. The cross-twin correlation for MZ twins (rMZ) represents the upper bound for heritability. If the heritability estimate ever exceeds rMZ then nonadditive sources of genetic variance contribute to the phenotypic variance. For a more detailed discussion see: Plomin, R., Chipuer, H., & Loehlin, J. (1990). Behavioral genetics and personality. In L. Pervin (Ed.), *Handbook of personality theory and research*. New York: Guilford.

7. Not all of the effects subsumed under h^2 are due purely to genetic factors and not all of the effects subsumed under c^2 and e^2 are purely environmental. Heritability estimates also include the effects of gene X environment interactions, where genetic factors interact with shared environmental factors. In addition, heritability estimates also include the effects of gene X environment correlations, where genetic factors are correlated with nonshared environmental factors. Shared environmental estimates also include the effects of gene X environment correlations between genetic factors and shared environmental factors. Nonshared environmental estimates also include measurement error as well as the effects of gene X environment interactions between genetic factors and nonshared environmental factors. Chapter 3 will discuss gene X environment interactions and gene X environment correlations. For details see: Purcell, S. (2002). Variance components models for gene-environment interaction in twin analysis. *Twin Research, 5*, 554–571.

8. Moffitt, T. E. (2005). Genetic and environmental influences on antisocial behaviors: Evidence from behavioral-genetic research. *Advances in Genetics, 55,* 41–104.

9. Mason, D. A., & Frick, P. J. (1994). The heritability of antisocial behavior: A meta-analysis of twin and adoption studies. *Journal of Psychopathology and Behavioral Assessment, 16,* 301–323; Miles, D. R., & Carey, G. (1997). Genetic and environmental architecture of human aggression. *Journal of Personality and Social Psychology, 72,* 207–217; Rhee, S. H., & Waldman, I. D. (2002). Genetic and environmental influences on antisocial behavior: A meta-analysis of twin and adoption studies. *Psychological Bulletin, 128,* 490–529.

10. For a great overview of the genetic influences on all different types of crime correlates see: Baker, L. A., Bezdjian, S., & Raine, A. (2006). Behavioral genetics: The science of antisocial behavior. *Law and Contemporary Problems, 69,* 7–46.

11. Arseneault, L., Moffitt, T. E., Caspi, A., Taylor, A., Rijsdijk, F. V., Jaffee, S. R., Ablow, J. C., & Measelle, J. R. (2003). Strong genetic effects on cross-situational antisocial behaviour among 5-year-old children according to mothers, teachers, examiner-observers, and twins' self-reports. *Journal of Child Psychology and Psychiatry, 44,* 832–848; Baker, L. A., Jacobson, K. C., Raine, A., Lozano, D. I., & Bezdjian. (2007). Genetic and environmental bases of childhood antisocial behavior: A multi-informant twin study. *Journal of Abnormal Psychology, 116,* 219–235.

12. Lyons, M. J., True, W. R., Eisen, S. A., Goldberg, J., Meyer, J. M., Faraone, S. V., Eaves, L. J., & Tsuang, M. T. (1995). Differential heritability of adult and juvenile antisocial traits. *Archives of General Psychiatry, 52,* 906–915.

13. Moffitt, T. E. (2005). The new look of behavioral genetics in developmental psychopathology: Gene-environment interplay in antisocial behaviors. *Psychological Bulletin, 131,* 533–554.

14. Gunderson, E. P., Tsai, A. L., Selby, J. V., Caan, B., Mayer-Davies, E. J., & Risch, N. (2006). Twins of mistaken zygosity (TOMZ): Evidence for genetic contributions to dietary patterns and physiologic traits. *Twin Research and Human Genetics, 9,* 540–549; Kendler, K. (1983). Overview: A current perspective on twin studies of schizophrenia. American Journal of Psychiatry, 140, 1413–1425. Kendler, K. S., Neale, M. C., Kessler, R. C., Heath, A. C., & Eaves, L. J. (1993). A test of the equal-environment assumption in twin studies of psychiatric illness. *Behavior Genetics, 23,* 21–27.

15. Cronk, N. J., Slutske, W. S., Madden, P. A., Bucholz, K. K., Reich, W., & Heath, A. C. (2002). Emotional and behavioral problems among female twins: An evaluation of the equal environments assumption. *Journal of the American Academy of Child and Adolescent Psychiatry, 41,* 829–837; Morris-Yates, A., Andrews, G., Howie, P., & Henderson, S. (1990). Twins: A test of the equal environments assumption. *Acta Psychiatrica Scandinavica, 81,* 322–326.

16. Horwitz, A. V., Videon, T. M., Schmitz, M. F., & Davis, D. (2003). Rethinking twins and environments: Possible social sources for assumed genetic influences in twin research. *Journal of Health and Social Behavior, 44,* 111–129.

17. Miele, F. (2002). *Intelligence, race, and genetics: Conversations with Arthur R. Jensen.* Boulder, CO: Westview, p. 98.

18. Schachter, F. F., & Stone, R. K. (1985). Difficult sibling, easy sibling: Temperament and wth within-family environment. *Child Development, 56,* 1335–1344.

19. Raine, A. (2002). The biological basis of crime. In J. Q. Wilson & J. Petersilia (Ed.), *Crime: Public policies for crime control.* Oakland, CA: ICS Press, p. 45.

20. Krueger, R. F., Moffitt, T. E., Caspi, A., Bleske, A., & Silva, P. A. (1998). Assortative mating for antisocial behavior: Developmental and methodological implications. *Behavior Genetics, 28,* 173–186.

21. Wright, L. (1997). *Twins and what they tell us about who we are.* New York: John Wiley and Sons, pp. 44; 47.

22. With MZAs, h^2 can be calculated by estimating a cross-twin correlation. According to some researchers, this cross-twin correlation (rMZA) is the heritability estimate. For a discussion of why rMZA equals heritability see: Lykken, D. T. (1995). *The antisocial personalities.* Hillsdale, NJ: Lawrence Erlbaum Associates; Rowe, D. C. (1994). *The limits of family influence: Genes, experience, and behavior.* New York: Guilford.

23. Tellegen, A., Lykken, D. T., Bouchard, T. J., Wilcox, K. J., Segal, N. L., & Rich, S. (1988). Personality similarity in twins reared apart and together. *Journal of Personality and Social Psychology, 54,* 1031–1039.

24. Bouchard, T. J., Lykken, D. T., McGue, M., Segal, N. L., & Tellegen, A. (1990). Source of human psychological differences: The Minnesota Study of Twins Reared Apart. *Science, 250,* 223–228; Bouchard, T. J., & McGue, M. (1990). Genetic and rearing environmental influences on adult personality: An analysis of adopted twins reared apart. *Journal of Personality, 58,* 263–292.

25. Mednick, S. A., Gabrielli, W. F., & Hutchings, B. (1984). Genetic influences in criminal convictions: Evidence from an adoption cohort. *Science, 224,* 891–894.

26. van den Oord, E. J. C. G., Boomsma, D. I., & Verhulst, F. C. (1994). A study of problem behaviors in 10- to 15-year old biologically related and unrelated international adoptees. *Behavior Genetics, 24,* 193–205.

27. See Mednick et al. (1984).

28. Raine, A. (1993). *The psychopathology of crime: Criminal behavior as a clinical disorder.* San Diego, CA: Academic Press.

29. Kaplan, J. M. (2000). *The limits and lies of human genetic research: Dangers for social policy.* New York: Routledge.

30. Evans, D. M., & Martin, N. G. (2000). The validity of twin studies. *GeneScreen, 1,* 77–79.

31. Segal, N. L. (1999). *Twins and what they tell us about human behavior.* New York: Dutton.

32. Plomin, R., DeFries, J. C., McClearn, G. E., & McGuffin, P. (2008).

33. Walsh (2002), p. 44.

34. Rowe, D. C. (2002). *Biology and crime.* Los Angeles, CA: Roxbury.

35. Mielke, J. H., Konigsberg, L. W., & Relethford, J. H. (2006). *Human biological variation.* New York: Oxford University Press; Redon, R., Ishikawa, S., Fitch, K. R., Feuk, L., Perry G. H. et al. (2006). Global variation in copy number in the human genome. *Nature, 444,* 444–454.

36. More specifically, a gene is considered a polymorphism if the rarer allele is inherited at least 1 percent of the time.

37. The environment also affects human phenotypes as well, a topic that will be covered in greater detail in Chapters 3 and 4.

38. Plomin, R., DeFries, J., Craig, I., & McGuffin, P. (2001). *Behavioral genetics.* Fourth edition. New York: Worth Publishers.

39. Genes also interact with the environment to produce phenotypic variance, a topic to which we will explore in Chapter 3. In the current chapter, we are only exploring the relationship between genotypic variance and phenotypic variance. This is not meant to imply that the environment it is unimportant, it simply is a way of introducing the important genetic background, background that most criminologists are lacking.

40. Ellis, L., & Walsh, A. (2000). *Criminology: A global perspective.* Boston, MA: Allyn and Bacon.

41. Beaver, K. M., Wright, J. P., & Walsh, A. (2008). A gene-based evolutionary explanation for the association between criminal involvement and number of sex partners. *Social Biology.* Forthcoming.

42. Beaver, K. M., Wright, J. P., DeLisi, M., & Vaughn, M. (2008). Gene-environment interplay and delinquent involvement: Evidence of direct, indirect, and interactive effects. *Journal of Adolecent Research.* Forthcoming.

43. A candidate gene is a gene that is thought to be involved in the development of a particular phenotype—in this case, antisocial phenotypes.

44. Dowling, J. E. (1998). *Creating mind: How the brain works.* New York: W. W. Norton; Kotulak, R. (1997). *Inside the brain: Revolutionary discoveries of how*

the mind works. Kansas City, MO: Andrews McMeel; LeDoux, J. (1996). *The emotional brain: The mysterious underpinnings of emotional life.* New York: Simon and Schuster.

45. Morley, K. I., & Hall, W. D. (2003). Is there a genetic susceptibility to engage in criminal acts? *Trends and Issues in Crime and Criminal Justice, 263,* 1–6.

46. This does not mean that these three systems of genes are the most important to antisocial behaviors or that other genes are not involved in the etiology of antisocial phenotypes. Rather, these genes are among the most studied thus providing an empirical support for the association between these genes and certain antisocial outcomes.

47. Clark, W. R., & Grunstein, M. (2000). *Are we hardwired? The role of genes in human behavior.* New York: Oxford University Press; Hamer, D., & Copeland, P. (1998). *Living with our genes: Why they matter more than you think.* New York: Doubleday.

48. Niehoff, D. (1999). *The biology of violence: How understanding the brain, behavior, and environment can break the vicious circle of aggression.* New York: The Free Press.

49. Raine (1993).

50. Swanson, J. M., Flodman, P., Kennedy, J., Spence, M. A., Moyzis, R., Schuck, S., Murias, M., Moriarity, J., Barr, C., Smith, M., & Posner, M. (2000). Dopamine genes and ADHD. *Neuroscience and Biobehavioral Reviews, 24,* 21–25.

51. Beaver, Wright, & Walsh (2008); Guo, G., Roettger, M. E., & Shih, J. C. (2007). Contributions of the DAT1 and DRD2 genes to serious and violent delinquency among adolescents and young adults. *Human Genetics, 121,* 125–136.

52. Burt, S. A., & Mikolajewski, A. J. (2008). Preliminary evidence that specific candidate genes are associated with adolescent-onset antisocial behavior. *Aggressive Behavior, 34,* 1–9.

53. Uhl, G., Blum, K., Noble, E., & Smith, S. (1993). Substance abuse vulnerability and D2 receptor genes. *Trends in Neuroscience, 16,* 83–88.

54. Munafo, M. R., Roberts, K., Johnstone, E. C., Walton, R. T., & Yudkin, P. L. (2005). Association of serotonin transporter gene polymorphism with nicotine dependence: No evidence of an interaction with trait neuroticism. *Personality and Individual Differences, 38,* 843–850.

55. Comings, D. E., Gade-Andavolu, R., Gonzalez, N., Wu, S., Muhleman, D., Chen, C., Koh, P., Farwell, K., Blake, H., Dietz, G., MacMurray, J. P., Lesieur, H. R., Rugle, L. J., & Rosenthal, R. J. (2001). The additive effect of neurotransmitter genes in pathological gambling. *Clinical Genetics, 60,* 107–116.

56. Beaver, K. M., Wright, J. P., DeLisi, M., Daigle, L. E., Swatt, M. L., & Gibson, C. L. (2007). Evidence of a gene x environment interaction in the creation of victimization: Results from a longitudinal sample of adolescents. *International Journal of Offender Therapy and Comparative Criminology, 51*, 620–645.

57. Beaver, K. M., Wright, J. P., DeLisi, M., Walsh, A., Vaughn, M. G., Boisvert, D., & Vaske, J. (2007). A gene x gene interaction between DRD2 and DRD4 is associated with conduct disorder and antisocial behavior in males. *Behavioral and Brain Functions, 3*, 30; Guo, Roettger, & Shih (2007).

58. For reviews see: Beaver, K. M. (2008). *The nature and nurture of antisocial outcomes.* New York: LFB Scholarly; Morley & Hall (2003).

59. Beaver, K. M. (2009). The biochemistry of violent crime. In C. J. Ferguson (Ed.), *Violent crime: Clinical and social implications.* Thousand Oaks, CA: Sage. Forthcoming; Raine, A. (1993).

60. Raine, A. (1993).

61. Moore, T. M., Scarpa, A., & Raine, A. (2002). A meta-analysis of serotonin metabolite 5-HIAA and antisocial behavior. *Aggressive Behavior, 28*, 299–316.

62. Lesch, K.-P., Bengel, D., Heils, A., Sabol, S. Z., Greenberg, B. D., Petri, S., Benjamin, J., Muller, C. R., Hamer, D. H., & Murphy, D. L. (1996). Association of anxiety-related traits with a polymorphism in the serotonin transporter gene regulatory region. *Science, 274*, 1527–1531.

63. Cadoret, R. J., Langebehn, D., Caspers, K., Troughton, E. P., Yucuis, R., Sandhu, H. K., & Philibert, R. (2003). Associations of the serotonin transporter promoter polymorphism with aggressivity, attention deficit, and conduct disorder in an adoptee population. *Comprehensive Psychiatry, 44*, 88–101.

64. Munafo, M. R., Roberts, K., Johnstone, E. C., Walton, R. T., & Yudkin, P. L. (2005). Association of serotonin transporter gene polymorphism with nicotine dependence: No evidence of an interaction with trait neuroticism. *Personality and Individual Differences, 38*, 843–850.

65. Herman, A. I., Philbeck, J. W., Vasilopoulos, N. L., & Depetrillo, P. B. (2003). Serotonin transporter promoter polymorphism and differences in alcohol consumption behaviour in a college student population. *Alcohol and Alcoholism, 38*, 446–449.

66. Cadoret, R. J., Langbehn, D., Caspers, K., Troughton, E. P., Yucuis, R., Sandhu, H. K., & Philibert, R. (2003).

67. Haberstick, B. C., Smolen, A., & Hewitt, J. K. (2006). Family-based association test of the 5HTTLPR and aggressive behavior in a general population sample of children. *Biological Psychiatry, 59*, 836–843.

68. Retz, W., Retz-Junginger, P., Supprian, T., Thome, J., & Rosler, M. (2004). Association of serotonin transporter promoter polymorphism with violence:

Relation with personality disorders, impulsivity, and childhood ADHD psychopathology. *Behavioral Sciences and the Law, 22*, 415–425.

69. Liao, D. L., Hong, C. J., Shih, H. L., & Tsai, S. J. (2004). Possible association between serotonin transporter promoter region polymorphism and extremely violent crime in Chinese males. *Neuropsychobiology, 50*, 284–287.

70. Beaver, K. M. (2006). *The intersection of genes, the environment, and crime and delinquency: A longitudinal study of offending.* University of Cincinnati. Unpublished dissertation.

71. Hawi, Z., Dring, M., Kirley, A., Foley, D., Kent, L., Craddock, N., Asherson, P., Curran, S. Gould, A., Richards, S., Lawson, D., Pay, H., Turic, D., Langley, K., Owen, M., O'Donovan, M., Thapar, A., Fitzgerald, M., & Gill, M. (2002). Serotonergic system and attention deficit hyperactivity disorder (ADHD): A potential susceptibility locus at the 5-HT(1B) receptor gene in 273 nuclear families from a multi-centre sample. *Molecular Psychiatry, 7*, 718–725; Morley, K. I., & Hall, W. D. (2003); Quist, J. F., Barr, C. L., Schachar, R., Roberts, W., Malone, M., Tannock, R., Basile, V. S., Beitchman, J., & Kennedy, J. L. (2000). Evidence for the serotonin HTR2A receptor gene as a susceptibility factor in attention deficit hyperactivity disorder (ADHD). *Molecular Psychiatry, 5*, 537–541.

72. Tang, G., Ren, D., Xin, R., Qian, Y., Wang, D., & Jiang, S. (2001). Lack of association between the tryptophan hydroxylase gene A218C polymorphism and attention-deficit hyperactivity disorder in Chinese Han population. *American Journal of Medical Genetics, 105*, 485–488.

73. New, A. S., Gelernter, J., Yovell, Y., Trestman, R. L., Nielsen, D. A., Silverman, J., Mitropoulou, V., & Siever, L. J. (1998). Tryptophan hydroxylase genotype is associated with impulsive-aggression measures: A preliminary study. *American Journal of Medical Genetics, 81*, 13–17; Staner, L., Uyanik, G., Correa, H., Tremeau, F., Monreal, J., Crocq, M. A., Stefos, G., Morris-Rosendahl, D. J., & Macher, J. P. (2002). A dimensional impulsive-aggressive phenotype is associated with the A218C polymorphism of the tryptophan hydroxylase gene: A pilot study in well-characterized impulsive inpatients. *American Journal of Medical Genetics, 114*, 553–557.

74. Rujescu, D., Giegling, I., Gietl, A., Hartmann, A. M., & Moller, H.-J. (2003). A functional single nucleotide polymorphism (V158M) in the COMT gene is associated with aggressive personality traits. *Biological Psychiatry, 54*, 34–39.

75. Jones, G., Zammit, S., Norton, N., Hamshere, M. L., Jones, S. J., Milham, C., Sanders, R. D., McCarthy, G. M., Jones, L. A., Cardno, A. G., Gray, M., Murphy, K. C., & Owen, M. J. (2001). Aggressive behaviour in patients with schizophrenia is associated with catechol-O-methyltransferase genotype. *British Journal of Psychiatry, 179*, 351–355; Volavka, J., Bilder, R., & Nolan, K. (2004). Catecholamines and aggression: The role of COMT and MAO polymorphisms. *Annals of the New York Academy of Sciences, 1036*, 393–398.

76. Beaver, K. M. (2008). Molecular genetics and crime. In Walsh, A., & Beaver, K. M. (Eds.), *Biosocial criminology: New directions in theory and research.* New York: Routledge, pp. 50–72.

77. Kim-Cohen, J., Caspi, A., Taylor, A., Williams, B., Newcombe, R., Craig, I. W., & Moffitt, T. E. (2006). MAOA, maltreatment, and gene-environment interaction predicting children's mental health: New evidence and a meta-analysis. *Molecular Psychiatry, 11,* 903–913.

Gene-Environment
Interplay Explained

Introduction

The previous chapter discussed behavioral genetic research, where samples of siblings are analyzed to decompose phenotypic variance into genetic and environmental components. This line of research might leave the impression that genes and the environment are independent from each other and work in relative isolation. This simply is not the case, and the separation of genetic effects from environmental effects is an artificial bifurcation that does not adequately reflect reality.[1] Instead, the prevailing consensus among biosocial criminologists is that genes and the environment are mutually reinforcing and co-dependent. According to this line of reasoning, phenotypic variance, including variance in antisocial phenotypes, is created by the co-occurrence of genetic and environmental factors, a phenomenon that has come to be known as gene-environment interplay. This chapter will discuss three main types of gene environment interplay—gene X environment interactions, gene X environment correlations, and epigenetics—and examine how each one is linked to antisocial phenotypes.

Gene X Environment Interactions

Exposure to the same environments often produces a wide range of heterogeneous responses. Children exposed to neglectful and abusive environments, for example, are at risk for displaying antisocial behaviors later in life, but most abused children will mature into prosocial adults. Adolescents living in crime-ridden, impoverished neighborhoods are at risk for being arrested for serious violent offenses, but most will never have contact with the criminal justice system. Some parents, despite being loving and caring, will raise offspring who ultimately turn out to be criminal, while most children who are raised by detached, unresponsive parents will never be arrested for a crime. Even siblings raised in the same household turn out quite differently despite being exposed to many of the same environments. One child, for instance, may lead a life of crime, while their sibling may become a successful businessperson. Why do we see time and again the same environments produce very different outcomes? This is a particularly pressing question that is difficult for purely environmental explanations to answer. After all, if the environment is so powerful, we should see people exposed to the same environmental stimuli display very similar responses. This simply is not borne out.

The concept of gene X environment interaction (GxE), however, can shed some much-needed insight into why people do not always respond to the same environments in the same way. At the heart of GxE lies the fact that all people have their own unique genotype, and these unique genotypes produce different genetic predispositions. These predispositions, in turn, are responsible for creating differential susceptibilities to the same environments. A health-related example will help to make this point clearer. Smoking cigarettes is a major environmental risk factor for developing lung cancer, but not all people who smoke will be diagnosed with lung cancer. So, why are some smokers resilient to lung cancer, while others are susceptible? The answer appears to be found in genotype. Alleles of some single-nucleotide polymorphisms (SNPs) have been found to affect the odds of developing lung cancer, where smokers who possess certain alleles for these SNPs are at greater risk for developing lung cancer than smokers who do not carry these alleles.[2] It is the combination of environmental risk (e.g., smoking cigarettes) and genetic risk (e.g., having certain alleles) that leads to differential outcomes (e.g., developing or not developing lung cancer).

This same logic can be applied to antisocial phenotypes to understand why exposure to criminogenic environments will not inevitably lead to crime and why genetic risk will also not inevitably lead to crime. It appears as though genotype structures differential responses to environments, meaning that criminogenic environments have their strongest effect when they are paired with a genotype that is susceptible to antisocial phenotypes. Remove the vulnerable genotype and replace it with a not-so-vulnerable genotype, and the effect of the criminogenic environment will not be nearly as strong. Conversely, take someone with a vulnerable genotype, remove them from a high-risk environment and place them in a low-risk environment, and the effect of genotype will either evaporate or not be as strong. Now we are in position to state a formal definition of GxEs: the effect of the environment depends on the presence of genotype and the effect of genotype depends on the presence of the environment. From a GxE perspective it is easy to see why the same environments produce different outcomes—because some genotypes are more sensitive to the environment than are other genotypes.

Figure 3.1 provides a graphical depiction of GxEs. The left-hand circle in the figure represents genetic risk, while the right-hand circle represents environmental risk. The overlap between the two circles represents people who have both genetic risk and environmental risk for antisocial phenotypes, while the non-overlapping areas of the circle represent people who have only genetic risk or only environmental risk. As can be seen, antisocial phenotypes are most likely to surface for people who have both risk factors—precisely what is meant by GxEs.

The earliest research that attempted to test for GxEs on antisocial phenotypes used samples that consisted of adopted children. By using an adoption-based research design (see Chapter 2) researchers are able to compare the adoptee to their biological parent and to their adoptive parent. Genetic risk is present where the biological parent was arrested and environmental risk is present where the adoptive parent was arrested. The results of adoption-based studies have revealed that adoptees that have a biological parent who was arrested *and* an adoptive parent who was arrested are at greatest risk for becoming criminal.[3] These findings provided initial support for the role of GxEs in the development of antisocial phenotypes. Additional evidence for GxEs has also come from studies conducted by behavioral geneticists, where they calculate heritability estimates for samples that are exposed to different

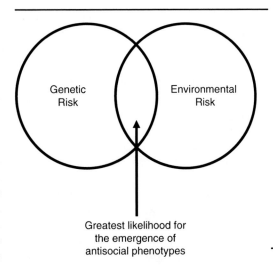

Figure 3.1
Depiction of gene x environment interactions in the production of antisocial phenotypes.

environments. For example, perhaps a research team was interested in determining whether there was an interaction between genetic factors and being reared by abusive parents in the prediction of antisocial behavior. To answer this question, the sample would be divided into two groups: one group would consist of persons who were reared by abusive parents and the other group would consist of persons who were not raised by abusive parents. Heritability estimates would then be calculated separately for each group. Evidence in support of a GxE would be garnered if the heritability estimates were larger for one group (e.g., the group of people who were raised by abusive parents) than for the other group (e.g., the group of people who were not raised by abusive parents). Behavioral genetic research designs have been important in highlighting the importance of GxEs in human phenotypes, but there is a drawback to this line of research: genetic risk is modeled as a latent factor, meaning that we do not know the specific genes that are implicated in the GxE.

In the past decade, researchers have moved away from modeling genetic risk as a latent factor and have begun to examine the effects that measured genetic polymorphisms have on behavioral phenotypes in the presence and absence of certain environmental stimuli. For example, suppose we were interested in examining whether a hypothetical gene, say Gene B, was associated with criminal offending. Suppose further that we also were interested in examining whether the effect of this gene varied depending on whether the person lived in a disadvantaged area or a non-disadvantaged area. Pretend that we found that Gene B was associated with criminal offending for people living in disadvantaged areas, but the effect of Gene B was not associated with criminal offending for people living in non-disadvantaged areas. Such a finding would be supportive of a GxE because the effect of Gene B was confined to persons residing in disadvantaged areas. This is the same type of analyses that researchers have used to test for GxEs in the production of antisocial phenotypes.[4]

Avshalom Caspi and his colleagues conducted the first study to detect a GxE between a measured gene and a measured environment on a behavioral phenotype.[5] They were interested in determining why childhood maltreatment produced antisocial behavior in some children, but not in others. They hypothesized that a polymorphism in the promoter region of the monoamine oxidase A (MAOA) gene (i.e., the gene that produces the enzyme, MAOA, which breaks down neurotransmitters) would affect susceptibility to childhood maltreatment. Different alleles of the MAOA gene have been linked to the production of differential activity levels of MAOA. One group of MAOA alleles codes for the production of high MAOA activity, while another group of MAOA alleles codes for the production of low MAOA activity. Caspi and his research team hypothesized that alleles that code for the production of low MAOA activity would be associated with displaying antisocial phenotypes. But there was a catch: they hypothesized that the effect of MAOA on antisocial phenotypes would only be observed for males who had been maltreated as a child—in other words, the MAOA gene would have no effect on antisocial phenotypes for non-abused males.

The reason that the effect of MAOA was thought to affect males but not females is because the MAOA gene is located on the X chromosome. Remember that males have one X chromosome, while females have two X chromosomes. As a result, males have only one copy of the MAOA gene, while females have two copies. What this means then is that if males inherit an allele that codes for the production of low MAOA activity, they do not have a "backup" copy to compensate for it. Females, in contrast, have two copies so even if they inherit an allele that codes for the production of low MAOA activity they have a "backup" copy that may code for the production of high MAOA activity.

Caspi et al. tested their hypothesis by analyzing data drawn from the Dunedin Multidisciplinary Health and Development Study. The results of their statistical models revealed that MAOA did not have a significant direct effect on the antisocial phenotype measures. However, the analyses did reveal that alleles that coded for the production of low MAOA activity increased antisocial problems for males who had been maltreated as children. In other words, there was a GxE between MAOA and childhood maltreatment, where the effect of MAOA only surfaced for maltreated males. The effect was relatively staggering: although only 12 percent of the sample had the low MAOA activity genotype *and* had been maltreated, they accounted for 44 percent of all violent convictions and 85 percent of them displayed antisocial phenotypes.

A number of follow-up studies have since been conducted to determine whether the GxE between MAOA and maltreatment would be observed in different samples. The results from some of these studies have upheld the MAOA X maltreatment interaction[6], but other studies have failed to find support for this GxE.[7] These divergent findings spawned Julia Kim-Cohen and her associates to conduct a meta-analysis of studies testing the MAOA X maltreatment interaction.[8] The results of this meta-analysis revealed that across five independent studies, the GxE between MAOA and maltreatment was a statistically significant predictor of antisocial phenotypes. Kim-Cohen and colleagues concluded by stating that "These findings provide the strongest evidence to date suggesting that the MAOA gene influences vulnerability to environmental stress, and that this biological process can be initiated early in life."[9]

Researchers have also tested for GxEs that involve genes other than MAOA and that involve environments other than maltreatment. The results garnered from these studies have provided even more support for the importance of GxEs in the etiology of antisocial phenotypes. Table 3.1 summarizes some of the studies that have detected statistically significant GxEs on antisocial phenotypes. The format of this table is relatively straightforward: the far left-hand column contains the polymorphism (i.e., the G in the GxE) that was studied, the middle column contains the environment (i.e., the E in the GxE), and the right-hand column contains the phenotypic outcome that was predicted by the GxE. In some situations, there was more than one environment that interacted with the polymorphism. As a result, each environment is numbered (for each polymorphism) and so too is each phenotypic outcome. The numbers can then be matched together to determine the phenotypic outcome that was predicted by the GxE. For example, look at DAT1. We can see that DAT1 interacted with alcoholic father (environment #1) to predict alcohol problems (phenotypic outcome #1). Similarly, we also see that DAT1 interacted with delinquent peers (environment #2) to predict number of police contacts and violence (phenotypic outcome #2) and DAT1 also interacted with family adversity (environment #3) to predict ADHD (phenotypic outcome #3).

It should also be noted that not all research shows that genetic effects are more powerful in high-risk as opposed to low-risk environments. Kevin Beaver and his colleagues, for example, examined the effect of DRD2 on adolescent victimization and found that the A1 allele increased victimization, but only among white males who had relatively few delinquent peers; there was no effect of DRD2 on victimization for white males who were exposed to a lot of delinquent friends.[10] Other studies have also detected stronger genetic effects in low-risk rather than high-risk environments.[11]

One of the most common explanations to these seemingly counterintuitive findings is that high-risk environments are so dominant that they can overshadow the effects that genes have on phenotypes. Take, for instance, the study by Beaver and associates showing that DRD2 did not have an effect on victimization for respondents with a relatively high number of delinquent peers. It is quite obvious that being in constant, daily contact with delinquent peers increases the odds of being victimized regardless of individual characteristics and genotype. However, in other situations, where a person is not exposed to delinquent peers as frequently, other factors are more likely to come into play (e.g., their temperament), and these other factors—many of which are genetically influenced—ultimately affect the chances of being victimized. Just keep in mind that the study of GxEs remains in its infancy and much more empirical research is needed to determine the complex ways in which certain genes interact with certain environments to create phenotypic variance.

Table 3.1   The effects of some gene X environment interactions on antisocial phenotypes

Polymorphism	Environment(s)	Phenotypic Outcome
DAT1	1. Alcoholic father 2. Delinquent peers 3. Family adversity	1. Alcohol problems[51] 2. Number of police contacts; violence[52] 3. ADHD[53]
DRD2	1. Delinquent peers 2. Religiosity 3. Family risk 4. Marital status 5. Marital stability 6. Criminal father	1. Victimization[54] 2. Violent delinquency[55] 3. Early-onset offending[56] 4. Desistance from delinquency[57] 5. Childhood ADHD[58] 6. Antisocial phenotypes[59]
DRD4	1. Marital status 2. Maternal insensitivity	1. Desistance from delinquency[60] 2. Externalizing behaviors[61]
5-HTTLPR	1. Delinquent peers 2. Antisocial parents	1. Number of police contacts[62] 2. Externalizing behaviors[63]
COMT	1. Birth weight	1. Early-onset antisocial behavior[64]
MAOA	1. Maltreatment 2. Neuropsychological deficits 3. Marital status	1. Antisocial phenotypes; conduct disorder[65] 2. Delinquency; low self-control[66] 3. Desistance from delinquency[67]

Gene X Environment Correlations

Gene X environment correlation (rGE) is the second type of gene-environment interplay. Where GxEs refer to the processes by which genes and the environment combine to produce phenotypic variance, rGEs capture the processes by which genotype structures differential exposure to environments.[12] This is a foreign concept to most criminologists because environmental measures are assumed to be purely social and not influenced by genetic factors. It seems somewhat odd to think that an environment could be due, in part, to genetic factors, but this is exactly what a line of quantitative research has revealed. Virtually every environment, from parental socialization to peer interactions, is partially influenced by genetic factors.[13] Below we will explore how genes and environment are correlated, but for now realize that there is reason to believe that rGEs may be more common than GxEs.[14] Lisabeth DiLalla added to this when she opined that "These correlations [rGEs] probably occur with most of the behaviors that we study, but they are extremely difficult to measure."[15] Before moving into a discussion of the literature bearing on rGEs, let us first discuss the three different types of rGEs: passive rGE, evocative rGE, and active rGE.

Passive rGEs are the result of biological parents passing along genotype and an environment to their children. Figure 3.2 shows that since genotype and the rearing environment are derived from the same source (i.e., parents) that the two will be positively correlated (as the double-headed arrow reveals). For example, suppose a child is born to two parents, both of whom are highly aggressive and antisocial. This child is at risk for being raised in an abusive and neglectful environment and, at the same time, they are also at risk for inheriting genetic predispositions for antisocial phenotypes. The end result is that the child's environment (i.e., abuse and neglect) is correlated with their genetic tendencies (i.e., genetic tendencies for displaying antisocial phenotypes).

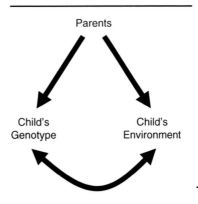

Evocative rGEs arise from genotype eliciting certain reactions from the environment and these reactions are positively correlated with genetic predisposition. Of course, genotype does not directly elicit reactions from the environment. Instead, and as Figure 3.3 depicts, genes influence the environment indirectly via phenotypes. The environmental reaction, which is a response to the phenotype, is then correlated with genotype (as depicted with the double-headed arrow). For example, suppose that a child has been diagnosed with conduct disorder (CD), a disorder which has been shown to be highly heritable.[16] Conduct disordered children are likely to evoke harsh discipline from their parents and they are also likely to be rejected by their same-age peers. As a result, the child's genetic predispositions (e.g., genetic factors for CD) are positively correlated with their environment (e.g., harsh discipline and peer rejection). Evocative rGEs probably can explain part of the reason why people with antisocial propensities tend to have difficulties in many spheres of their lives, such as relationship problems, employment and educational problems, economic problems, and so on.

Active rGEs refer to the integral role that genotype plays in the selection of environments that are compatible with genetic tendencies and that allow optimal genetic expression. Figure 3.4 contains a representation of an active rGE and shows that genotype will influence the choice and selection of one environment over another.[17] Why do musically inclined youths join the choir? Why do athletically talented adolescents play sports? Why do quiet and reserved adults veer away from loud, boisterous parties? Part of the reason is because genetically influenced traits (e.g., being a good singer, being a good athlete, and being shy) propel people into

Figure 3.2
Portrayal of a passive gene x environment correlation.

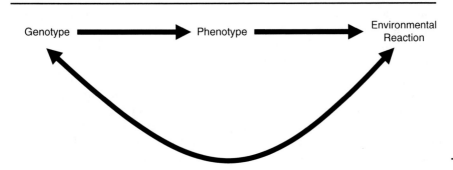

Figure 3.3
Portrayal of an evocative gene x environment correlation.

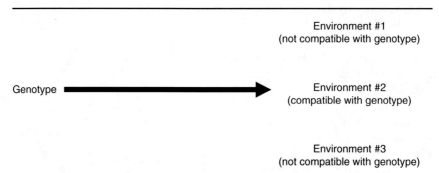

Figure 3.4
Depiction of an active gene x environment correlation.

or away from certain environments. In this way, genotype plays an active role in carving out niches that are compatible with genetic predispositions.

The formation of peer groups is also partially a function of rGEs. Some adolescents, for example, prefer to associate with delinquent peers, others prefer to associate with athletes, and still others prefer to associate with band members. How are these friendship networks formed? This is obviously a complex question, but we do know that peers tend to befriend other peers who share similar talents, interests, and beliefs—all of which are partially influenced by genetic factors. When a person chooses another friend on the basis of shared traits (which are genetically influenced), they are really choosing other friends on the basis of genetic factors. This necessarily translates into meaning that genotype is centrally involved in the formation of peer groups.

A criminological example with delinquent peers will help to make the concept of active rGE clearer. One of the strongest correlates to adolescent delinquency is affiliating with antisocial friends. There is debate among criminologists over whether contact with antisocial peers causes delinquency or whether delinquents seek out other delinquents to befriend. The evidence seems to indicate that both processes are at work, but it is the latter process—where delinquents befriend other delinquents—that can be explained by active rGEs. Why? Because we know that antisocial phenotypes are genetically influenced and we also know that delinquent peers befriend other delinquent peers. Consequentially, the genetic factors that are partially responsible for antisocial behavior are the same genetic factors that are driving delinquent youths to befriend each other.

An impressive body of research has examined rGEs on a wide array of environments. The most common way of testing for rGEs is by employing environmental measures as dependent variables. Heritability estimates are then calculated for these environments in the same way that heritability is calculated for behavioral phenotypes (see Chapter 2). In this case, it is possible to calculate, for example, the percentage of variance in an environment that is accounted for by genetic factors. rGEs are detected when the environment is found to be at least partially heritable. Once again, however, these types of studies model heritability as a latent factor, which tells us nothing about the particular genes that might be involved in the rGE. Recent rGE research has overcome this limitation and examined whether certain genetic polymorphisms explain a significant amount of variance in environmental measures. Below we will review both of these lines of literature, but let us begin with the results garnered from behavioral genetic research and then we will move into a discussion of the molecular genetic studies that have tested for rGEs.

There are simply too many behavioral genetic studies that have examined the heritability to environmental measures to be covered here. A recent review of the behavioral genetic literature by Kenneth Kendler and Jessica Baker, however, provides a thorough overview of the findings in respect to rGEs and will be the basis for our discussion.[18] Kendler and Baker reviewed fifty-five studies that had estimated the heritability of different environments. They divided the studies into different groupings based on the type of environment that was being examined. Four of these groupings are of particular relevance to criminological research: parenting behaviors, family environment, peer interactions, and stressful life events.

Parental socialization occupies a fundamental position within criminological scholarship. Almost every single criminological theory includes some aspect of parenting behaviors and most empirical-based research includes measures of parental socialization. Rarely, however, do criminologists ever entertain the idea that the parenting measures are genetically influenced. A line of behavioral genetic research has explored this possibility and Kendler and Baker's review examined 19 of them. These studies had estimated the genetic basis to dimensions of the parent-child relationship, including maternal and paternal warmth, maternal and paternal negativity, maternal and paternal control, and maternal and paternal monitoring. The studies revealed moderate heritabilities for these parenting environments with heritability estimates ranging between .12 and .37. Kendler and Baker also examined the heritability of family environments that extended beyond parenting behaviors. The environments that fell into this category included such measures such as family cohesion, family conflict, and family control. Once again, they found that the average heritabilities for these environments ranged between .18 and .30.

The next group of studies that were included in the review examined the heritability of peer interactions. Peer networks are of utmost importance to some of the major criminological theories, especially social learning theory, but criminologists have been slow to examine the heritability of peer groups. Kendler and Baker's review included six studies that had examined the genetics of peer interaction and overall they reported that the average heritability across studies was .21. It should be pointed out, however, that these studies indexed various dimensions of peer relationships, not necessarily contact with antisocial peers. There have been a number of studies conducted that estimate the heritability of delinquent peer exposure. The results from most of the studies have revealed heritability estimates of about .40 or higher[19], although it should be noted that at least one sample revealed a heritability estimate of only .03.[20]

Last, Kendler and Baker reviewed the studies that had examined the heritability of stressful life events. Stressful life events have been linked to various maladaptive outcomes, but within criminology, Robert Agnew's general strain theory focuses on different sources of strain, including stressful events, and how they facilitate antisocial behaviors.[21] Agnew's theory has accrued a good deal of empirical support[22], but again, criminologists have never examined the genetic underpinnings to stressful situations. A total of 10 studies examining the heritability of stressful life events were included in the review and the heritability estimates ranged between .24 and .47, with an average weighted heritability that was equal to .28.

The above evidence appears to indicate beyond a shadow of doubt that most environments are genetically influenced, or in the words of Kendler and Baker, "Genetic influences on measures of the environment are pervasive in extent and modest to moderate in impact."[23] The next step in the study of rGEs is to identify the precise genes that are associated with differential exposure to various environments. A small but ever-expanding body of research has begun to explore this issue and the results have revealed that genes involved in neurotransmission are correlated with different environments, including criminogenic environments.

The first study to report an rGE between a measured gene and a measured environment was conducted by Danielle Dick and her colleagues.[24] In this study, they were interested in examining the associations among marital status, alcohol dependence, and the GABRA2 gene (a gene which is involved in the transmission of the inhibitory neurotransmitter, GABA). The results of their analysis revealed that GABRA2 was related to alcohol dependence. Most importantly was that GABRA2 was also linked with marital status, where a SNP in GABRA2 was associated with the odds of being married. This latter finding was direct evidence of an rGE, most likely an active rGE.

Marital status has taken on great importance for life-course criminologists, where research has shown that offenders who marry are more likely to desist from crime than are offenders who remain single.[25] Although marriage is known to be a non-random event, where people choose to marry or not to marry (i.e., an active rGE), criminologists have never taken into consideration the role that genetic factors play in the decision to marry.[26] As with most criminological research, SSSMs are employed to examine the relationship between marital status and desistance, which leaves open the possibility that the marriage-desistance association is spurious, owing to unmeasured genetic factors.

The family environment has also been of interest to molecular genetic studies testing for rGEs. For example, Michael Lucht and his colleagues examined whether a polymorphism in the DRD2 gene was associated with negative paternal parenting.[27] The results of their study indicated an empirical link between alleles of the DRD2 gene and negative paternal parenting, where certain alleles corresponded to more paternal rejection. Another study, conducted by Kevin Beaver and John Shutt, also reported a link between dopaminergic genes and parenting behaviors.[28] More specifically, they examined the association between DAT1, DRD2, and DRD4 and maternal negativity, paternal negativity, and childhood maltreatment. The results of their analysis revealed that DRD2 was related to maternal negativity, paternal negativity, and childhood maltreatment, while DAT1 was associated with maternal negativity. DRD4 was unrelated to all of the parenting measures.

The results of these two studies could be interpreted as support for evocative rGEs, where children are equipped with genotypes that elicit certain responses from the environment—in this case, the environment would be parental socialization. The dopaminergic genes that were found to be involved in rGEs have also been found to confer an increased risk to developing antisocial phenotypes, such as ADHD and delinquency (see Chapter 2). Children and adolescents displaying these antisocial phenotypes, in turn, are likely to be difficult to manage and evoke harsh discipline and punishment from their parents. The findings could also be interpreted as support for passive rGEs, where parents who are excessively negative, harsh, and neglectful pass on genotypes that make their offspring difficult and taxing. The research designs employed by Lucht et al. and Beaver and Shutt, however, make it nearly impossible to disentangle evocative rGEs from passive rGEs.

Another study carried out by Lee Butcher and Robert Plomin employed a genome-wide scan to examine the association between 41 SNPs and a measure of family chaos.[29] The results of their study failed to detect any significant associations (beyond those that would have occurred by chance) between the SNPs and family chaos. However, Butcher and Plomin did not interpret these findings as evidence against rGEs. As they explained:

> The evidence for the heritability of measures of the family environment such as family chaos is persuasive, which implies that differences in DNA sequence are ultimately responsible for the heritability. It is likely that the DNA differences responsible for this heritability have such small or subtle effects that even more powerful strategies will be needed to detect them. Identifying genes associated with environmental measures will be worth the effort because they will foster research on an active model of experience in which individuals select, modify, and create environments on the basis of their genetic proclivities. In other words, genetic effects on behavior do not stop at the skin—genetic effects need to be considered in relation to an 'extended phenotype' that includes effects on individuals' environments.[30]

The last study to detect an rGE was published by Kevin Beaver and his colleagues.[31] They were interested in examining whether alleles of a polymorphism in the DAT1 gene were associated with differential exposure to delinquent peers. They analyzed data from the Add Health and found that DAT1 was predictive of delinquent peers for male adolescents. This finding provided the first empirical evidence linking a genetic polymorphism to the formation of delinquent peer groups, an example of an active rGE. What was also of particular interest in this study was that the effect of DAT1 on delinquent peers was only observed for males from high-risk families, not for males from low-risk families. This latter finding represents a GxE because the genetic effect (i.e., the effect of DAT1) was observed in one environment (i.e., high-risk families), but not in the other (i.e., low-risk families).

Beaver et al.'s research revealed that GxEs and rGEs can both be working simultaneously to create phenotypic variance. In fact, GxEs and rGEs are probably linked together in most phenotypes that are studied. To see how this is possible, let's revisit the three types of rGEs. First, and as Figure 3.5 shows, passive rGEs equip children with a genotype and with environment, both of which are likely to be

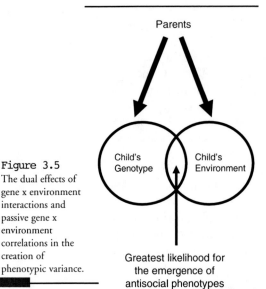

Figure 3.5
The dual effects of gene x environment interactions and passive gene x environment correlations in the creation of phenotypic variance.

correlated. But note that since genotype and environment are correlated, children will often be hit with a "double whammy" where they receive genetic risk and environmental risk. When both risk factors are present, then interactions between the two are likely to occur, which, in turn, may produce antisocial phenotypes.

Figure 3.6 shows the dual effect of GxEs and evocative rGEs in the creation of phenotypic variance. Remember that with evocative rGEs genotype is partially responsible for producing phenotypes and these phenotypes in turn elicit responses from the environment. For example, imagine a child with a genotype that produces serious violence during early adolescence. This youth, because of their antisocial behaviors, has problems at school and is eventually expelled. In short, their genotype was responsible for school failure, including the expulsion (i.e., an environmental reaction to their behavior), which underscores the logic of evocative rGEs. Being expelled from school likely places the antisocial youth in environments where they are not supervised and where they may be hanging out with other youths who have also been expelled. As a result, the adolescent will be in a criminogenic environment, one that is likely to interact with their genotype to produce even more antisocial phenotypes.

Last, Figure 3.7 depicts the dual effects of GxEs and active rGEs. Remember that with active rGEs genotype is partially responsible for nudging a person into environments that allow genetic expression. Chronic offenders, for example, are likely to select criminogenic environments, such as gangs and high-crime neighborhoods. Once in these criminogenic environments, the person's genotype is likely to interact with the environment to produce antisocial phenotypes. The important point to bear in mind is that GxEs and rGEs are not mutually exclusive but rather work simultaneously in the etiology of most human phenotypes, including antisocial phenotypes.

Figure 3.6
The dual effects of gene x environment interactions and evocative gene x environment correlations in the creation of phenotypic variance.

Genotype ➡ Phenotype ➡

Environmental Reaction   Vulnerable Genotype

Greatest likelihood for the emergence of antisocial phenotypes

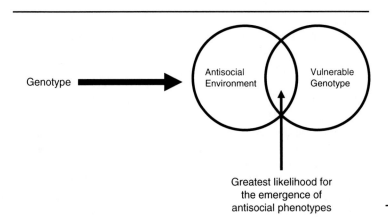

Genotype

Antisocial
Environment

Vulnerable
Genotype

Greatest likelihood for
the emergence of
antisocial phenotypes

Figure 3.7
The dual effects of
gene x environment
interactions and
active gene x
environment
correlations in the
creation of
phenotypic variance.

Epigenetics

The human genome consists of all the genes contained on the 23 pairs of chromosomes. Although genes provide the necessary instructions for humans to form, develop, and live, they need additional information to tell them when and where to code for proteins. Remember that DNA is found in the nucleus of every cell except red blood cells. This means that the DNA found in kidney cells is the same DNA found in liver cells. What, then, separates kidney cells from liver cells and what separates all other cells from each other? The answer to this question is relatively straightforward: only those genes that are needed for the functioning of the kidney (liver) are expressed (meaning that they actually code for the production of proteins), while all of the other genes are silenced (meaning that they do not code for the production of proteins). How does the human genome know which genes should be expressed and which genes should be silenced? This information is not contained in DNA, but rather in the epigenome.

The epigenome consists of chemical markers that are situated along the strands of DNA. These chemical markers affect gene activity because they alter the ability of DNA to be duplicated onto RNA. Some of these chemical markers enhance gene activity, whereas other chemical markers decrease or silent gene activity. Unlike the human genome that is immutable once formed, the chemical markers on the epigenome can actually be changed throughout life in response to the environment, and these epigenetic modifications can alter genetic expression. Since the epigenome partially controls the expression of the human genome, the epigenome is also partially responsible for producing phenotypes. Perhaps even more interesting is that these epigenetic modifications can be passed along from generation-to-generation.[32] This means that environmental stimuli can change a person's epigenome today and these epigenetic changes can be passed on to future generations.[33] If we return back to our original question, where we asked what separates a liver cell from a kidney cell, it appears as though the answer is found in the epigenome, where chemical markers direct genes to be "switched on" or "turned off" depending on the particular cell.

Epigenetic mechanisms thus alter DNA activity without altering DNA sequences.[34] There are numerous different epigenetic processes, but we will focus on two: DNA methylation and histone acetylation. Let us begin by discussing DNA methylation. Remember that epigenetic processes are partially responsible for why some genes are expressed in some cells (e.g., liver cells) but not in other cells (e.g., kidney cells). The silencing of genes is accomplished because an enzyme, called DNA methyltransferase, attaches a group of atoms, known as a methyl group (CH3), to the nucleotide cytosine (C in the genetic alphabet). But methylation is not likely to occur on all cytosine bases. There are blocks of DNA that are primarily made up of cytosine (C) bases and guanine (G) bases, and these dinucleiotide DNA sequences are referred to as CpG islands (the "p" indicates that the CG bases are held together by a phosphodiester bond). It is here, on cytosines on CpG islands, where methylation is most likely to occur. To understand why this is the case, it is important to note that certain sections of genes, known as promoter regions, act as switches that are able to turn genes "on" or "off" and CpG islands are located near those switches. These switches are turned on by special proteins called transcription factors. However, when a methyl group is attached to a cytosine base, the transcription factors are discouraged from turning the gene on. As a result, the transcription of DNA into RNA is prevented. If DNA cannot be transcribed into RNA, then the central dogma of biology does not occur. As a result, the protein specified by the particular gene will never be produced and that gene is turned "off" or silenced.[35] DNA methylation, in other words, is responsible for turning genes "off."

Histone acetylation is the second type of epigenetic process that we will discuss. In order to understand this epigenetic process, it is first necessary to point out that if DNA was uncoiled and stretched out it would measure about six feet in length. DNA needs to be packaged very efficiently in order to fit into the nucleus of each cell. This is accomplished with the help of histones. Histones can be thought of as spools around which DNA is wound very tightly. The tighter the DNA is wound, the less likely genes are to be expressed. Think of this: transcription factors are needed in order for a gene to be transcribed into RNA. When DNA is tightly wound around histones, transcription factors are not as easily able to access genes. As a result, genes that are inaccessible to transcription factors are unable to be decoded into proteins.

Histone acetylation occurs when acetyltransferase enzymes tack a group of atoms, known as an acetyl group (CH3CO), to the histone. This process loosens the DNA from the histone, which necessarily translates into transcription factors being able to access genes more readily. As a consequence of acetylation, genes are more likely to be turned "on" and expressed. Acetyl groups can be removed from histones via deacetylase enzymes, which results in the DNA becoming more tightly wound around the histone. And guess what this means? It means that genes are more likely to be turned "off" because transcription factors are less likely to be able to access the genes.

Let us recap four main points about epigenetics. First, epigenetic modifications can alter gene activity by turning genes "on" or "off." As a result, two people could have the exact same alleles for a gene, but due to epigenetic differences, the genes may be differentially expressed. Second, and as will be discussed in greater detail below, epigenetic modifications can occur in response to environments that are experienced from conception to death.[36] Diet and nutrition, smoking, and prenatal exposure to toxins are just a sampling of the many environments that are thought to result in epigenetic alterations. The important point to remember is that the environment by way of altering the epigenome may actually be responsible for turning genes "on" and "off." Third, these epigenetic modifications can be inherited. This is a particularly fascinating finding because it means that the environment can change the epigenome and these changes can actually be passed across generations. Fourth, epigenetic modifications are reversible and thus are particularly attractive targets for different types of interventions for certain diseases, such as cancer.[37]

So how do epigenetic modifications relate to human phenotypes, especially antisocial phenotypes? This is a difficult question to answer because no research has directly examined the connection between epigenetics and criminal outcomes.[38] But, the existing research does seem to indicate that a wide range of environments—some of which are studied by criminologists—are responsible for altering the epigenome. In a ground-breaking study, Ian Weaver and his colleagues studied maternal nurturing among rats.[39] They divided mother rats into two groups: those that licked and groomed their newborn pups and that engaged in arched-back nursing (the high-nurturing group) and those that rejected their newborn pups (the low-nurturing group). The newborn pups were then placed into stressful environments to see how they would react. The pups from the high-nurturing group were relatively calm and responsive, while those from the low-nurturing group were skittish and not as adaptive.

These findings, while interesting, left unanswered whether the association between nurturing and behavior was due to genetic factors, environmental factors, or both. So Weaver and associates then cross-fostered rats, where rat pups born to low-nurturing mothers and rat pups born to high-nurturing mothers were switched at birth. Cross-fostering is similar to the adoption-based research design and it helps to separate genetic from environmental effects. The cross-fostering experiment revealed that newborn pups resembled their "adoptive" mother more than their biological mother.

Most social scientists would have stopped there and concluded that these findings provided cold, hard evidence that socialization trumped genetics. Weaver et al., however, were cautious against making such a hasty conclusion and began to examine the methylation patterns of these rat pups. Their findings were striking: pups raised by high-nurturing mothers had less methylation of glucocorticoid receptor genes when compared to pups raised by low-nurturing mothers. Glucocorticoid receptors found in the hippocampus shape behavioral responses to stressful situations, and, in general, animals with less methylation of glucocorticoid receptor genes are better equipped to deal with stressful environments. Acetylation differences were also detected in genes associated with nerve growth in the hippocampus. These epigenetic differences emerged during the first week of life and persisted into adulthood. In some pups, Weaver and colleagues reversed the epigenetic patterns of the low-nurtured pups by administering a drug (trichostatin). Remarkably, the behavioral differences between low- and high-nurtured pups disappeared after the epigenetic patterns were equalized. In a

Figure 3.8
The possible
interrelationships
among criminogenic
environmets,
epigenetic
modifications, and
antisocial phenotypes.

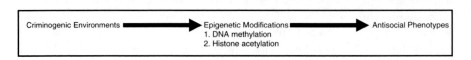

follow-up study this same research team identified more than 900 genes that were regulated by maternal care.[40]

These findings have direct bearing on criminology because most criminological theories identify nurturing and parental socialization as important factors implicated in the etiology of crime and delinquency. In a recent study, for example, Lee Ellis and his colleagues surveyed 1,218 criminologists worldwide about what they thought causes crime.[41] Parenting- and family-level factors, such as an unstable family life and lack of supervision and monitoring, ranked near the top. And, as was discussed in Chapter 1, most criminologists interpret the relationship between parent-level factors and antisocial phenotypes as evidence in favor of socialization. The study conducted by Weaver et al. casts doubt on such a simplistic one-to-one relationship and instead points to the likelihood that parents and other environments may exert their effects on antisocial phenotypes via changing the epigenome (see Figure 3.8). Criminologists have yet to take this idea seriously.

Studies using human samples have also detected epigenetic modifications by analyzing monozygotic (MZ) twin pairs. Even though MZ twins share 100 percent of their DNA, they often display divergent phenotypes. This is even true for genetically driven disorders, such as schizophrenia and autism. One of the more dominant explanations for divergent outcomes between MZ twins is that they are exposed to different nonshared environment and these nonshared environments may interact with genotype. If a pair of MZ twins is genetically predisposed to heart disease and one smokes but the other does not, then the smoker is much more likely to develop heart disease. From this example it is relatively easy to see that exposure to different environments led to genetic susceptibilities being triggered in one twin but not the other.

Epigeneticists, however, have offered a new twist for why MZ twins may turn out differently. According to them, exposure to different environments may actually alter the epigenome and these alterations may cause certain genes to be differentially expressed producing phenotypic differences.[42] Partial evidence in favor of this hypothesis was gathered by Mario Fraga and associates when they examined epigenetic differences in a sample of MZ twin pairs who were of different ages.[43] Young MZ twin pairs had virtually identical epigenetic patterns. Older MZ twin pairs, however, had 2.5 times as many epigenetic differences (as measured by DNA methylation patterns) as younger MZ twin pairs. These findings are particularly important because they indicate that for one reason or another epigenetic patterns change throughout the life course, and remember that these changes can affect gene expression.

The study by Fraga and colleagues was important because it showed that MZ twins, although genetically identical, may have their genes differentially expressed because of epigenetic modifications that arise throughout life. These epigenetic differences *could* lead to phenotypic differences, but Fraga's research team did not directly examine this possibility. The findings of some studies have, however, revealed that epigenetic differences are linked to phenotypic differences. A study by Arturas Petronis and associates, for example, explored the relationship between epigenetic modifications and schizophrenia in two pairs of MZ twins.[44] One pair of twins was concordant for schizophrenia (i.e., both twins had developed schizophrenia) and the other pair was discordant for schizophrenia (i.e., one twin had developed schizophrenia and one twin had not developed schizophrenia). They analyzed epigenetic patterns on the DRD2 gene in both sets of twins and their findings were truly amazing: the twin with schizophrenia (from the discordant twin pair) was epigenetically more similar to the two twins from the concordant twin pair (where both twins had schizophrenia) than they were to their own co-twin (who did not have schizophrenia). Additional studies have revealed that epigenetic modifications may be related to risk-taking behaviors[45], ADHD[46], childhood asthma[47], autism and other neurodevelopmental disorders[48], and bipolar disorder.[49]

Whether these findings could be extended to antisocial phenotypes remains unknown and as Anthony Walsh explains: "It is too early in the epigenetic game to go much beyond speculation, but for my money the possibilities are about as exciting and intriguing as anything that has come along in the behavioral sciences in the past 50 years."[50] If Walsh is correct, then the study of epigenetic modifications may prove to be especially valuable to criminologists in the 21st century.

Summary

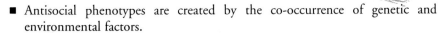

There is widespread recognition among biosocial criminologists that a complex arrangement of genetic and environmental factors work in tandem to produce variance in antisocial phenotypes. The close nexus between genes and the environment has become known as gene-environment interplay, and there are three main types of gene-environment interplay. The first, GxE, occurs when genetic effects only surface when paired with certain environments or when environmental effects only surface when paired with certain genetic factors. The second, rGE, occurs when genotype and the environment are correlated. The last type of gene-environment interplay is epigenetics, where the expression of genes is altered without altering DNA sequences. It is likely that all three of these processes work simultaneously to create phenotypic variance, including variance in antisocial phenotypes.

Key Points

- Antisocial phenotypes are created by the co-occurrence of genetic and environmental factors.
- People respond to the same environments in different ways because they have unique genotypes.

- Gene X environment interactions (GxEs) occur when the effect of genotype is contingent on the presence of a particular environment or when the effect of a particular environment is contingent on genotype.

- Findings from empirical research have underscored the importance of GxEs in the production of antisocial phenotypes.

- Gene X environment correlations (rGE) occur when genotype structures differential exposure to environments.

- Passive rGEs arise because parents pass along genotype and an environment to their children, both of which are positively correlated.

- Evocative rGEs arise when genotype elicits certain responses from the environment.

- Active rGEs arise when genotype is partially responsible for choosing environments that allow optimal genetic expression.

- A growing body of research has revealed that rGEs have direct application to the field of criminology.

- GxEs and rGEs are not mutually exclusive and both can occur simultaneously in the etiology of antisocial phenotypes.

- Epigenetic modifications alter the expression of genes without altering DNA sequences.

- The environment can cause changes to chemical markers on the epigenome.

- DNA methylation reduces the likelihood of genetic expression while histone acetylation makes genes more likely to be expressed.

- Although epigenetic changes have been connected to phenotypic outcomes, it is unknown exactly how epigenetics may relate to the development of antisocial phenotypes.

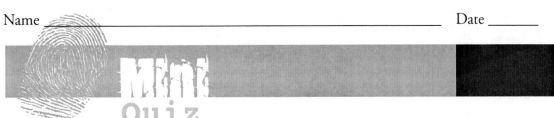

1. Antisocial phenotypes are created by _____.

    a) environmental factors only
    b) genetic factors only
    c) environmental and genetic factors
    d) none of the above

2. Genetic factors sometimes only have an effect on a phenotype when they are paired with certain environments. This is an example of a(n) _____.

    a) passive gene X environment correlation
    b) evocative gene X environment correlation
    c) active gene X environment correlation
    d) gene X environment interaction

3. At birth a child's genotype and their environment are often correlated. What concept best explains why this occurs?

    a) passive gene X environment correlation
    b) evocative gene X environment correlation
    c) active gene X environment correlation
    d) gene X environment interaction

4. _____ gene X environment correlations can partially explain the formation of delinquent peer groups.

    a) Passive   b) Evocative   c) Active   d) Epigenetic

5. _____ can partially explain why exposure to the same environments often produces different responses.

    a) Passive gene X environment correlations
    b) Evocative gene X environment correlations
    c) Active gene X environment correlations
    d) Gene X environment interactions

6. The environment _____ genetic expression via epigenetic modifications.

    a) can alter   c) always changes
    b) cannot alter   d) never changes

7. DNA methylation _____ genetic expression, while histone acetylation _____ genetic expression.

    a) reduces, reduces   c) increases, reduces
    b) increases, increases   d) reduces, increases

8. Epigenetic modifications alter genetic expression _____ DNA sequences.

    a) without changing   c) neither of the above
    b) by changing   d) both of the above

9. Gene X environment interactions and gene X environment correlations _____.

    a) are mutually exclusive
    b) are not mutually exclusive
    c) are unrelated to antisocial phenotypes
    d) none of the above

10. Antisocial phenotypes are most likely to surface for people _____.

    a) with genetic risk
    b) with environmental risk
    c) with both genetic and environmental risk
    d) none of the above

1. Describe gene X environment interactions. Be sure to discuss how gene X environment interactions can be applied to the study of criminal and delinquent behaviors.

2. Describe gene X environment correlations. Be sure to discuss how gene X environment correlations can be applied to the study of criminal and delinquent behaviors.

3. Explain the differences among passive gene X environment correlations, evocative gene X environment correlations, and active gene X environment correlations.

4. Discuss the different ways that gene X environment interactions and gene X environment correlations can simultaneously work to produce antisocial phenotypes.

5. What is epigenetics? Describe DNA methylation and histone acetylation.

Further Reading

Deater-Deckard, K., & Petrill, S. A. (2001). *Gene-environment processes in social behaviors and relationships.* New York: The Haworth Press.

Hernandez, L. M., & Blazer, D. G. (2006). *Genes, behavior, and the social environment: Moving beyond the nature/nurture debate.* Washington, DC: National Academies Press.

Jablonka, E., & Lamb, M. J. (2005). *Evolution in four dimensions: Genetic, epigenetic, behavioral, and symbolic variation in the history of life.* Cambridge, MA: MIT Press.

Plomin, R., & McClearn, G. E. (1993). *Nature and nurture and psychology.* Washington, DC: American Psychological Association.

Ridley, M. (2003). *Nature via nurture: Genes, experience, and what makes us human.* New York: Harper Collins.

Rutter, M. (2006). *Genes and behavior: Nature-nurture interplay explained.* Malden, MA: Blackwell.

End Notes

1. Ridley, M. (2003). *Nature via nurture: Genes, experience, and what makes us human.* New York: Harper Collins.

2. Hung, R. J., McKay, J. D., Gaborieau, V., Boffetta, P., Hashibe, M., et al. (2008). A susceptibility locus for lung cancer maps to nicotinic acetylcholine receptor subunit genes on 15q25. *Nature, 452*, 633–637.

3. Cadoret, R. J., Cain, C. A., & Crowe, R. R. (1983). Evidence for gene-environment interaction in the development of adolescent antisocial behavior. *Behavior Genetics, 13*, 301–310; Cadoret, R. J., Yates, W. R., Troughton, E., Woodworth, G., & Stewart, M. A. (1995). Genetic-environmental interaction in the genesis of aggressivity and conduct disorders. *Archives of General Psychiatry, 52*, 916–924; Mednick, S. A., Gabrielli, W. F., & Hutchings, B. (1984). Genetic influences in criminal convictions: Evidence from an adoption cohort. *Science, 224*, 891–894.

4. Perhaps the most common way of testing for GxEs is by calculating a multiplicative interaction term. However, it would be an erroneous assumption to equate GxEs with statistical interactions. Statistical interactions are one way to test for GxEs, but they are not the only way. See: Rutter, M., & Silberg, J. (2002). Gene-environment interplay in relation to emotional and behavioral disturbance. *Annual Review of Psychology, 53*, 463–490. In addition, not all GxE research examines a measured genetic polymorphism; some research has modeled genetic risk as a latent factor, and still other researchers have calculated heritability estimates for phenotypes in respondents who were differentially exposed to risky environments. We will discuss these issues at greater length in Chapter 7, but in this chapter we will focus only on those GxE studies that examined the effect of a measured gene on a behavioral phenotype.

5. Caspi, A., McClay, J., Moffitt, T. E., Mill, J., Martin, J., Craig, I. W., Taylor, A., & Poulton, R. (2002). Role of genotype in the cycle of violence in maltreated children. *Science, 297*, 851–854.

6. Foley, D. L., Eaves, L. J., Wormley, B., Silberg, J. L., Maes, H. H., Kuhn, J., & Riley, B. (2004). Childhood adversity, monoamine oxidase A genotype, and risk for conduct disorder. *Archives of General Psychiatry, 61*, 738–744.

7. Haberstick, B. C., Lessem, J. M., Hopfer, C. J., Smolen, A., Ehringer, M. A., Timberlake, D., & Hewitt, J. K. (2005). Monoamine oxidase A (MAOA) and antisocial behaviors in the presence of childhood and adolescent maltreatment. *American Journal of Medical Genetics Part B (Neuropsychiatric Genetics): 135B*, 59–64.

8. Kim-Cohen, J., Caspi, A., Taylor, A., Williams, B., Newcombe, R., Craig, I. W., & Moffitt, T. E. (2006). MAOA, maltreatment, and gene-environment interaction predicting children's mental health: New evidence and a meta-analysis. *Molecular Psychiatry, 11*, 903–913.

9. Kim-Cohen et al. (2006), p. 903.

10. Beaver, K. M., Wright, J. P., DeLisi, M., Daigle, L. E., Swatt, M. L., & Gibson, C. L. (2007). Evidence of a gene x environment interaction in the creation of victimization: Results from a longitudinal sample of adolescents. *International Journal of Offender Therapy and Comparative Criminology, 51*, 620–645.

11. DeLisi, M., Beaver, K. M., Wright, J. P., & Vaughn, M. G. (2008). The etiology of criminal onset: The enduring salience of nature *and* nurture. *Journal of Criminal Justice, 36*, 217–223; Rowe, D. C., Almeida, D. M., & Jacobson, K. C. (1999). School context and genetic influences on aggression in adolescence. *Psychological Science, 10*, 277–280.

12. Plomin, R. DeFries, J. C., & Loehlin, J. C. (1977). Genotype-environment interaction and correlation in the analysis of human behavior. *Psychological Bulletin, 84*, 309–322.

13. Jaffee, S. R., & Price, T. S. (2007). Gene-environment correlations: A review of the evidence and implications for prevention of mental illness. *Molecular Psychiatry, 12*, 432–442.

14. Plomin, R., & Davis, O. S. P. (2006). Gene-environment interactions and correlations in the development of cognitive abilities and disabilities. In J. MacCabe, O'Daly, O, Murray, R. M., McGuffin, P., & Wright, P. (Eds.), *Beyond nature and nurture: Genes environment and their interplay in psychiatry.* Andover, UK: Thomson.

15. DiLalla, L. F. (2002). *Behavior genetics of aggression in children: Review and future directions.* Developmental Review, 22, 593–622, p. 598.

16. Gelhorn, H. L., Stallings, M. C., Young, S. E., Corley, R. P., Rhee, S. H., & Hewitt, J. K. (2005). Genetic and environmental influences on conduct disorder: Symptom, domain, and full-scale analyses. *Journal of Child Psychology and Psychiatry, and Allied Disciplines, 46*, 580–591.

17. Scarr, S., & McCartney, K. (1983). How people make their own environments: A theory of genotype → environment effects. *Child Development, 54*, 424–435.

18. Kendler, K. S., & Baker, J. H. (2007). Genetic influences on measures of the environment: A systematic review. *Psychological Medicine, 37*, 615–626.

19. Cleveland, H. H., Wiebe, R. P., & Rowe, D. C. (2005). Sources of exposure to smoking and drinking friends among adolescents: A behavioral-genetic evaluation. *Journal of Genetic Psychology, 166*, 153–169; Fowler, T., Shelton, K., Lifford, K., Rice, F., McBride, A., Nivolov, I., Neale, M. C., Harold, G., Thapar, A., & van den Bree, M. B. M. (2007). Genetic and environmental

influences on the relationship between peer alcohol use and own alcohol use in adolescents. *Addiction, 102*, 894–903; Harden, K. P., Hill, J. E., Turkheimer, E., & Emery, R. E. (2008). Gene-environment correlation and interaction in peer effects on adolescent alcohol and tobacco use. *Behavior Genetics.* Forthcoming; Iervolino, A. C., Pike, A., Manke, B., Reiss, D., Hetherington, E. M., & Plomin, R. (2002). Genetic and environmental influences in adolescent peer socialization. Evidence from two genetically sensitive designs. *Child Development, 73*, 162–174; Kendler, K. S., Jacobson, K. C., Gardner, C. O., Gillespie, N., Aggen, S. A., & Prescott, C. A. (2007). Creating a social world: A developmental twin study of peer-group deviance. *Archives of General Psychiatry, 64*, 958–965.

20. Iervolino, A. C., Pike, A., Manke, B., Reiss, D., Hetherington, E. M., & Plomin, R. (2002). Genetic and environmental influences in adolescent peer socialization. Evidence from two genetically sensitive designs. *Child Development, 73*, 162–174.

21. Agnew, R. (1992). Foundation for a general strain theory of crime and delinquency. *Criminology, 30*, 47–87.

22. Agnew, R. (2006). General strain theory: Current status and directions for further research. In Cullen, F. T., Wright, J. P., & Blevins, K. R. (Eds.), *Taking stock: The status of criminological theory.* New Brunswick, NJ: Transaction.

23. Kendler, K. S., & Baker, J. H. (2007), p. 615.

24. Dick, D. M., Agrawal, A., Schuckit, M. A., Bierut, L. et al. (2006). Marital status, alcohol dependence, and GABRA2: Evidence for gene-environment correlation and interaction. *Journal of Studies on Alcohol, 67*, 185–194.

25. Sampson, R. J., & Laub, J. H. (1993). *Crime in the making: Pathways and turning points through life.* Cambridge, MA: Harvard University Press.

26. Some criminologists have tried to examine the marriage-desistance association after taking into account selection effects, such as by using propensity-score matching (PSM). While PSM is likely to capture some genetic effects, it cannot control for all genetic factors. See: King, R. D., Massoglia, M., & MacMillan, R. (2007). The context of marriage and crime: Gender, the propensity to marry, and offending in early adulthood. *Criminology, 45*, 33–66.

27. Lucht, M., Barnow, S., Schroeder, W., Grabe, H. J., Finckh, U., John, U., Freyberger, H. J., & Herrmann, F. H. (2006). Negative perceived paternal parenting is associated with dopamine D2 receptor exon 8 and GAB(A) alpha 6 receptor variants: An explorative study. *American Journal of Medical Genetics Part B (Neuropsychiatric Genetics), 141B*, 167–172.

28. Beaver, K. M., & Shutt, J. E. (2008). Evidence of gene x environment correlations between dopaminergic genes and parental negativity and maltreatment. Unpublished manuscript.

29. Butcher, L. M., & Plomin, R. (2008). The nature of nurture: A genomewide association scan for family chaos. *Behavior Genetics*, 38, 361–371.

30. Butcher & Plomin, 2008, p. 370.

31. Beaver, K. M., Wright, J. P., & DeLisi, M. (2008). Delinquent peer group formation: Evidence of a gene x environment correlation. *The Journal of Genetic Psychology, 169*, 227–244.

32. Holliday, R. (2006). Epigenetics: A historical review. *Epigenetics, 1/2,* 76–80.

33. Jablonka, E., & Lamb, M. J. (2005). *Evolution in four dimensions: Genetic, epigenetic, behavioral, and symbolic variation in the history of life.* Cambridge, MA: MIT Press.

34. Lopez-Rangel, E., & Lewis, M. E. S. (2006). Loud and clear evidence for gene silencing by epigenetic mechanisms in autism spectrum and related neurodevelopmental disorders. *Clinical Genetics, 69*, 21–25.

35. Corwin, E. J. (2004). The concept of epigenetics and its role in the development of cardiovascular disease: Commentary on "new and emerging theories of cardiovascular disease." *Biological Research for Nursing, 6*, 11–16.

36. Jaenisch, R., & Bird, A. (2003). Epigenetic regulation of gene expression: How the genome integrates intrinsic and environmental signals. *Nature Genetics (supplement), 33*, 245–254.

37. Fang, M. Z., Wang, Y., Ai, N., Hou, Z., Sun, Y., Lu, H., Welsh, W., Yang, C. S. (2003). Tea polyphenol (-)-epigallocatechin-3-gallate inhibits DNA methyltransferase and reactivates methylation-silenced genes in cancer cell lines. *Cancer Research, 63*, 7563–7570; Verma, M., & Srivastava, S. (2002). Epigenetics in cancer: Implications for early detection and prevention. *Lancet Oncology, 3*, 755–763.

38. Walsh, A. (2008). Criminal behavior from heritability to epigenetics: How genetics clarifies the role of the environment. In Walsh, A., & Beaver, K. M. (Eds.), *Biosocial criminology: New directions in theory and research.* New York: Routledge.

39. Weaver, I. C. G., Cervoni, N., Champagne, F. A., D'Alessio, A. C., Sharma, S., Seckl, J. R., Dymov, S., Szyf, M., & Meaney, M. J. (2004). Epigenetic programming in maternal behavior. *Nature Neuroscience, 7*, 847–854.

40. Weaver, I. C. G., Meaney, M. J., & Szyf, M. (2006). Maternal care effects on the hippocampal transcriptome and anxiety-mediated behaviors in the off-spring that are reversible in adulthood. *Proceedings of the National Academy of Sciences, 103*, 3480–3485.

41. Ellis, L., Cooper, J. A., & Walsh, A. (2008). Criminologists' opinions about causes and theories of crime and delinquency: A follow-up. *The Criminologist, 33*, 23–26.

42. Wong, A. H. C., Gottesman, I. I., & Petronis, A. (2005). Phenotypic differences in genetically identical organisms: The epigenetic perspective. *Human Molecular Genetics, 14*, R11–R18.

43. Fraga, M. F., Ballestar, E., Paz, M. F., Ropero, S., Setien, F., et al. (2005). Epigenetic differences arise during the lifetime of monozygotic twins. *Proceedings of the National Academy of Sciences, 102*, 10604–10609.

44. Petronis, A., Gottesman, I. I., Kan, P., Kennedy, J. L., Basile, V. S., Paterson, A. D., & Popendikyte, V. (2003). Monozygotic twins exhibit numerous epigenetic differences: Clues to twin discordance? *Schizophrenia Bulletin, 29*, 169–178.

45. Kaminsky, Z., Petronis, A., Wang, S.-C., Levine, B., Ghaffar, O., Floden, D., & Feinstein, A. (2008). Epigenetics of personality traits: An illustrative study of identical twins discordant for risk-taking behavior. *Twin Research and Human Genetics, 11*, 1–11.

46. Mill, J., & Petronis, A. (2008). Pre- and peri-natal environmental risks for attention-deficit hyperactivity disorder (ADHD): The potential role of epigenetic processes in mediating susceptibility. *The Journal of Child Psychology and Psychiatry*. Forthcoming.

47. Li, Y.-F., Langholz, B., Salam, M. T., & Gilliland, F. D. (2005). Maternal and grandmaternal smoking patterns are associated with early childhood asthma. *Chest, 127*, 1232–1241.

48. Lopez-Rangel, E., & Lewis, M. E. S. (2006). Loud and clear evidence for gene silencing by epigenetic mechanisms in autism spectrum and related neurodevelopmental disorders. *Clinical Genetics, 69*, 21–25.

49. Mill, J., Tang, T., Kaminsky, Z., Khare, T., Yazdanpanah, S., et al. (2008). Epigenomic profiling reveals DNA-methylation changes associated with major psychosis. *American Journal of Human Genetics, 82*, 696–711.

50. Walsh, A. (2008). Criminal behavior from heritability to epigenetics: How genetics clarifies the role of the environment. In Walsh, A., & Beaver, K. M., (Eds.), *Biosocial criminology: New directions in theory and research*. New York: Routledge, p. 45.

51. Vaske, J., Beaver, K. M., Wright, J. P., Boisvert, D., & Schnupp, R. (2008). An interaction between DAT1 and having an alcoholic father predicts serious alcohol problems in a sample of males. *Drug and Alcohol Dependence*. Forthcoming.

52. DeLisi, M., Beaver, K. M., Wright, J. P., & Vaughn, M. G. (2008). DAT1 and 5HTT are associated with pathological criminal behavior in a nationally representative sample of youth. Unpublished manuscript.

53. Laucht, M., Skowronek, M. H., Becker, K., Schmidt, M. H., Esser, G., Schulze, T. G., & Rietschel, M. (2007). Interacting effects of the dopamine

transporter gene and psychosocial adversity on attention-deficit/hyperactivity disorder symptoms among 15-year-olds from a high-risk community sample. *Archives of General Psychiatry, 64*, 585–590.

54. Beaver, K. M., Wright, J. P., DeLisi, M., Daigle, L. E., Swatt, M. L., & Gibson, C. L. (2007). Evidence of a gene x environment interaction in the creation of victimization: Results from a longitudinal sample of adolescents. *International Journal of Offender Therapy and Comparative Criminology, 51*, 620–645.

55. Beaver, K. M., Gibson, C. L., Jennings, W., & Ward, J. T. (2008). A gene x environment interaction between DRD2 and religiosity in the prediction of adolescent delinquent involvement in a sample of males. Unpublished manuscript.

56. DeLisi, M., Beaver, K. M., Wright, J. P., & Vaughn, M. G. (2008). The etiology of criminal onset: The enduring salience of nature *and* nurture. *Journal of Criminal Justice, 36*, 217–223.

57. Beaver, K. M., Wright, J. P., DeLisi, M., & Vaughn, M. G. (2008). Desistance from delinquency: The marriage effect revisited and extended. *Social Science Research, 37*, 736–752.

58. Waldman, I. D. (2007). Gene-environment interactions reexamined: Does mother's marital stability interact with the dopamine receptor D2 gene in the etiology of childhood attention-deficit/hyperactivity disorder? *Development and Psychopathology, 19*, 1117–1128.

59. DeLisi, M., Beaver, K. M., Wright, J. P., & Vaughn, M. G. (2008). Gene x environment interaction between DRD2 and father arrest is associated with six antisocial phenotypes. Unpublished manuscript.

60. Beaver, K. M., Wright, J. P., DeLisi, M., & Vaughn, M. G. (2008). Desistance from delinquency: The marriage effect revisited and extended. *Social Science Research, 37*, 736–752.

61. Bakermans-Kranenburg, M. J., & van IJzendoorn, M. H. (2006). Gene-environment interaction of the dopamine D4 receptor (DRD4) and observed maternal insensitivity predicting externalizing behavior in preschoolers. *Development and Psychobiology, 48*, 406–409.

62. DeLisi, M., Beaver, K. M., Wright, J. P., & Vaughn, M. G. (2008). DAT1 and 5HTT are associated with pathological criminal behavior in a nationally representative sample of youth. Unpublished manuscript.

63. Cadoret, R. J., Langbehn, D., Caspers, K., Troughton, E. P., Yucuis, R., Sandhu, H. K., & Philibert, R. (2003). Associations of the serotonin transporter promoter polymorphism with aggressivity, attention deficit, and conduct disorder in an adoptee population. *Comprehensive Psychiatry, 44*, 88–101.

64. Thapar, A., Langley, K., Fowler, T., Rice, F., Turic, D., Whittinger, N., Aggleton, J., Van den Bree, M., Owen, M., & O'Donovan, M. (2005). Catechol O-methyltransferase gene variant and birth weight predict early-onset antisocial behavior in children with attention-deficit/hyperactivity disorder. *Archives of General Psychiatry, 62*, 1275–1278.

65. Kim-Cohen et al. (2006).

66. Beaver, K. M., DeLisi, M., Vaughn, M. G., & Wright, J. P. (2008). The intersection of genes and neuropsychological deficits in the prediction of adolescent delinquency and low self-control. *International Journal of Offender Therapy and Comparative Criminology.* Forthcoming.

67. Beaver, K. M., Wright, J. P., DeLisi, M., & Vaughn, M. G. (2008). Desistance from delinquency: The marriage effect revisited and extended. *Social Science Research, 37*, 736–752.

An Introduction
To the Brain

Introduction

Chapters 2 and 3 explored the various ways that biological and environmental factors influence the development of antisocial phenotypes. Missing from this discussion, however, was the potential role that the brain plays in the production of human behaviors, including criminal and delinquent conduct. Over the past two decades or so, there has been an explosion of scientific research attempting to uncover the ways in which brain structure and brain functioning are connected to emotions, personality traits, and behaviors. This body of research has provided a tremendous amount of evidence indicating that the brain is involved in the etiology of almost every imaginable antisocial phenotype from violent aggression[1] to drug addiction[2] and from psychopathy[3] to sexual offending.[4] Even in the face of all this brain-based research, most sociological criminologists have failed to take seriously the effect that the brain may have on various criminal and delinquent outcomes.

The current chapter is designed to serve as an introduction to the brain and how it is related to antisocial phenotypes. Toward this end, the chapter will be laid out in four main sections. First, a brief overview of the anatomy of the brain will be provided, paying particular attention to those areas of the brain that might be implicated in antisocial phenotypes. Second, the imaging techniques that are used to examine the structure and function of the brain will be discussed. Third, the connection between the brain and antisocial phenotypes will be explored in detail. Fourth, the ways in which the brain can be applied to criminological research will be examined by using the examples of age and gender.

Anatomy of the Brain

Although weighing only a mere three pounds, the brain is the most infinitely complex entity in existence. It governs every thought, action, and feeling and it is also responsible for processing every bit of information encountered in the social world. Genetically speaking, the brain is "expensive," as more than 60 percent of the entire human genome codes for this single organ. Some of the genes that code for the brain are polymorphisms, and different alleles for some of these polymorphisms have been found to correspond to variation in specific regions of the brain. This is particularly important because, as will be discussed below, different regions of the brain are responsible for different tasks and functions. What all of this means, then,

Figure 4.1
The possible
connection among
genetic variation,
variation in the brain,
and phenotypic
variation.

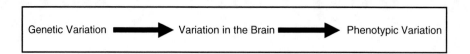

is that genetic polymorphisms, including the polymorphisms discussed in the previous chapters, may exert their influence on phenotypes indirectly by altering brain structure and functioning. Stated differently, genetic variation may cause variation in the brain, which, in turn, may lead to variation in antisocial phenotypes. Figure 4.1 shows this process graphically. Below we begin to explore the potential connection between the brain and antisocial outcomes by identifying and briefly describing the limbic system and the cerebral cortex (see Figure 4.2)—two of the main regions of the brain that have the most direct application to antisocial phenotypes. Later in the chapter, we will discuss the research tying some of these brain regions to antisocial phenotypes.

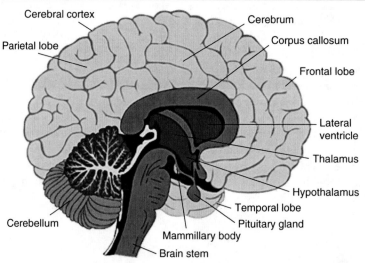

Figure 4.2
Cross-section of the
human brain.

Source: National Institute on Alcohol Abuse and Alcoholism of the National Institutes of Health

The limbic system. The limbic system has been identified as having a potentially very important role in the emergence of antisocial phenotypes. Located on top of the brainstem, the limbic system consists of primitive brain structures that are involved in a wide array of processes, especially generating emotions. When we encounter a scary stimulus, it is our limbic system that generates the emotion of fear, which sometimes causes us to flee without thinking. The limbic system works by affecting the endocrine system and the autonomic nervous system. More specifically, an environmental stimulus, such as seeing a masked-man, causes the limbic system to release hormones and other chemicals that alter the physiology of the body. This sudden influx of biochemicals produces different emotions and feelings which primes us to act in a particular way, such as running away from danger or preparing to fight. As we will see, however, the emotions that derive from the limbic system can be kept in check by the prefrontal cortex.

The limbic system is also implicated in long-term memory, including forming memories about specific stimuli that cause fear. For example, suppose that you walked down a dark alley and were attacked. Thanks to your limbic system, the next time you walk down a dark alley you will probably be anxious and fearful because of the memory of what had happened to you previously. The limbic system consists of a number of different structures, some of which are associated with antisocial phenotypes. One of the structures of the limbic system that is thought to be vitally important to aggression and other antisocial phenotypes is the amygdala.

The amygdala, an almond-shaped structure, is considered the emotional hub of the brain and is responsible for generating feelings such as anger, rage, and fear. The amygdala is extensively interconnected with other regions of the brain, including the prefrontal cortex, the brainstem, and the hypothalamus. Importantly, the amygdala is involved in emotional learning and fear conditioning. Emotional learning and fear conditioning refer to the processes whereby the presence of a stimulus is paired with a response. Over time, the presence of the stimulus will automatically produce the response. For example, suppose that every time you answered your phone you were given a small shock. After a few times of answering the phone and being shocked, you would come to anticipate a shock when picking up the phone. Fear conditioning also can explain the previous example with the dark alley, where encountering a dark alley (stimulus) brings about feelings of fear and anxiety (response).

Another component of the limbic system is the hippocampus. The hippocampus is an elongated structure that is primarily involved in the formation of long-term or declarative memories. The hippocampus does not store memories per se, but rather is vitally important in the laying down of new memories. What this means is that damage to the hippocampus will not erase memories (e.g., amnesia), but it will preclude the ability to form new ones. Persons who have their hippocampus removed are unable to create new memories, but they are able to remember events that had occurred prior to the surgery. Like the amygdala, the hippocampus is also involved in emotional learning and fear conditioning. Damage or insult to the hippocampus may impair memory formation, may result in cognitive impairments, and may interfere with normal human development.

The last two main structures of the limbic system are the thalamus and the hypothalamus. The thalamus is considered the brain's "relay station" because it receives incoming messages from systems throughout the body, it organizes and prioritizes those messages, and it then dispatches them to the cerebral cortex, where they are processed. Directly underneath the thalamus is the hypothalamus, which is involved in the regulation of visceral functions, including the modulation of body temperature. The hypothalamus has extensive connections with the hippocampus, and like the hippocampus, is involved in the production of long-term memories.

Also of importance is that the hypothalamus works in conjunction with the pituitary gland to release biochemicals, including stress hormones, such as cortisol, and sex hormones, such as testosterone. These chemicals, in turn, are partially responsible for how we view, interpret, and react to the social world. The ways in which the body responds to stress is also governed, in part, by what is known as the hypothalamic-pituitary-adrenal (HPA) axis. When stressful situations are encountered, the hypothalamus emits the hormone, corticotrophin releasing factor (CRF). CRF triggers the pituitary gland to release the adrenocorticotropic hormone (ACTH). Last, ACTH stimulates the adrenal glands to produce cortisol, which is the main stress hormone. Cortisol has a number of physiological effects on the body, including increasing blood pressure and blood sugar and impairing memory formation. Chronic stress can result in higher-than-normal cortisol levels and these elevated levels can persist over prolonged periods of time.

The cerebral cortex. The cerebral cortex, often referred to as the cerebrum or the neocortex, accounts for approximately two-thirds of the brain's volume. The cerebrum is divided in half by a large fissure that runs from the back of the brain to the middle of the forehead. This fissure separates the left hemisphere from the right hemisphere. The two hemispheres are connected to each other by a large bundle of fibers called the corpus callosum. The corpus callosum allows the two hemispheres to communicate with each other. When the corpus callosum is damaged or severed (a procedure sometimes employed to alleviate seizures in epileptics) information cannot be transferred from one hemisphere to the other.

The cerebral cortex, as well as other parts of the brain (e.g., the hypothalamus and the thalamus), consists of two types of matter: gray matter and white matter. To understand the difference between the two realize that gray matter refers to neuronal cell bodies and their synaptic connections. When cells are densely packed they create a grayish color—hence, the term gray matter. Gray matter is often used as a measure of the density of cells that are found in particular regions of the brain, and gray matter has been found to be positively correlated with cognitive abilities and skills, including intelligence.[5] White matter, in contrast, consists of myelinated axons. Myelinated axons are axons that are covered with a fatty sheath that increases the speed with which information is processed in the brain. Axons that are myelinated produce a whitish tint—hence, the term white matter. In very general terms, gray matter can be thought of as where information processing occurs, while white matter can be thought of as the means by which information is transferred throughout the brain.

The cerebral cortex is divided into four lobes: the occipital lobe, the parietal lobe, the temporal lobe, and the frontal lobe. Although all four lobes are critical to human functioning, we will spend most of our time discussing the frontal lobe. Briefly, the occipital lobe is located in the very back of the brain and is mainly responsible for vision. The parietal lobe is located in the center of the cerebral cortex and governs voluntary motor skills. The temporal lobe is found above the ears and is largely implicated in hearing and language. While there is some evidence linking these three lobes to maladaptive behaviors[6], biosocial criminologists have drawn particular attention to the role of the frontal lobe.[7]

The frontal lobe is found directly behind the forehead and is responsible for higher-order cognitive functions. In the most anterior part of the frontal lobe is found the prefrontal cortex. The prefrontal cortex accounts for about 30 percent of the human brain and is considered the CEO or executive controller of the brain. The prefrontal cortex is interconnected with the limbic system and is largely responsible for modulating the emotions that are generated from limbic system structures. One of the main reasons why we do not act on every emotion is because the prefrontal cortex curtails or suppresses emotionally charged behaviors. For example, suppose you were at a party and someone insulted you. Immediately your limbic system would probably generate the feelings of rage and anger, which would prime the body for a physical fight. Most of the time, however, a fight would not ensue because our prefrontal cortex would act as a "check" on these feelings and limit a behavioral response.

The prefrontal cortex is subdivided into three different regions.[8] The first region of the prefrontal cortex is the dorsolateral prefrontal cortex (DLPFC), which is located in the lateral part of the prefrontal cortex. The DLPFC is implicated in behavioral regulation, is involved in information-processing, and is necessary for working memory.[9] The DLPFC is also interconnected with the orbitofrontal cortex (OFC), which is the second region of the prefrontal cortex. The OFC is involved in goal-oriented behaviors, decision-making processes, and is thought to play an important role in the regulation of emotions. The third region of the prefrontal cortex is the medial prefrontal cortex (MPFC), which is found deep in the brain and is interconnected with the hypothalamus, the amygdala, and the DLPFC. The MPFC is implicated in activities that require a significant amount of attention and concentration.[10]

Although the DLPFC, OFC, and MPFC all perform slightly different functions, in reality they are tightly interconnected and work collaboratively. Together, the functions carried out by the entire prefrontal cortex are called "executive functions." Although definitions vary as to exactly what the executive functions entail, executive functions can be thought of as being involved in the ability to delay gratification, to anticipate the consequences of actions, to control impulses, and process complex information. Sharon Ishikawa and Adrian Raine[11] also advanced a description of executive functions when they stated that "Executive functions refer to a cluster of higher order cognitive processes involving initiation, planning, cognitive flexibility, abstraction, and decision making that allow the execution of contextually appropriate behavior." Terrie Moffitt, one of the leading experts on the brain-antisocial behavior link, described executive functions in the following passage:

> The normal functions of the frontal lobes of the brain include sustaining attention and concentration, abstract reasoning and concept formation, goal formulation, anticipation and planning, programming and initiation of purposive sequences of motor behavior, effective self-monitoring of behavior and self-awareness, and inhibition of unsuccessful, inappropriate, or impulsive behaviors, with adaptive

shifting to alternative behaviors. These functions are commonly referred to as 'executive functions,' and they hold consequent implications for social judgment, self-control, responsiveness to punishment, and ethical behavior.[12]

The above discussion underscores the importance of executive functions to behavioral control and emotional regulation. This is particularly important because acts of violence are often impulsive and unplanned, and criminals, moreover, are often characterized as lacking restraint and forethought, having low levels of self-control, and being impulsive. What this appears to mean is that the executive functions of criminals are not as efficient as the executive functions of non-criminals. "Executive dysfunction," according to Ishikawa and Raine, "is hypothesized to relate to antisocial and/or aggressive behavior by decreasing behavioral inhibition and impairing one's ability to generate socially acceptable responses in challenging situations."[13]

A meta-analysis conducted by Alex Morgan and Scott Lilienfeld revealed strong empirical support in favor of this claim.[14] They found, across 39 studies, that respondents who were classified as antisocial scored significantly worse on tests of executive function.[15] Exactly what accounts for variation in executive functions (i.e., why do criminals have reduced executive functions?) appears to be found in the human genome. A recent study by Naomi Friedman and colleagues, for example, analyzed a sample of twins and found a heritability estimate of .99 for executive functions, meaning that virtually all of the variation in executive functions was accounted for by genetic factors and that the environment explained none of the variation.[16] These findings add credence to the likelihood that genes exert their influences on phenotypes via the brain.

It should also be noted that the limbic system and the cerebrum are extensively interconnected and it is likely the interaction between the two that produces antisocial phenotypes. Tatia Lee and colleagues provided a succinct explanation of how the two systems may work together in the etiology of violence. According to them:

> The suppression of negative emotion is achieved via an inhibitory connection between the frontal and limbic regions. Therefore, any functional or structural abnormalities in one or more of these regions or their interconnections would be expected to increase the propensity for impulsive behavior due to the unsuccessful suppression of negative emotion...a combination of subcortial hyperactivity to negative affect stimuli combined with insufficient prefrontal regulatory resources results in emotion dysregulation and a predisposition to reactive aggression.[17]

In other words, if the limbic system generates strong negative emotions and if the prefrontal cortex is unable (for whatever reason) to control those emotions, then violence is a likely outcome.

Brain-Imaging Techniques

Researchers studying the brain and its relation to human behavioral phenotypes have made tremendous progress within the past few decades. Much of this progress can be traced to sophisticated brain-imaging (also called neuroimaging) techniques that are able to map brain structure and brain function. Brain structure refers to the size, length, volume, and any other quantifiable features of the brain and of the brain's structures. For example, it is possible to estimate the width of the corpus callosum and to measure the amount of gray matter in the frontal lobe. Brain functioning, in contrast, refers to the *processes* carried out by the brain. For example, researchers are able to examine how active different regions of the brain are when presented with certain stimuli. Biosocial criminologists are interested in determining whether variation in brain structure and variation in brain function correspond to variation in antisocial phenotypes. To understand how it is possible to examine the connection between the brain and behavior, it is first necessary to present an overview of the main neuroimaging techniques. We will begin by discussing the neuroimaging techniques used to assess brain structure, followed by a discussion of the neuroimaging techniques used to assess brain function.

The oldest brain imaging technique is the computerized tomography (CT) scan (also referred to as computed axial tomography [CAT] scan). Developed in the 1970s, and typically used to appraise brain injuries, CT scans assess the structure of the brain. With CT scans, X-rays are taken of the brain at more than 150 angles. A computer then measures the amount of radiation that is absorbed by the brain. This information is then processed to create a digitized picture of the brain, where denser brain structures are depicted as lighter. In this way, researchers are able to gain an estimate of the tomography of the brain. Although CT scans are relatively inexpensive, they are host to a number of limitations, including exposing subjects to X-rays and being ineffective at mapping the smaller brain structures. Most of the early research examining the link between the brain and antisocial phenotypes used CT scans.[18]

The second commonly employed brain-imaging technique used to assess brain structure is magnetic resonance imaging (MRI). Unlike CT scans that rely solely on X-rays, MRIs use radio waves and magnetic fields to produce high-resolution images of brain structure. To understand how MRIs work, it is first necessary to point out that brains consist of nuclei that are randomly distributed. The first step with an MRI is to organize the nuclei. This is accomplished by exposing the brain to high-powered magnets that cause the nuclei to align with the magnetic field. Radio waves are then transmitted to the brain which causes some of the nuclei to move differentially depending on the type of tissue (e.g., gray matter, white matter, blood, etc.). Finally, the transmission of radio waves is suspended which causes the nuclei to migrate back into alignment with the magnetic field. When the nuclei realign, a voltage in the magnetic field is created. Sensors are then used to measure these voltages and a computer processes the information to create a high-quality image of the brain.

MRIs can only assess the structure of the brain, but there have been recent developments in magnetic resonance technology that allow the *function* of the brain to be studied as well. A newer technique, known as functional magnetic resonance imaging (fMRI), measures brain function by assessing brain blood flow that is associated with neural activity. Neurons that are active consume oxygen and in order to replenish this oxygen more blood needs to be pumped to those areas.

Oxygenated blood and deoxygenated blood respond differentially to magnetic signals (magnetic signals repel oxygenated blood, while deoxygenated blood is attracted to magnetic fields) and these differences can be mapped using different methods. Areas of the brain that are active tend to have increased brain blood flow which typically corresponds to increased oxygenated blood in those brain regions. fMRI scanners then use this information to produce high-resolution images of brain function measured via brain blood flow.

The second imaging technique that can be used to analyze brain function is positron emission tomography (PET). When administering a PET scan, the patient is first injected with a radiotracer (i.e., flurodeoxyglucose), which contains a glucose analog and an isotope. Areas of the brain that are active expend energy and thus burn glucose (the only source of energy in the brain). The radiotracer is absorbed in greater quantities in those regions of the brain that are active. The isotope in the radiotracer emits gamma rays that are then analyzed by computers to produce images of metabolic activity. The isotope reveals where in the brain glucose is being burned and, by implication, what regions of the brain are active. PET scans are usually used to assess brain activity during fixed tasks.

Single photon emission tomography (SPECT) is another neuroimaging technique designed to assess the function of the brain. SPECT is used to measure regional cerebral blood flow (RCBF), which is an indirect way of indexing the activity level of regions of the brain. In general, the areas of the brain that are the most active have the greatest RCBF. With SPECT, patients typically inhale a radioactive gas that contains an isotope. Sensors are then affixed at various points around the patient's head. These sensors measure the amount of time it takes for the radioactive gas to reach various regions of the brain. The radioactive gas should reach the most active areas of the brain first because more blood is being pumped to those regions. Using this procedure it is then possible to construct a three-dimensional image of the activity level of the brain.

Variation in the Brain and Genetic Imaging

The brain-imaging techniques described above have provided a wealth of information about the structure and the function of the brain. One of the more interesting findings to emerge from this line of research is that there is much variability in brain structure as well as brain functioning. The prefrontal cortex, in particular, shows a high degree of person-to-person differences. Recently, brain science researchers have attempted to figure out whether variation in brain structure and brain function is under genetic control. To do so, they have used neuroimaging techniques in samples of monozygotic (MZ) and dizygotic (DZ) twins. Genetic influences on brain structure and function are detected when the brains of MZ twins are more similar to each other than the brains of DZ twins (see Chapter 2). The results of these studies have unequivocally shown that brain structure is largely influenced by genetic factors.

In a landmark study, Paul Thompson and his colleagues analyzed brain structure in a sample that consisted of MZ twins, DZ twins, and unrelated subjects.[19] Thompson et al. then compared the brains of MZ twins (from the same twin pair), the brains of DZ twins (from the same twin pair), and the brains of unrelated subjects (randomly paired together). The results of their study revealed that MZ twins' brains were more similar than DZ twins' brains and DZ twins' brains were more similar than the brains of unrelated subjects. Astonishingly, MZ twins had virtually identical patterns of gray matter. Taken together, these results provided empirical evidence of a strong genetic basis to brain structure. In the words of Thompson et al.: "A 95–100% correlation was revealed between MZ twins in frontal, linguistic, and parieto-occipital association cortices, suggesting individual differences in these regions can be largely attributed to genetic factors."[20] These results are mirrored by those garnered in additional studies showing that other brain structures, such as the corpus callosum[21], are also highly heritable.[22]

This unique approach of integrating a behavioral genetic research design into neuroimaging research has provided rich information showing that genetic influences are the dominant source of variation in the human brain. As with all behavioral genetic research, however, these findings are unable to provide any information about which particular genes are important. During the past decade, an emerging line of inquiry known as genetic imaging has overcome this limitation by examining whether particular alleles of certain polymorphisms are associated with differences in brain structure and brain functioning. In other words, genetic-imaging studies are interested in determining whether certain polymorphisms may be able to explain variation in the brain.

Recall that most of the candidate genes that are thought to play a role in the development of antisocial phenotypes are involved in neurotransmission (see Chapter 2). Genetic imaging researchers have examined these same genes to explore the association between dopaminergic, serotonergic, and enzymatic degradation genes and variation in brain structure and functioning.[23] The results of these studies have been quite revealing. To illustrate, Philip Shaw and colleagues examined the association between the dopamine D4 receptor (DRD4) gene, the dopamine D1 receptor (DRD1) gene, and the dopamine transporter (DAT1) gene and brain structure.[24] The results of their study indicated that persons who carried at least one copy of the seven-repeat allele of the DRD4 gene had thinning in regions of the brain (e.g., the orbitofrontal cortex) that are associated with attention and behavioral regulation. DAT1 and DRD1 were unrelated to brain structure. Similar results were garnered in another study where DRD4 was associated with gray matter volume in the prefrontal cortex.[25] This same study also reported that DAT1 was associated with variations in brain structure.

There is also some evidence tying a polymorphism in the serotonin transporter gene (5-HTTLPR) to variation in brain structure and brain function. Genetic-imaging studies have indicated that carriers of the short allele of the 5-HTTLPR polymorphism have reduced gray matter volume in limbic system structures, such as the amygdala[26], have more neuronal inputs into the limbic system[27], and have reduced gray matter volume in the cerebellum.[28] Functional brain differences, especially in the limbic system, have also been detected for the 5-HTTLPR polymorphism. For example, Ahmad Hariri and associates examined whether the 5-HTTLPR polymorphism was associated with amygdala activity levels in subjects who were presented with fearful stimuli.[29] The results of this study revealed greater activity in the amygdala (as measured by fMRIs) for subjects who carried at least one short allele of the 5-HTTLPR polymorphism. Other genomic-imaging studies have revealed similar findings, where carriers of the short allele have been found to have increased amygdala activation in response to a range of stimuli, including public speaking[30] and exposure to aversive images.[31]

Genetic-imaging studies have also examined whether variation in brain structure and function vary as a function of two enzymatic breakdown genes—the catechol-O-methyltransferase (COMT) gene and the monoamine oxidase A (MAOA) gene—both of which have been tied to antisocial phenotypes. The COMT gene, for example, has been found to be associated with differential activation of the prefrontal cortex during tasks that demand the use of executive functions,[32] during decision-making processes[33], and during the activation of working memory.[34] The MAOA gene has also been linked to brain function as well as brain structure. A study conducted by Andreas Meyer-Lindenberg and colleagues found that the low MAOA activity allele (the same allele that has been linked to antisocial phenotypes; see Chapter 2) was associated with reduced limbic volume, greater amygdala activation, and reduced prefrontal cortex activity.[35] For males, the MAOA genotype was also associated with orbitofrontal volume and activity levels in the amygdala and hippocampus. Taken together, these genetic-imaging studies provide empirical support linking certain polymorphisms to variation in brain structure and function. In the next section, we explore whether variation in the structure and functioning of the brain is linked to antisocial phenotypes.

The Brain and Antisocial Phenotypes

The neuroimaging techniques described above have been used to test the connection between the structure and function of the brain and antisocial phenotypes. In these studies, researchers typically compare the brains of a group of offenders to the brains of a control group. The brains of these two groups are then analyzed to determine if there are any differences (either structural or functional differences depending on the neuroimaging technique used). When a difference is detected, the conclusion usually drawn is that there is an association between the brain and antisocial behavior. This approach has been employed in an impressive amount of research to examine whether brain structure and functioning are related to a range of antisocial phenotypes from murder to pathological lying.[36] The following discussion, however, will focus on only two broad groups of offenders: murderers and psychopaths.

Adrian Raine and his colleagues conducted the first study to use neuroimaging techniques to explore brain functioning in murderers.[37] They scanned the brains of

22 murderers who pleaded not guilty by reason of insanity and compared them to the brains of 22 non-murderers who were matched on sex and age. The results of the PET scans revealed that murderers, in comparison with the control group, had lower metabolic activity in the prefrontal cortex. Another study, also conducted by Adrian Raine, compared the brain structure and function of 41 murderers who pleaded not guilty by reason of insanity to 41 non-murderers matched on age and gender.[38] Once again, the PET scans indicated that the murderers had reduced metabolic activity in the prefrontal cortex as well as the corpus callosum and areas of the brain implicated in behavioral regulation. They also reported structural differences in the amygdala, thalamus, and medial temporal lobe between the murderers and the control group.

The next study published by Adrian Raine examined brain functioning in a sample of 15 predatory murderers, nine affective murderers, and 41 controls.[39] Predatory murderers, generally speaking, are murderers who proactively seek out their victims and murder in cold blood. Affective murderers, in contrast, are murderers who are hot-headed and impulsive and typically murder in an act of rage. Raine and colleagues hypothesized that affective murderers, in comparison with predatory murderers, would have lower prefrontal cortex activity and higher limbic system activity. They speculated that an overactive limbic system would produce intense emotions, such as rage and anger, while an under-active prefrontal cortex would be less able to control these emotions. For example, suppose someone insulted you. You most likely would be angry, but your prefrontal cortex typically prevents you from acting on this rage. Pretend, however, that your limbic system was overly active. Now, this insult would produce even more intense anger and rage. And also pretend that your prefrontal cortex was not as active and thus was not as able to control your anger and rage. This is precisely the type of situation that would lead to affective murders. Predatory murder, however, requires planning and forethought, which necessarily means that predatory murderers should not have deficits in the prefrontal cortex. The results of the PET scans largely substantiated this hypothesis, where affective murderers, in contrast to predatory murderers and controls, had generally lower prefrontal cortex activity, while having higher limbic system activity.

These studies provided strong evidence that brain structure and function are associated with murder, but as Chapters 2 and 3 made clear, the environment is also important in the emergence of violent behaviors. Adrian Raine et al. took this into account by examining brain functioning in two groups of murderers: those who were reared in criminogenic environments (e.g., abuse, neglect, etc.) and those who were reared in "normal" environments.[40] This research team then compared the brain functioning of these two groups. The results were quite striking: murderers reared in normal environments had lower prefrontal cortex activity in comparison with murderers who were reared in criminogenic environments. Raine and colleagues speculated that criminogenic environments can produce violent offenders in the absence of biological predispositions. Persons reared in non-criminogenic environments, however, need a biological predisposition to become a violent offender. In this way, Raine's research emphasizes the importance of biology and the environment in the understanding of violent offending.

A number of studies have also used neuroimaging techniques to examine the brain structure and function of psychopaths. Psychopaths are among the most serious violent and dangerous offenders. They lie, steal, cheat, rape, rob, and otherwise prey on society. They are often described as lacking empathy, being egocentric and narcissistic, and they are pathological liars. Although estimates vary as to the prevalence of psychopathy, research tends to indicate that psychopaths are over-represented in prisons and they are disproportionately involved in the most physically violent crimes. This group of offenders thus represents some of the worse offenders.[41]

Brain-imaging researchers have analyzed samples of psychopaths and, similar to murderers, have found structural and functional impairments in the prefrontal cortex.[42] Raine and colleagues, for example, reported an 11 percent reduction in gray matter volume in the prefrontal cortex of 21 psychopaths in comparison with two control groups.[43] Other studies have detected functional differences in the prefrontal cortex of psychopaths, where metabolic activity in the prefrontal cortex tends to be lower in psychopaths than in controls.[44] In an innovative study, Yaling Yang et al. examined prefrontal gray matter volume in a sample of 16 unsuccessful psychopaths (i.e., they were caught and convicted of a crime), 13 successful psychopaths (i.e., they were not caught for their criminal behaviors), and 23 controls. MRIs revealed that unsuccessful psychopaths, in comparison with the control group, had reduced prefrontal gray matter in the prefrontal cortex. There was no difference in gray matter volume between successful psychopaths and the control group. The results of this study were explained by Yang and colleagues in the following way:

> Relatively intact prefrontal structure may provide successful psychopaths with both the cognitive resources to manipulate and con others successfully, as well as sufficiently good decision-making skills in risky situations to avoid legal detection and capture. In contrast, prefrontal structural deficits may render unsuccessful psychopaths particularly susceptible to poor decision making; interpersonally inappropriate, impulsive, disinhibited, unregulated, reward-driven antisocial behavior; and reduced sensitivity to environmental cues signaling danger and capture—factors placing them more prone to legal detection and conviction.[45]

In a different study, Raine's research team also used neuroimaging techniques to examine the structure and function of the corpus callosum in psychopaths.[46] Compared to controls, psychopaths had a 22.6 percent increase in white matter volume in the corpus callosum and a 6.9 percent increase in length, yet had a 15.3 percent reduction in the thickness of the corpus callosum. Why the corpus callosum is different in psychopaths is not known, but it appears as though the structural differences in psychopaths' corpus callosum may reflect some type of neurodevelopmental abnormality.

Neuroimaging studies have also detected structural and functional differences between psychopaths and non-psychopaths in the limbic system. For example, fMRIs have indicated that psychopaths, when compared to non-psychopaths, have reduced activity levels in the amygdala and in the hippocampus.[47] In addition to these functional differences, studies have also revealed structural differences in the hippocampi[48] and perhaps even the amygdala of psychopaths.[49]

Also of relevance are two additional neuroimaging studies that did not examine samples of psychopaths per se, but did examine behaviors that are common among psychopaths. In the first study, Yaling Yang and colleagues used MRIs to examine brain structure in a sample of 12 pathological liars and two control groups.[50] The results of their imaging analysis revealed that pathological liars, in comparison to subjects from the control groups, had increased white matter volume. The precise reasons for this relationship are not well understood, but it may be the case "that increased prefrontal white matter developmentally provides the individual with the capacity to lie."[51] In the second study, brain functioning was examined in a sample of spouse abusers. fMRIs indicated that spouse abusers, in comparison with non-spouse abusers, had more active limbic systems and less activity in the prefrontal cortex. According to the study authors, "The findings give rise to the provisional hypothesis that when exposed to aggressive stimuli, batterers have inadequate prefrontal resources to exercise top-down regulatory control over the excessive limbic activation generated by negative stimuli."[52]

Collectively, the results of these neuroimaging studies provide strong empirical evidence supporting the notion that brain structure and brain function are associated with antisocial phenotypes, especially violence. More specifically, the findings across these studies consistently revealed that compared to non-criminals, criminals had reduced activity in the prefrontal cortex and increased activity in the limbic system. These findings largely substantiate the claim that antisocial phenotypes are partially the result of an under-active prefrontal cortex and an overactive limbic system. We next turn to a discussion of how the brain can be integrated into criminology by showing its application to two of the most studied crime correlates: age and gender.

Applications to Criminology

Two of the strongest predictors of criminal and delinquent involvement are age and gender. In almost every sample, regardless of the country of origin and the historical time period, adolescents and males are overrepresented in acts of crime, especially in acts of serious violence.[53] Although numerous explanations have been advanced to explain the relationship between age and crime and the relationship between gender and crime, very little is known about how age and gender are linked to antisocial phenotypes, including crime. Below a rough sketch is presented showing that integrating the brain into criminology can provide some much needed insight into how and why age and gender are associated with antisocial outcomes.

Age and crime. One of the most robust correlates to antisocial behavior is age. Across virtually every study, age emerges as a statistically significant predictor of criminal and delinquent involvement. A wealth of research has indicated that delinquent behavior ceases to exist until around the age of 12 or 13 where it begins a sharp and steady incline. During adolescence, almost all youth engage in at least minor forms of delinquency, such as petty theft and underage drinking. By around the age of 18 or 19, the prevalence of delinquency begins a very sharp downward trend so that by the mid-to-late twenties most people have "aged out" of crime and no longer are delinquent. This general age-graded pattern of offending has been dubbed the "age-crime curve." Although much criminological scholarship has been devoted to studying and trying to explain the age-crime curve, criminologists have been unable to provide any "hard-and-fast" evidence on the causes of this phenomenon. But, as some biosocial researchers have pointed out, the brain may be the key to unlocking the underlying mechanisms that can explain the age-crime curve.[54] To understand how, let us explore brain development, paying particular attention to the adolescent brain.

Adolescents are, on average, poor decision makers. They skip school, they use drugs, they engage in unsafe sexual practices, they drive recklessly, they engage in delinquency and so on and so forth.[55] Numerous explanations have been advanced to explain these behaviors, ranging from peer pressure to the need for autonomy. While each of these explanations may hold a kernel of truth, they all fall short of providing a full-blown (and believable) account of why everywhere adolescents are more troublesome, aggressive, and impulsive than any other age-group. Recently, however, neuroscientific research has provided a compelling account for these age-graded behaviors: the brain.

Brain-imaging techniques have been used to plot the development of the brain from childhood through adulthood. The results of these studies have indicated that brain development does not commence during childhood or adolescence as once was believed, but instead continues to develop well into adulthood. At the onset of puberty, the adolescent's body and brain is flooded with chemicals and hormones, including testosterone, all of which stimulate certain parts of the brain. The amygdala, for example, is stimulated by testosterone and other chemicals produced in high concentrations during puberty, all of which are partially responsible for bringing about unstable emotional states. This is why adolescents may be calm and complacent one moment and yelling and screaming the next. But it is not just the influx of these biochemicals that explains youthful misconduct; the brain is also changing structurally. In particular, the limbic system, where emotions and feelings are generated, is fully developed by adolescence. Sex hormones (i.e., testosterone and estrogen) are overly active in the limbic system. What this means is that with the sudden influx of biochemicals, the limbic system is working overtime.

Usually the emotions flowing from the limbic system are controlled by the prefrontal cortex. But, guess what? The prefrontal cortex is not fully developed in adolescents; in fact, it does not finish developing until the mid-to-late twenties. This means that adolescents have an overactive limbic system (due to the surge of hormones) superimposed on a prefrontal cortex that is not structurally developed, all of which amounts to a recipe for disaster.[56] Perhaps Richard Restak, the eminent neurologist, said it best when he said that "the immaturity of the adolescent's behavior is perfectly mirrored by the immaturity of the adolescent's brain."[57] Some sociological criminologists are even finding it difficult to ignore the importance of the brain any longer. For example, Michael Benson, who is a sociologist by training, recognized the importance of the brain in adolescent delinquency when he opined:

> The teenage brain has a lot to do with teenage delinquency. When it comes to managing their behaviors, teenagers lack more than just experience and education; they also lack some of the mental equipment necessary to make sound judgments and to act responsibly. At the outset of the teenage years, our emotional inner life takes on a vividness that we have never experienced before and that our brain is not yet fully ready to handle. From a developmental perspective, the misperceptions, bad decisions, and emotional overreactions of teenagers are to a certain degree biologically programmed. Conformity is simply more difficult for teenagers than adults.[58]

Adolescent delinquency typically passes as quickly as it emerged. By the mid-to-late twenties, criminal and delinquent involvement is almost nonexistent. Perhaps not coincidentally, this is about the same age range in which the prefrontal cortex finishes developing. The prefrontal cortex, in other words, finishes maturing around the same age that criminal and delinquent involvement drop off considerably. The findings from these neuroimaging studies hint at the very real possibility that brain development may be the answer to the elusive question of what accounts for the relationship between age and crime.

The adolescent brain and the adult brain are not only different structurally, but they are also different neurochemically. In comparison with the adult brain, the adolescent brain has different baseline levels of certain neurotransmitters, some of which have been linked to antisocial phenotypes. Levels of serotonin (a neurotransmitter thought to inhibit criminal behavior; see Chapter 2) increase with age which necessarily means that concentrations of serotonin are lower in adolescents than in adults. Moreover, norepinephrine and dopamine, both of which are thought to facilitate antisocial behaviors, are found at relatively higher levels in adolescents than in adults. Perhaps part of the reason for why adults are better than adolescents at controlling their impulses and thus regulating their behaviors is because their levels of serotonin are higher, while their norepinephrine and dopamine levels are lower.[59] This remains pure speculation, however, because empirical research has yet to examine whether the age-graded fluctuations in these neurotransmitters are able to explain the age-graded fluctuations in delinquent and criminal behavior. Nonetheless, the neuroscientific research discussed above provides a new and refreshing explanation for why there is such a strong, consistent, and robust association between age and crime.

Gender and crime. A brute fact flowing from criminological research is that males are much more likely to engage in crime, especially violent crime, than are females. This gender effect has been observed in every country ever studied and at every time period.[60] Still, what causes males to be over-represented in violence and aggression remains unknown. One of the more common explanations advanced by sociological criminologists is that males and females are socialized differently. According to this line of reasoning, males are socialized to be dominant, assertive, aggressive, and violent. Females, in contrast, are socialized to be passive, docile, loving, empathetic, and caring. As a result of these different socialization patterns, males turn out to be more violent and criminal, while females turn out to be more coddling and affectionate. In keeping with their academic training, sociological criminologists also argue that biology plays virtually no role in creating these gender differences. The prevailing consensus among sociological criminologists, then, is that male-female differences in antisocial behavior are the result of differential socialization, not differences in biology. There is a problem with this explanation: there is not a shred of evidence to support it.

Consider, for example, the argument that culture shapes behavior, including criminal behavior. If this is true, then why are males more violent than females in every society ever studied? Surely, there should be some places where males are socialized to be passive and demure, while females are socialized to be aggressive and violent. This simply is not the case. Males are always and everywhere more violent and aggressive than females.[61] Still, sociological criminologists cling to their sociological roots and argue that parents socialize boys and girls differently, and these differences are what ultimately produce gender disparities in crime. Is there any empirical evidence to support this claim? Well, Hugh Lytton and David Romney set out to answer this question by examining whether parents actually socialize boys differently than girls.[62] To do so, they conducted a meta-analysis of 122 studies that had analyzed parental socialization in children. They looked at 19 different dimensions of parental socialization, including physical punishment, discouragement of aggression, and warmth, nurturance, and responsiveness. The results of their meta-analysis revealed that only one dimension of parental socialization—the encouragement of sex-typed activities—was significantly different between boys and girls. These findings are decimating to criminological theories that argue that the environment, including the family environment, is responsible for producing male-female differences in criminal involvement.

Criminologists have shied away from exploring the possibility that the brain may be able to explain the gender gap in offending behaviors. Part of the reason is because criminologists are not trained in neuroscience, and part of the reason is because it is a political minefield to talk of gender-based brain differences. As was pointed out in Chapter 1, however, scientific knowledge is accumulated by exploring all hypotheses, not just those that are politically correct or dovetail with the current ideology. With that said, it is interesting to learn that there is a considerable amount of research indicating that the brains of males and females are structurally and functionally different.[63] These differences, in turn, may be able to account—at least in part—for the overrepresentation of males in violent, aggressive, and antisocial phenotypes. Although morphological differences have been detected on various regions of the brain, we will focus on differences in the limbic system and differences in the prefrontal cortex.

Not surprisingly, structures in the limbic system, including the amygdala[64] and the hypothalamus[65], are relatively larger in males than in females, and these size differentials may partially explain why males are more likely to react to negative stimuli with physical violence.[66] Functional differences between males and females have also been observed for the amygdala. One study, for example, examined amygdala activity levels via PET scans. The results revealed that different regions of the amygdala were more active in males versus females and vice versa.[67] Neuroscience research has also explored gender-based differences in the prefrontal cortex. The results of these studies have revealed that females, on average, have relatively larger prefrontal cortexes than do males. But it is not just the size that matters; females also have greater activity levels in the prefrontal cortex, including the orbitofrontal cortex.[68] Taken together, the neuroscience research shows that males, when compared to females, have relatively larger limbic system structures coupled to a relatively smaller prefrontal cortex, which, according to some neuroscientists, "may explain gender differences in emotional behavior, particularly aggression."[69]

There is also some evidence indicating that levels of neurotransmitters are different between genders. Females tend to have higher levels of whole blood serotonin[70] and they also tend to have more serotonin receptors[71] than males. This is particularly important because remember that high levels of serotonin have been found to reduce antisocial phenotypes (see Chapter 2). Another neurotransmitter, -aminobutyric (GABA), also thought to inhibit violence and aggression, is found at higher concentrations in females.[72] Interestingly, there is some evidence to indicate that dopamine, a neurotransmitter thought to facilitate antisocial behaviors, is found at lower, not higher, levels in males than females.[73] It remains to be seen whether these gender differences in neurotransmitter levels are able to account for gender differences in criminal offending.

Summary

This chapter took us on an exploration of the brain and discussed the various ways in which the limbic system and the prefrontal cortex may contribute to the development of antisocial phenotypes. The limbic system is where emotions, such as anger, fear, and rage, are generated. The prefrontal cortex is responsible for controlling the emotions engendered by the limbic system and the prefrontal cortex is also responsible for the so-called executive functions, such as planning, judgment, and behavioral regulation. Neuroimaging research suggests that criminals suffer from an overactive limbic system and from an under-active prefrontal cortex. There is also reason to believe that the brain may be able to explain, at least in part, the age-crime curve and the gender gap in aggression and violence. These are exciting possibilities and ones that hopefully encourage criminologists to seek out additional ways that the brain may be involved in the development of antisocial phenotypes.

Key Points

- The brain is the most complex entity in existence.
- Emotions, such as fear, anger, and rage, are generated in the limbic system.
- The amygdala is part of the limbic system and is considered the emotional hub of the brain.
- The hippocampus is part of the limbic system and is implicated in the formation of memories.
- The thalamus is part of the limbic system and is considered the brain's "relay station."
- The hypothalamus is part of the limbic system and is involved in the regulation of visceral functions.
- The cerebral cortex, also called the cerebrum or the neocortex, accounts for about two-thirds of the brain's volume.
- The cerebral cortex is divided in half by a large fissure running from the back of the head to the middle of the forehead.
- The corpus callosum is a large bundle of fibers that allows the brain's two hemispheres to communicate.
- The brain consists of two types of matter: gray matter and white matter.
- The frontal lobe is located directly behind the forehead and is responsible for higher-order cognitive functions.
- The prefrontal cortex is found in the anterior of the frontal lobe.
- The prefrontal cortex is the CEO of the brain and modulates the emotions generated from the limbic system.
- The prefrontal cortex is responsible for the so-called "executive functions."
- Executive functions refer to a multitude of tasks including the ability to control impulses, the ability to delay gratification, and the ability to anticipate the consequences of actions.
- Criminals suffer from executive dysfunctions.
- Variation in executive functions is due mostly to genetic factors.
- Neuroimaging techniques allow researchers to examine brain structure and brain function.
- Genetic imaging research uses neuroimaging techniques to examine the association between genetic polymorphisms and brain structure and function.
- Variation in the brain structure and function is due, in large part, to genetic factors.

- Criminals tend to have an over-active limbic system and a sub-active prefrontal cortex.
- The prefrontal cortex is the last area of the brain to develop and it is not finished maturing until the mid- to late-twenties.
- There are structural and functional differences between the brains of females and males.

Name _____ Date _____

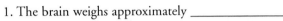

Mini
Quiz

1. The brain weighs approximately _____

    a) one pound   c) three pounds
    b) two pounds   d) four pounds

2. Approximately _____ percent of all genes code for the brain

    a) 20   b) 30   c) 60   d) 80

3. Emotions are generated in the _____.

    a) prefrontal cortex   c) orbitofrontal cortex
    b) limbic system   d) none of the above

4. The amygdala is the _____.

    a) emotional hub of the brain
    b) rational decision maker of the brain
    c) structure that controls impulses
    d) structure that holds memories

5. The cerebral cortex consists of _____ lobes.

    a) zero   b) two   c) four   d) eight

6. The prefrontal cortex is responsible for _____.

    a) controlling emotions   c) both a and b
    b) executive functions   d) neither a nor b

7. Variation in executive functions is due mostly to _____.

    a) environmental factors   c) genetic factors
    b) epigenetic factors   d) all of the above

8. Genes likely influence phenotypes by influencing _____.

    a) brain structure   c) both a and b

    b) brain function   d) neither a nor b

9. Brain imaging techniques can be used to examine _____.

    a) brain structure   c) both a and b

    b) brain function   d) neither a nor b

10. The brain does not finish developing until the mid-to-late twenties. What is the last area of the brain to mature?

    a) the limbic system   c) the prefrontal cortex

    b) the amygdala   d) the thalamus

11. Murderers tend to have an overactive _____ and an underactive _____.

    a) prefrontal cortex, limbic system

    b) limbic system, prefrontal cortex

    c) amygdala, thalamus

    d) thalamus, amygdala

12. In comparison to females, males tend to have a relatively larger _____ and a relatively smaller _____.

    a) prefrontal cortex, amygdala   c) amygdala, thalamus

    b) amygdala, prefrontal cortex   d) thalamus, amygdala

13. During adolescence, the _____ has already developed, but the _____ has not finished maturing.

    a) limbic system, amygdala

    b) prefrontal cortex, amygdala

    c) amygdala, hypothalamus

    d) limbic system, prefrontal cortex

14. Parents tend to socialize boys and girls _____.

    a) differently   c) identically

    b) similarly   d) none of the above

15. According to empirical research, the gender gap in offending behaviors can be explained by which of the following?

    a) parental socialization   c) both a and b

    b) cultural factors   d) neither a nor b

1. Describe the functions of the limbic system and of the prefrontal cortex.

2. Discuss how the limbic system and the prefrontal cortex are involved in the production of antisocial phenotypes.

3. Define and discuss what is meant by executive functions.

4. Explain how the brain can be used to explain the well-known age-crime curve.

5. Explain how the brain can be used to explain the gender gap in offending behaviors.

Further Reading

Blair, J., Mitchell, D., & Blair, K. (2005). *The psychopath: Emotion and the brain.* Malden, MA: Blackwell.

Brizendine, L. (2006). *The female brain.* New York: Morgan Road Books.

Damasio, A. (1994). *Descartes' error: Emotion, reason, and the human brain.* New York: Penguin Books.

DeLisi, M., & Conis, P. J. (2008). *Violent offenders: Theory, research, public policy, and practice.* Boston, MA: Jones and Bartlett.

Goldberg, E. (2001). *The executive brain: Frontal lobes and the civilized mind.* New York: Oxford University Press.

Marcus, G. (2004). *The birth of the mind: How a tiny number of genes creates the complexities of human thought.* New York: Basic Books.

Restak, R. (2001). *The secret life of the brain.* New York: Dana Press and Joseph Henry Press (co-publishers).

Robinson, M. B. (2004). *Why crime? An integrated systems theory of antisocial behavior.* Upper Saddle River, NJ: Pearson Prentice Hall.

Wright, J. P., Tibbetts, S. G., & Daigle, L. E. (2008). *Criminals in the making: Criminality across the life course.* Thousand Oaks, CA: Sage.

End
Notes

1. Wong, M. T. H., Lumsden, J., Fenton, G. W., & Fenwick, P. B. C. (1994). Electroencephalography, computed tomography and violence ratings of male patients in a maximum-security mental hospital. *Acta Psychiatrica Scandinavica, 90,* 97–101.

2. Ruden, R. A., & Byalick, M. (1997). *The craving brain: The biobalance approach to controlling addictions.* New York: HarperCollins.

3. Blair, J., Mitchell, D., & Blair, K. (2005). *The psychopath: Emotion and the brain.* Malden, MA: Blackwell Publishing.

4. Wright, P., Nobrega, J., Langevin, R., & Wortzman, G. (1990). Brain density and symmetry in pedophilic and sexually aggressive offenders. *Sexual Abuse: A Journal of Research and Treatment, 3,* 319–328.

5. Haier, R. J., Jung, R. E., Yeo, R. A., Head, K., & Alkire, M. T. (2004). Structural brain variation and general intelligence. *NeuroImage, 23,* 425–433.

6. Wright, J. P., Tibbetts, S. G., & Daigle, L. E. (2008). *Criminals in the making: Criminality across the life course.* Thousand Oaks, CA: Sage.

7. Beaver, K. M., Wright, J. P., & DeLisi, M. (2007). Self-control as an executive function: Reformulating Gottfredson and Hirschi's parental socialization thesis. *Criminal Justice and Behavior, 34,* 1345–1361.

8. Ishikawa, S. S., & Raine, A. (2003). Prefrontal deficits and antisocial behavior: A causal model. In Lahey, B. B., Moffitt, T. E., & Caspi, A. (Eds.), *Causes of conduct disorder and juvenile delinquency.* New York: Guilford Press.

9. MacDonald, A., Cohen, J. D., Stenger, V. A., & Carter, C. S. (2000). Disassociating the role of the dorsolateral prefrontal and anterior cingulate cortex in cognitive control. *Science, 288,* 1835–1838.

10. Simpson, J. R., Snyder, A. Z., Gusnard, D. A., & Raichle, M. E. (2001). Emotion-induced changes in human medial prefrontal cortex: I. During cognitive task performance. *Proceeding of the National Academy of Sciences of the United States of America, 98,* 683–687.

11. Ishikawa & Raine, 2003, p. 281.

12. Moffitt, T. E. (1990). The neuropsychology of juvenile delinquency: A critical review. In Tonry, M., & Morris, N. (Eds.), *Crime and justice: An annual review of research.* Chicago: University of Chicago Press, p. 115.

13. Ishikawa & Raine, 2003, p. 282.

14. Morgan, A. B., & Lilienfeld, S. O. (2000). A meta-analytic review of the relation between antisocial behavior and neuropsychological measures of executive function. *Clinical Psychology Review, 20,* 113–136.

15. Specifically, antisocial persons scored .62 standard deviations below non-antisocial persons on tests of executive functions.

16. Friedman, N. P., Myake, A., Young, S. E., DeFries, J. C., Corley, R. P., & Hewitt, J. K. (2008). Individual differences in executive functions are almost entirely genetic in origin. *Journal of Experimental Psychology, 137,* 201–225.

17. Lee, T. M. C., Chan, S. C., & Raine, A. (2008). Strong limbic and weak frontal activation to aggressive stimuli in spouse abusers. *Molecular Psychiatry, 13,* 655–656.

18. Raine, A. (1993). *The psychopathology of crime: Criminal behavior as a clinical disorder.* San Diego, CA: Academic Press.

19. Thompson, P. M., Cannon, T. D., Narr, K. L., van Erp, T. et al. (2001). Genetic influences on brain structure. *Nature Neuroscience, 4,* 1253–1258.

20. Thompson, P. M., Cannon, T. D., Narr, K. L., van Erp, T. et al., p. 1254.

21. Scamvougeras, A., Kigar, D. L., Jones, D., Weinberger, D. R., & Witelson, S. F. (2003). Size of the human corpus callosum is genetically determined: An MRI study in mono and dizygotic twins. *Neuroscience Letters, 338,* 91–94.

22. Pennington, B. F., Filipek, P. A., Lefly, D., Chhabildas, N., Kennedy, D. N., Simon, J. H., Filley, C. M., Galaburda, A., & DeFries, J. C. (2000). A twin MRI study of size variations in the human brain. *Journal of Cognitive Neuroscience, 12,* 223–232.

23. Meyer-Lindenberg, A., & Weinberger, D. R. (2006). Intermediate phenotypes and genetic mechanisms of psychiatric disorders. *Nature Reviews Neuroscience, 7,* 818–827.

24. Shaw, P., Gornick, M., Lerch, J., Addington, A., et al. (2007). Polymorphisms of the dopamine D4 receptor, clinical outcome, and cortical structure in attention-deficit/hyperactivity disorder. *Archives of General Psychiatry, 64,* 921–931.

25. Durston, S., Fossella, J. A., Casey, B. J., Hulshoff Pol, H. E., et al. (2005). Differential effect of DRD4 and DAT1 genotype on fronto-striatal gray matter volumes in a sample of subjects with attention deficit hyperactivity disorder, their unaffected siblings, and controls. *Molecular Psychiatry, 10,* 678–685.

26. Pezawas, L., Meyer-Lindenberg, A., Drabant, E. M., Verchinski, B. A., et al. (2005). 5-HTTLPR polymorphism impacts human cingulated-amygdala interactions: A genetic susceptibility mechanism for depression. *Nature Neuroscience, 8,* 828–834.

27. Young, K. A., Holcomb, L. A., Bonkale, W. L., Hicks, P. B., Yazdani, U., & German, D. C. (2007). 5HTTLPR polymorphism and enlargement of the

pulvinar: Unlocking the backdoor to the limbic system. *Biological Psychiatry, 61*, 813–818.

28. Canli, T., Omura, K., Haas, B. W., Fallgatter, A., Constable, R. T., & Lesch, K. P. (2005). Beyond affect: A role for genetic variation of the serotonin transporter in neural activation during a cognitive attention task. *Proceedings of the National Academy of Sciences, 102*, 12224–12229.

29. Hariri, A. R., Mattay, V. S., Tessitore, A., Kolachana, B., Fera, F., Goldman, D., Egan, M. F., & Weinbeger, D. R. (2002). Serotonin transporter genetic variation and the response of the human amygdala. *Science, 297*, 400–403.

30. Furmark, T., Tillfors, M., Garpenstrand, H., Marteinsdottir, I., Långström, B., Oreland, L., & Fredrikson, M. (2004). Serotonin transporter polymorphism related to amygdala excitability and symptom severity in patients with social phobia. *Neuroscience Letters, 362*, 189–192; Tillfors, M., Furmark, T., Marteinsdottir, I., Fischer, H., Pissiota, A., Långström, B, & Fredrikson, M. (2001). Cerebral blood flow in subjects with social phobia during stressful speaking tasks: A PET-study. *American Journal of Psychiatry, 158*, 1220–1226.

31. Heinz, A., Braus, D. F., Smolka, M. N., Wrase, J., Puls, I., Hermann, D., et al. (2005). Amygdala-prefrontal coupling depends on a genetic variation of the serotonin transporter. *Nature Neuroscience, 8*, 20–21.

32. Egan, M. F., Goldberg, T. E., Kolachana, B. S., Callicott, J. H., Mazzanti, C. M., Straub, R. E., Goldman, D., & Weinberger, D. R. (2001). Effect of COMT Val[108/158] Met genotype on frontal lobe function and risk for schizophrenia. *Proceedings of the National Academy of Sciences, 98*, 6917–6922.

33. Boettiger, C. A., Mitchell, J. M., Tavares, V. C., Robertson, M., Joslyn, G., D'Esposito, M., & Fields, H. L. (2007). Immediate reward bias in humans: Fronto-parietal networks and a role for the catechol-O-methyltransferase 158[val/val] genotype. *The Journal of Neuroscience, 27*, 14383–14391.

34. Meyer-Lindenberg, A., Nichols, T., Callicott, J. H., Ding, J., Kolachana, B., Buckholtz, J., Mattay, V. S., Egan, M., & Weinberger, D. R. (2006). Impact of complex genetic variation in COMT on human brain function. *Molecular Psychiatry, 11*, 867–877.

35. Meyer-Lindenberg, A., Buckholtz, J. W., Kolachana, B., Hariri, A. R., et al. (2006). Neural mechanisms of genetic risk for impulsivity and violence in humans. *Proceedings of the National Academy of Sciences, 103*, 6269–6274.

36. Yang, Y., Raine, A., Lencz, T., Bihrle, S., LaCasse, L., & Colletti, P. (2005). Prefrontal white matter in pathological liars. *British Journal of Psychiatry, 187*, 320–325.

37. Raine, A., Buchsbaum, M. S., Stanley, J., Lottenberg, S., Abel, L., & Stoddard, J. (1994). Selective reductions in prefrontal glucose metabolism in murders. *Biological Psychiatry, 36*, 365–373.

38. Raine, A., Buchsbaum, M., & LaCasse, L. (1997). Brain abnormalities in murderers indicated by positron emission tomography. *Biological Psychiatry, 42,* 495–508.

39. Raine, A., Meloy, J. R., Bihrle, S., Stoddard, J., LaCasse, L., & Buchsbaum, M. S. (1998). Reduced prefrontal and increased subcortical brain functioning assessed using positron emission tomography in predatory and affective murderers. *Behavioral Sciences and the Law, 16,* 319–332.

40. Raine, A., Stoddard, J., Bihrle, S., & Buchsbaum, M. (1998). Prefrontal glucose deficits in murderers lacking psychosocial deprivation. *Neuropsychiatry, Neuropsychology, and Behavioral Neurology, 11,* 1–7.

41. DeLisi, M., Vaughn, M. G. (2008). Still psychopathic after all these years. In DeLisi, M., & Conis, P. J. (Eds.), Violent offenders: Theory, research, public policy, and practice. Boston, MA: Jones and Bartlett; Walsh, A., & Wu, H.-H. (2008). Differentiating antisocial personality disorder, psychopathy, and sociopathy: Evolutionary, genetic, neurological, and sociological considerations. *Criminal Justice Studies, 21,* 135–152.

42. Damasio, A. (1994). *Descartes' error: Emotion, reason, and the human brain.* New York: Penguin Books.

43. Raine, A., Lencz, T., Bihrle, S., LaCasse, L., & Colletti, P. (2000). Reduced prefrontal gray matter volume and reduced autonomic activity in antisocial personality disorder. *Archives of General Psychiatry, 57,* 119–127.

44. Volkow, N. D., & Tancredi, L. (1987). Neural substrates of violent behaviour: A preliminary study with positron emission tomography. *British Journal of Psychiatry, 151,* 668–673; Volkow, N. D., Tancredi, L. R., Grant, C., Gillespie, H., Valentine, A., Mullani, N., Wang, G.-J., & Hollister, L. (1995). Brain glucose metabolism in violent psychiatric patients: A preliminary study. *Psychiatry Research, 61,* 243–253.

45. Yang, Y., Raine, A., Lencz, T., Bihrle, S., LaCasse, L., & Colletti, P. (2005). Volume reduction in prefrontal gray matter in unsuccessful criminal psychopaths. *Biological Psychiatry, 57,* 1103–1108, p. 1107.

46. Raine, A., Lencz, T., Taylor, K., Hellige, J. B., Bihrle, S., LaCasse, L., Lee, M., Ishikawa, S., & Colletti, P. (2003). Corpus callosum abnormalities in psychopathic antisocial individuals. *Archives of General Psychiatry, 60,* 1134–1142.

47. Kiehl, K. A., Smith, A. M., Hare, R. D., Mendrek, A., Forster, B. B., Brink, J., & Liddle, P. F. (2001). Limbic abnormalities in affective processing by criminal psychopaths as revealed by functional magnetic resonance imaging. *Biological Psychiatry, 50,* 677–684.

48. Raine, A., Ishikawa, S. S., Arce, E., Lencz, T., Knuth, K. H., Bihrle, S., LaCasse, L., & Colletti, P. (2004). Hippocampal structural asymmetry in unsuccessful psychopaths. *Biological Psychiatry, 55,* 185–181.

49. Blair, R. J. R. (2003). Neurobiological basis of psychopathy. *British Journal of Psychiatry, 182*, 5–7; Blair, J., Mitchell, D., & Blair, K. (2005). *The psychopath: Emotion and the brain*. Malden, MA: Blackwell.

50. Yang, Y., Raine, A., Lencz, T., Bihrle, S., LaCasse, L., & Colletti, P. (2005). Prefrontal white matter in pathological liars. *British Journal of Psychiatry, 187*, 320–325.

51. Yang, Y., Raine, A., Lencz, T., Bihrle, S., LaCasse, L., & Colletti, P. (2005). Prefrontal white matter in pathological liars. *British Journal of Psychiatry, 187*, 320–325, p. 323.

52. Lee, T. M. C., Chan, S. C., & Raine, A. (2008). Strong limbic and weak frontal activation to aggressive stimuli in spouse abusers. *Molecular Psychiatry, 13*, 655–660.

53. Archer, J. (2004). Sex differences in aggression in real-world settings: A meta-analytic review. *Review of General Psychology, 8*, 291–322.

54. Collins, R. E. (2004). Onset and desistance in criminal careers: Neurobiology and the age-crime relationship. *Journal of Offender Rehabilitation, 39*, 1–19; Spear, L. P. (2000). The adolescent brain and age-related behavioral manifestations. *Neuroscience and Biobehavioral Reviews, 24*, 417–463; Walsh, A. (2009). Crazy by design: A biosocial approach to the age-crime curve. In Walsh, A., & Beaver, K. M. (Eds.), *Biosocial criminology: New directions in theory and research*. New York: Routledge.

55. Steinberg, L. (2004). Risk taking in adolescence. *Annals of the New York Academy of Sciences, 1021*, 51–58.

56. Giedd, J. N. (2004). Structural magnetic resonance imaging of the adolescent brain. *Annals of the New York Academy of Sciences, 1021*, 77–85; Giedd, J. N., Blumenthal, J., Jeffries, N. O., Castellanos, F. X., Liu, H. et al. (1999). Brain development during childhood and adolescence: A longitudinal MRI study. *Nature Neuroscience, 2*, 861–863; Gogtay, N., Giedd, J. N., Lusk, L., Hayashi, K. M., Greenstein, D., et al. (2004). Dynamic mapping of human cortical development during childhood through early adulthood. *Proceedings of the National Academy of Sciences, 101*, 8174–8179.

57. Restak, R. (2001). *The secret life of the brain*. New York: Dana Press and Joseph Henry Press (co-publishers), p. 76.

58. Benson, M. L. (2002). *Crime and the life course: An introduction*. Los Angeles, CA: Roxbury, p. 70.

59. Collins, R. E. (2004). Onset and desistance in criminal careers: Neurobiology and the age-crime relationship. *Journal of Offender Rehabilitation, 39*, 1–19.

60. Campbell, A. (2009). Gender and crime: An evolutionary perspective. In Walsh, A., & Beaver, K. M. (Eds.), *Biosocial criminology: New directions in theory and research*. New York: Routledge.

61. Campbell, A. (2009).

62. Lytton, H., & Romney, D. M. (1991). Parents' differential socialization of boys and girls: A meta-analysis. *Psychological Bulletin, 109,* 267–296.

63. Cosgrove, K. P., Mazure, C. M., & Staley, J. K. (2007). Evolving knowledge of sex differences in brain structure, function, and chemistry. *Biological Psychiatry, 62,* 847–855.

64. Caviness, V. S., Kennedy, D. N., Richelme, C., Rademacher, J., & Filipek, P. A. (1996). The human brain age 7–11 years: A volumetric analysis based on magnetic resonance images. *Cerebral Cortex, 6,* 726–736.

65. LeVay, S. (1991). A difference in hypothalamic structure between heterosexual and homosexual men. *Science, 253,* 1034–1037.

66. Brizendine, L. (2006). *The female brain.* New York: Morgan Roads Books.

67. Kilpatrick, L. A., Zald, D. H., Pardo, J. V., & Cahill, L. F. (2006). Sex-related differences in amygdala functional connectivity during resting conditions. *NeuroImage, 30,* 452–461.

68. Andreason, P., Zametkin, A., Guo, A., Baldwin, P., & Cohen, R. (1993). Gender-related differences in regional cerebral glucose metabolism in normal volunteers. *Psychiatry Research, 51,* 175–183.

69. Gur, R. C., Gunning-Dixon, F., Bilker, W. B., & Gur, R. E. (2002). Sex differences in temporo-limbic and frontal brain volumes of health adults. *Cerebral Cortex, 12,* 998–1003, p. 1002.

70. Ortiz, J., Artigas, F., & Gelpi, E. (1988). Serotonergic status in human blood. *Life Sciences, 43,* 983–990.

71. Parsey, R. V., Oquendo, M. A., Simpson, N. R., Ogden, T. R., Van Heertum, R.., Arango, V., & Mann, J. J. (2002). Effects of sex, age, and aggressive traits in man on brain serotonin 5-HT$_{1A}$ receptor binding potential measured by PET using [C-11]WAY-100635. *Brain Research, 954,* 173–182.

72. Sanacora, G., Mason, G. F., Rothman, D. L., Behar, K. L., et al. (1999). Reduced cortical γ- aminobutyric acid levels in depressed patients determined by proton magnetic resonance spectroscopy. *Archives of General Psychiatry, 56,* 1043–1047.

73. Cosgrove, K. P., Mazure, C. M., & Staley, J. K. (2007). Evolving knowledge of sex differences in brain structure, function, and chemistry. *Biological Psychiatry, 62,* 847–855.

Environmental
Influences on
Antisocial Phenotypes

Introduction

The previous chapters demonstrated the biosocial basis to antisocial phenotypes, where genetic factors, the brain, and the environment combine together to produce criminal and delinquent outcomes. Much of the discussion thus far, however, has focused primarily on biology and genetics, with the environment receiving secondary emphasis. The current chapter addresses this gap and explores the environmental underpinnings to antisocial behavior in greater detail. Before proceeding, a point of clarification is in order: When most criminologists think of environmental influences, they think of parents, peers, neighborhoods, culture, and other social factors that are encountered in everyday life. Biosocial criminologists, in contrast, define environmental influences more broadly and conceptualize the environment as any non-genetic influence.[1] As we will see, many of these environments are biological in nature (but not genetic per se), which ultimately means that the environments studied by biosocial criminologists are sharply different from the environments typically studied by sociological criminologists.

There are two main reasons why biosocial criminologists are not interested in the same environments as other criminologists. First, most of the environments analyzed by criminologists are shared environments (e.g., families, neighborhoods, culture), but behavioral genetic research has shown that these environments explain little to no variation in antisocial phenotypes (see Chapter 2). Second, and as Figure 5.1 shows, there is good reason to believe that environments exert their influence on human phenotypes by affecting brain development.[2] Yet, most of the environments analyzed by criminologists are not recognized as having salient effects on brain development. In light of these serious limitations, the current chapter will not examine the environments that are usually of interest to criminologists, but instead will pay particular attention to those environments that affect the developing brain. Specifically, three groups of environmental influences will be explored: prenatal environmental influences, perinatal environmental influences, and environmental influences during infancy and early childhood.

Prenatal Environments

The gestation period in humans spans approximately nine months, but is often divided into three trimesters. The first trimester begins at conception and runs

Figure 5.1
The possible connection among environmental influences, variation in the brain, and phenotypic variation.

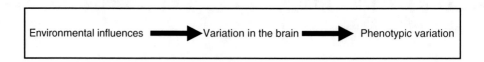

through the third month of pregnancy, the second trimester refers to the fourth, fifth, and six months of pregnancy, and the third trimester spans from the seventh month through birth. During gestation, fetal development follows a precisely timed schedule where organs form and develop at specific time periods. The heart, for example, usually begins to beat about three weeks after conception, while the fingers and toes form approximately six weeks after conception. Most importantly to biosocial criminologists, however, is the development of the brain.

The brain begins to form almost immediately after conception and continues to grow and mature throughout the entire pregnancy. This is particularly important because after organs are finished developing, they are usually not affected by prenatal environments. But, the brain, since it develops from conception to birth, can be affected almost every single day of the entire pregnancy. Exactly what types of prenatal environments can affect fetal development is the topic of the current section. We will explore four different prenatal environments that alter brain development and that have been found to be related to later life antisocial phenotypes: prenatal exposure to testosterone, prenatal exposure to toxins, prenatal malnutrition, and prenatal exposure to stress. While reading this section, keep in mind that Chapter 4 discussed the role that brain structure and brain function played in the development of antisocial phenotypes. It is likely that the environments that are to be discussed here are associated with criminal and aggressive behaviors because they are partially responsible for creating variation in the brain.

Prenatal exposure to testosterone.   When most people think of the relationship between testosterone and antisocial behavior, they think of circulating testosterone levels in adolescent or adult males. There is good reason to believe, however, that prenatal levels of testosterone, in comparison with circulating levels of testosterone, have a much stronger influence on behaviors and personality traits. To understand why, it is necessary to discuss how males and females develop in utero. All fetuses—whether they are to become males or females—begin with undifferentiated sex organs. Around the fifth week of pregnancy, the SRY gene, which is a gene located on the Y chromosome (remember that males have one Y chromosome and females have zero Y chromosomes), causes the gonads to develop into testes. After the testes have formed, they begin to produce the hormone, testosterone, which masculinizes the sex organs causing the penis, the scrotum, and the internal ducts to develop. If the SRY gene is absent (i.e., females) then the gonads develop into ovaries, not testes. Without the testes, testosterone is not produced in high quantities and, as a result, female sex organs, such as the vagina, labia, and clitoris, form in place of the male sex organs.

Prenatal testosterone is often described as having organizing effects because it organizes different structures, including the sex organs as well as the brain.[3] Recall from Chapter 4 that different regions of the brain, including those that are involved in antisocial phenotypes, are structurally different between males and females. Emerging evidence indicates that a cause of these male-female brain differences is due to males being exposed to higher levels of prenatal testosterone than females.[4] The process of sex differentiation of the brain begins around the eighth week of pregnancy when the male brain is saturated with testosterone. This influx of testosterone causes some areas of the brain, especially those associated with aggression (e.g., the amygdala), to grow larger. Female brains, in contrast, are not doused in testosterone and thus their brains develop differently than males. For example, females have smaller brain regions that are tied to aggression and larger brain centers that are devoted to communication.

But to pretend that prenatal exposure to testosterone only explains male-female brain differences misses the mark; exposure to prenatal testosterone also varies within-sexes. What this means is that some males are exposed to very high levels of prenatal testosterone while others are exposed to abnormally low levels of prenatal testosterone and still other males are exposed to intermediate levels of prenatal testosterone. The same holds true for females. Of particular interest is that these varying levels of prenatal testosterone appear to have relatively salient effects that alter the developing brain and that can affect phenotypes. Allan Mazur provided an excellent statement on the effects of varying levels of prenatal testosterone when he noted "that early exposure to greater amounts of testosterone produces more male characteristics (masculinization) and fewer female characteristics (demasculinization), while less exposure to testosterone produces the reverse."[5] It makes logical sense, then, to hypothesize that persons who are exposed to relatively high levels of prenatal testosterone should be more aggressive and antisocial (i.e., more male-like behaviors) than persons who are exposed to relatively lower levels of prenatal testosterone.[6] Below three lines of research bearing on this hypothesis are discussed.

First, there is a body of research that has examined the association between prenatal testosterone levels and later-life phenotypes in clinical populations. Clinical populations contain subjects who are, for a variety of different reasons, exposed to abnormally high levels of testosterone in utero. These subjects are then compared to a control group (i.e., subjects who were exposed to normal levels of prenatal testosterone) to determine whether the two groups differ in respect to the phenotype of interest. If the particular phenotype differs between the two groups, then researchers typically conclude that prenatal testosterone levels are associated with these phenotypic differences. Among researchers interested in examining the effects of prenatal testosterone levels, the most commonly studied clinical population consists of people who were affected by congenital adrenal hyperplasia (CAH).

CAH is a family of autosomal recessive disorders that causes an overproduction of androgens, including testosterone, beginning very early in gestation and continuing until after birth.[7] Females with CAH are thus exposed to levels of testosterone in utero that exceed normal levels and, as a result, they are often born with ambiguous genitalia, including clitoral enlargement and labial infusion. CAH, simply put, masculinizes females. Females with CAH are typically identified at birth, treated with postnatal hormones, and undergo genital reconstructive surgery to feminize them. CAH provides a type of naturally occurring experiment, where females with CAH can be compared to females without CAH. If prenatal testosterone is involved in antisocial phenotypes or in other male-typical behaviors, then females with CAH should act more "male-like" than females without CAH. Males with CAH are also examined and compared to males without CAH, but it is difficult to isolate the effect of prenatal testosterone because all healthy male fetuses are exposed to relatively high levels of testosterone in utero. As a result, most studies that employ samples of people with CAH focus on females, giving males only secondary attention.

Studies that have examined the effects of CAH have found a number of phenotypic differences between CAH females and non-CAH females that begin to emerge very early in life. CAH girls, in comparison with non-CAH girls, are more likely to engage in male-like behaviors, such as rough-and-tumble playing, are more likely to be labeled "tomboys,"[8] are more likely to accept boys as friends[9], and are more likely to show a preference for boy toys, such as guns and cars, while simultaneously not showing as much interest in girl toys, including dolls.[10] Although it may be tempting to interpret these findings as evidence that prenatal testosterone is a cause of boy-like behaviors, some critics argue that the effects of CAH are due to socialization, not prenatal testosterone.[11] They argue that because girls with CAH are often born with ambiguous genitalia, their parents socialize them more similarly to boys. The end result, according to this line of reasoning, is that CAH girls act like boys because of parental socialization.

In a methodologically rigorous study, Vickie Pasterski and her colleagues tackled this criticism head-on and examined toy play in a sample of CAH girls ages three to 10 years old.[12] CAH girls along with their unaffected siblings were presented with a number of toys (some were typical boy toys and others were typical girl toys) and were asked to play with whatever toys they wanted. Their parents were also present. The CAH girls, when compared to their unaffected sisters, preferred to play with boy-typical behaviors. This preference was observed even though CAH girls were provided with more positive parental feedback for playing with girl-typical toys than their unaffected sisters. Stated differently, even though CAH girls were encouraged to play with girl toys more than unaffected girls, CAH girls still preferred to play with boy-typical toys. The findings from this study provide some of the strongest evidence to date that the effects of CAH are due to prenatal testosterone, not to parental socialization.

There is also a body of research indicating that adult CAH females differ from adult females without CAH. In a review of this literature, Celina Cohen-Bendahan and colleagues found that females with CAH, in comparison with females without CAH, have higher spatial ability skills, are less interested in infants, are less motherly, are less empathetic, and are more likely to be sexually attracted to females.[13] A close look at all of these differences reveals findings that are strikingly similar to what are found when males are compared to females. For instance, males, when compared to females (without CAH), have higher spatial ability skills, are less interested in infants, are less motherly, are less empathetic, and are more likely to be sexually attracted to females.[14] CAH females, in short, fall somewhere between females and males in terms of sex-typed behaviors.

Taken as a whole, the above discussion seems to indicate that CAH females display a variety of behaviors, attitudes, and preferences that are similar to males. While interesting, what does all of this have to do with antisocial phenotypes? Well, these studies provide initial evidence that exposure to prenatal testosterone may be partially responsible for male-typical phenotypes. And, given that violent crime and aggression are among the most male-typical behaviors, it stands to reason that CAH females should be more antisocial and aggressive than non-CAH females. A limited line of research testing this possibility has produced mixed results.

Interest in the potential relationship between CAH and aggression began to surface in the 1960s and 1970s with the publication of three studies that examined aggression in CAH females and unaffected females.[15] The results of these studies revealed that CAH females were not significantly more aggressive than non-CAH females. It should be pointed out, however, that these three studies were plagued by methodological limitations, including small sample sizes and unreliable measures of aggression.[16] A more recent study conducted by Sheri Berenbaum and Susan Resnick represented an improvement over these prior studies by employing two well-known and widely used standardized aggression scales (i.e., Multidimensional Personality Questionnaire and Reinisch's Aggression Inventory).[17] The results of the study indicated that CAH females were more aggressive than unaffected adult females. Interestingly, the differences in aggression were only observed in adolescents and adults, not in children.

The most methodologically sound study to examine the association between CAH and aggression was carried out by Vicki Pasterski and her colleagues.[18] This team of researchers examined aggression in a sample of 38 girls with CAH and 29 boys with CAH and their unaffected siblings. Not surprisingly, the results of their study revealed that boys without CAH were more aggressive than girls without CAH. Most importantly was that CAH girls were rated as more aggressive than their unaffected sisters. There was no difference in aggression between CAH boys and their unaffected brothers. Pasterski et al. concluded that these "results suggest that the prenatal elevation in androgen that is experienced by females with CAH is associated with increased aggressive behavior ... in childhood."[19]

The research reviewed above provides some tentative evidence that CAH females are more aggressive than non-CAH females, but there are at least two main shortcomings with the CAH literature. First, the results found with CAH females may not be generalizable to non-CAH subjects. In other words, while prenatal exposure to testosterone may masculinize CAH females perhaps causing them to act aggressively, this does not necessarily mean that prenatal testosterone is associated with aggression in non-CAH subjects. Second, when an association between CAH and aggression is observed, the effect tends to be confined to females, not males. Thus it remains an open-empirical question of whether variations in prenatal levels of testosterone can explain why some males are antisocial and others are not and why some females are antisocial and others are not. These issues cannot be addressed by using samples of CAH subjects, but instead are most reliably answered by examining prenatal testosterone levels in samples drawn from the general population.

The second body of research that has examined the association between levels of prenatal testosterone has used samples selected from the general population and measured prenatal testosterone levels *indirectly*. Indirectly measuring prenatal testosterone levels entails identifying some measurable characteristic that correlates with prenatal testosterone levels. Hypothetically speaking, if weight was positively correlated with prenatal testosterone levels, then it would be possible to use weight as an indirect measure of prenatal testosterone levels, where people who weigh more would have been exposed to more testosterone in utero. Although a number of different techniques are available to indirectly measure prenatal testosterone levels, one of the most widely used methods is the second to fourth finger ratio (2D:4D ratio).[20]

The ratio between the length of the second finger (also known as the index finger or the second digit; 2D) and the fourth finger (also known as the ring finger or the fourth digit; 4D) is sexually dimorphic. By around the fourteenth week of pregnancy the 2D:4D ratio is established and remains fixed throughout the remainder of life. In general, males have a low 2D:4D ratio, meaning that they have relatively shorter index fingers (2D) in comparison to their ring fingers (4D). The opposite is true for females, where they tend to have relatively longer index fingers (2D) in comparison to their ring fingers (4D). Evidence suggests that the 2D:4D ratio reflects the amount of prenatal testosterone exposure, where a lower 2D:4D ratio indicates greater exposure to prenatal testosterone and a greater 2D:4D ratio indicates less exposure to testosterone in utero.[21] The exact reason(s) for why the 2D:4D ratio is affected by prenatal testosterone is not well understood, but it might be due to the fact that the same set of genes, known as Homeobox genes (HoxA and HoxD), that are implicated in the formation of the gonads also affect the development of the fingers.[22]

Given that the 2D:4D ratio is a proxy indicator of prenatal testosterone exposure, researchers have examined whether the 2D:4D ratio is associated with a range of phenotypes. A lower 2D:4D ratio (i.e., more prenatal testosterone) has been found to be associated with more male-like behaviors. For example, in an innovative study, John Manning and Rogan Taylor found that professional football players had lower 2D:4D ratios when compared to a group of control males[23] and other studies have reported that relatively low 2D:4D ratios are associated with autism[24] and musical abilities.[25] Evidence also exists showing that 2D:4D ratios are correlated with cognitive abilities and are related to sexual orientation in both males and females.[26] In children, research has found that a relatively low 2D:4D ratio corresponds with more symptoms of hyperactivity and poorer social cognitive function in girls, while a relatively high 2D:4D ratio is associated with emotional problems in boys.[27]

Of particular interest, however, are the studies that have examined the relationship between 2D:4D ratio and antisocial phenotypes. Since relatively low 2D:4D ratios reflect greater prenatal testosterone exposure, it is generally assumed that low 2D:4D ratios would be associated with more antisocial phenotypes. A line of research has provided some support for this hypothesis. A study conducted by Elizabeth Austin and her colleagues, for example, examined the association between 2D:4D ratios and personality traits in a sample of males and females.[28] They found that females with lower 2D:4D ratios had significantly higher scores on measures of sensation seeking, psychoticism, and neuroticism. There was no relationship between 2D:4D ratio and personality measures for males.

Other studies have examined the association between the 2D:4D ratio and aggression during experimental conditions. Matthew McIntyre and his colleagues, for instance, observed males and females play a simulated war game. They found that subjects who had lower 2D:4D ratios were more likely to engage in an unprovoked attack during the simulation.[29] In another experiment, Kobe Millet and Siegfried Dewitte tested for an association between 2D:4D ratio and aggression in a sample of undergraduate male students.[30] Their analysis revealed that males with lower 2D:4D ratios were more aggressive, but only after they had viewed an aggressive music video—in other words, the association between 2D:4D ratio and aggression was dependent on being exposed to an aggressive video. In the last experiment, Zeynep Benderlioglu and Randy Nelson were interested in exploring the potential association between 2D:4D ratio and reactive aggression.[31] To do so, 100 subjects were instructed to call and ask for donations for a charity. Unbeknownst to them, the persons they called were confederates who refused to donate money and were confrontational. Reactive aggression was measured by how the subjects responded to the confrontations (e.g., the force with which they hung up the phone). The results of this study indicated a significant association between 2D:4D ratio and reactive aggression, where lower 2D:4D ratios corresponded to more reactive aggression. This effect, however, was only observed for females, not males.

The 2D:4D ratio has also been found to correlate with aggression in non-experimental studies. Allison Bailey and Peter Hurd employed a sample of 298 undergraduate male and female students and measured their 2D:4D ratio and also assessed their aggression by using a standardized aggression scale.[32] The analysis revealed a statistically significant correlation ($r = -.21$) between 2D:4D ratio and aggression, where a lower 2D:4D ratio was associated with higher scores on the aggression scale. This effect was confined to males as there was no relationship between the 2D:4D ratio and aggression for females. Most recently, Elizabeth Hampson and colleagues found evidence that a lower 2D:4D ratio was associated with more aggression and greater sensation seeking in females.[33] In males, their analysis revealed that lower 2D:4D ratios were related to greater sensation seeking and more verbal aggression. Collectively, the results of these studies seem to point to the likelihood that there is a relationship between the 2D:4D ratio and antisocial phenotypes, but the association is far from invariant and ebbs and flows from study-to-study.

The third way that researchers test for an association between prenatal testosterone levels and different phenotypes is by using direct measures of prenatal testosterone exposure. You might be wondering why researchers even use indirect measures of prenatal testosterone exposure if it is possible to measure prenatal testosterone directly. After all, directly measuring prenatal testosterone levels would produce more accurate and more precise estimates than indirect measures. To understand why direct measures are not used frequently, it is important to point out that directly measuring prenatal testosterone levels entails assaying testosterone levels from umbilical cord blood at birth, from maternal serum via venipuncture, or from amniotic fluid during an amniocentesis.[34] In addition to a host of ethical and practical obstacles, one of the major drawbacks to directly measuring prenatal testosterone, at least in relation to the study of antisocial phenotypes, is that the window of opportunity to directly measure prenatal testosterone is relatively short; after birth, only indirect measures can be used.

Suppose you were a researcher interested in examining the association between adolescent aggression and prenatal testosterone levels. You would have two choices. First, you could measure prenatal testosterone directly and then wait about 13 years to measure aggression. This would be the methodologically rigorous approach, but it is not always feasible. Second, you could measure prenatal testosterone indirectly (e.g., 2D:4D ratios) and aggression at the same time. In that way, you would be able to find out the association between prenatal testosterone and aggression immediately as opposed to waiting 13 years. Although indirectly measuring testosterone is more cost effective and produces quicker results than directly measuring testosterone, a small body of research has tested for an association between direct measures of prenatal testosterone and various phenotypic outcomes.

Findings from extant research tend to suggest that higher prenatal testosterone levels (measured directly) are associated with more male-like phenotypes. For example, there is some evidence of a positive association between prenatal testosterone and the preference for boy-typical toys in girls,[35] while elevated levels of prenatal testosterone have been found to reduce timidity in boys, but not girls.[36] There are also studies linking direct measures of prenatal testosterone exposure to gendered behaviors in adulthood (e.g., sex-typed activities, Bem Sex Role Inventory, etc.), where greater exposure to testosterone in utero in females corresponds to more male-like behaviors.[37] Whether these findings would extend to antisocial phenotypes is unknown because researchers have yet to examine the association between direct measures of prenatal testosterone and later life aggressive and violent behaviors.

The evidence presented above provides some support for the association between exposure to testosterone in utero and antisocial phenotypes later in life. This leaves us to ponder why prenatal levels of testosterone vary from person-to-person. Although this is a complex issue, as with most human traits it appears as though genetic factors are largely responsible.[38] This should not be taken to mean that the environment is unimportant; in fact, there is some reason to believe that nonshared environmental factors may also play a role in structuring prenatal exposure to testosterone. Birth order, in particular, appears to be a potentially important environmental variable that alters exposure to prenatal testosterone for males.[39] More specifically, there is circumstantial evidence to suggest that with each successive male birth, levels of prenatal testosterone exposure drop. But whatever the reasons, it is likely that variations in prenatal testosterone exposure are implicated—at least to some extent—in the development of antisocial phenotypes.[40]

Prenatal exposure to toxins. Prenatal exposure to toxins represents one of the most salient environmental factors that can interfere with normal brain development. Any substance, such as chemicals and drugs, that crosses the placenta and produces congenital malformations (i.e., a birth defect) are known as teratogens and some of these agents are neuroteratogens that target the central nervous system, including the brain. Prenatal exposure to toxins can cause physical deformities, but they can also often result in "soft" neurological damage (e.g., executive dysfunctions; see Chapter 4) which may lead to the development of antisocial phenotypes later in the life course. Despite the dramatic influence that prenatal exposure to toxins has on the developing brain, sociological criminologists have paid very little attention to this topic. The following section will address this gap in the criminological literature and present a brief overview to three groups of toxins that have been tied to antisocial phenotypes: prenatal exposure to cigarette smoke, prenatal exposure to alcohol, and prenatal exposure to industrial chemicals.

An alarming number of women continue to smoke while pregnant, with prevalence estimates ranging between 10 and 25 percent.[41] This translates into about one-half million US babies being exposed to tobacco prenatally each year.[42] Nicotine acts as both a teratogen and a neuroteratogen and thus can adversely affect the developing brain.[43] Studies conducted on rats have revealed that intrauterine exposure to nicotine alters the cerebral cortex and the hippocampus[44] and also affects the development of the serotonergic and dopaminergic systems.[45] These findings are largely mirrored by studies employing humans, where research using neuroimaging techniques has revealed that prenatal exposure to cigarette smoke[46] is associated with reductions in cortical gray matter as well as with other structural brain differences.[47] There is even evidence indicating that levels of prenatal testosterone are higher in mothers who smoke during pregnancy when compared to mothers who do not.[48]

Perhaps as a consequence of these neurodevelopmental problems, there is now a rich knowledge base linking prenatal exposure to cigarette smoke to a range of maladaptive outcomes including reduced cognitive abilities[49], poor academic performance[50], hyperactivity[51], and early-life antisocial behavioral phenotypes.[52] In a review of the literature that had studied the association between maternal smoking during pregnancy and severe antisocial behavior in their children, Lauren Wakschlag and her colleagues identified seven studies that had reported a link between prenatal exposure to tobacco and disruptive behaviors early in life, including conduct disorder and oppositional defiant disorder, as well as serious violence during adolescence and adulthood.[53]

Most noteworthy, however, are those studies that have examined the effect that prenatal exposure to cigarette smoke has on subsequent delinquent and criminal involvement. The results of these studies have indicated that maternal cigarette smoking during pregnancy is consistently related to offspring criminal behavior during adolescence and adulthood.[54] The strength of the association, however, tends to vary considerably from study-to-study. Some studies have detected a strong and robust relationship[55], whereas other studies have reported a small, but statistically significant association.[56] Spurred on by these varying effect sizes, Travis Pratt, Jean McGloin, and Noelle Fearn conducted a meta-analysis of 18 studies that had examined the nexus between prenatal exposure to cigarette smoke and criminal behaviors.[57] Their analysis revealed a statistically significant, yet relatively weak, relationship between maternal cigarette smoking during pregnancy and antisocial behavior in offspring.

One explanation for why prenatal exposure to cigarette smoke has been found to have relatively small effects on antisocial phenotypes is because most researchers have failed to examine potential interactions with environmental conditions. Recall that in Chapter 3 interactions were discussed within the context of gene X environment interactions (GxE). This discussion of GxEs revealed that genes may have their strongest effects when they are paired with criminogenic environments, such as childhood abuse and neglect. The same logic could extend to prenatal exposure to cigarette smoke, where the effects would be weak for persons from a "good" environment, but much stronger for persons from a "bad" environment. Chris Gibson and Stephen Tibbetts explored this possibility by examining the interrelationships among prenatal exposure to cigarette smoke, whether the father was present or absent from the household, and age of criminal onset.[58] The results of their study indicated that prenatal exposure to cigarette smoke interacted with the absence of the father to predict an early age of onset.[59] This type of interaction is referred to as a biosocial interaction because the environmental variable (e.g., father absence from household) interacts with the biological variable (e.g., prenatal exposure to cigarette smoke) to predict behavioral phenotypes.[60] We will revisit biosocial interactions later in this chapter.

Although the evidence reviewed above points to the likelihood that exposure to cigarette smoke in utero is, in some capacity, linked to later life behavioral problems, there exists a number of alternative interpretations. Most prominent is that the association between maternal cigarette smoke and offspring behavior is not causal, but is really due what is known as self-selection effects (sometimes referred to as a selection effect or a selection bias). Self-selection occurs when a characteristic or a suite of characteristics are responsible for driving people into one environment or another. In this case, it is possible that some characteristics, such as poverty and low IQ, may be associated with why some pregnant women smoke. These same characteristics may also be linked to the development of antisocial behavior in offspring. If this is occurring, then mothers who smoke while pregnant are different from mothers who do not smoke while pregnant. And it may be these preexisting differences (e.g., poverty and low IQ), and not cigarettes per se, that are causing their children to display antisocial phenotypes (meaning that the relationship is spurious).

Brian Boutwell and his colleagues addressed this possibility by analyzing data drawn from the Fragile Families and Child Wellbeing Study (FFCWS).[61] They used a statistical technique known as propensity score matching (PSM) which takes into account selection effects. Analysis of the FFCWS data revealed that the association between prenatal exposure to cigarette smoke and externalizing behavior problems vanished after taking into account selection effects for eleven factors (e.g., race, religiosity, poverty, maternal antisocial propensities, etc.). Boutwell et al. extended their analysis a step further to examine whether the amount of exposure to cigarettes was associated with behavioral problems. To do so, they divided the sample into those mothers who smoked more than a pack of cigarettes per day while pregnant and those mothers who smoked a pack or less per day while pregnant. They found that even after taking into account selection effects there was an association between being exposed to a large amount of tobacco in utero and childhood behavioral problems. The results of this study thus pointed to two main findings. First, the relationship between relatively low levels of prenatal cigarette smoke exposure and behavioral problems is spurious. Second, exposure to high levels of tobacco in utero has a direct effect on the offspring's odds of displaying behavioral problems.[62]

Another interpretation of the association between maternal smoking during pregnancy and subsequent antisocial behavior is that the relationship is spurious owing to unmeasured genetic factors. According to this perspective, mothers who smoke while pregnant possess genetic predispositions for antisocial phenotypes that mothers who do not smoke do not possess. As a result, these genetic predispositions are transmitted from mother-to-offspring among females who smoke, but they are not transmitted among females who do not smoke. If this is the case, then the result may be a spurious relationship between maternal cigarette smoking during pregnancy and antisocial behavior in offspring, owing to unmeasured genetic factors. This process is depicted in Figure 5.2.

Only a couple of studies have examined the association between maternal cigarette smoking during pregnancy and antisocial phenotypes while simultaneously controlling for genetic factors. In the first study, Barbara Maughan and colleagues analyzed twin pairs drawn from the Environmental Risk Longitudinal Twin Study.[63] Before controlling for genetic factors, they reported that maternal smoking during pregnancy was associated with increased conduct problems in children at ages five and seven years old. They then estimated a series of statistical models that controlled for genetic factors. The results of these analyses indicated that the effect of prenatal exposure to cigarette smoke, while still statistically significant, was attenuated. In the second study, Brian D'Onofrio and colleagues analyzed kinship pairs from the National Longitudinal Survey of Youth and found that after controlling for genetic factors the relationship between smoking during pregnancy and offspring externalizing problem behaviors evaporated.[64] In other words, the smoking during pregnancy-antisocial phenotypes association was spurious due to genetic factors. These studies highlight the complexity of the relationship between prenatal exposure to cigarette smoke and offspring antisocial behavior and point to the need for future research to examine this association in greater detail.

In addition to nicotine, alcohol is another prenatal toxin (i.e., a teratogen) that can affect the developing brain and that has been linked to later life antisocial

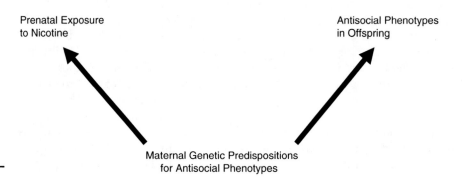

Figure 5.2
Comparison of a causal relationship between prenatal exposure to nicotine and antisocial phenotypes (top panel) and a spurious relationship due to genetic factors (bottom panel).

phenotypes. Surveys have indicated that about 15 percent of pregnant women consume at least some alcohol during pregnancy.[65] While it is unknown whether exposure to low levels of alcohol in utero has any deleterious and lasting effects on the fetus[66], high rates of exposure have consistently been linked to a broad range of maladaptive outcomes. For example, prenatal exposure to alcohol has been linked to reduced cognitive disabilities, learning and memory difficulties, and structural alterations to certain brain regions, such as the corpus callosum, the cerebellum, and the hippocampus.[67] Prenatal alcohol exposure also appears to impair executive functions[68], which as Chapter 4 discussed, are strongly implicated in the etiology of antisocial phenotypes. Given the strong effect that alcohol exposure in utero has on the developing brain, and given that brain structure and functioning are linked to behavioral phenotypes, there is good reason to suspect that prenatal exposure to alcohol (especially at high levels) is associated with antisocial phenotypes.

A wealth of research has examined the association between alcohol exposure in utero and a range of phenotypic outcomes. These studies have found a link between prenatal alcohol exposure and attention deficit hyperactivity disorder (ADHD)[69], poor social skills[70], depression, and suicide.[71] Additionally, research has also found that prenatal alcohol exposure is associated with externalizing problem behaviors, such as aggression, conduct problems, and delinquency.[72] What is of particular interest is that some research has indicated even exposure to very low levels of intrauterine alcohol (i.e., .5 ounces of absolute alcohol per day) may increase the odds of developing antisocial phenotypes, including behavioral problems, such as delinquency.[73]

The above set of findings suggests the existence of a relationship between prenatal alcohol exposure and behavioral problems later in life. Similar to the effects of prenatal exposure to cigarettes, keep in mind that this relationship could be being driven by self-selection (see discussion above). Brian D'Onofrio and his colleagues explored this possibility and found a statistically significant association between prenatal alcohol exposure and behavioral problems even after taking into account genetic and environmental factors.[74] This study provides some of the strongest evidence to date that alcohol exposure in utero is a contributor to childhood behavioral problems. Still, due to a paucity of research, it remains unresolved whether prenatal exposure to alcohol also has such strong and consistent effects on criminal behaviors during adolescence and adulthood.

Prenatal exposure to nicotine and alcohol are two teratogens that have been linked to behavioral phenotypes later in life. It would be a mistake, however, to assume that drugs that are intentionally ingested are the only toxins that can affect the developing fetus. Indeed, there are more than 200 industrial chemicals (many of which are unregulated) that are known to be neurotoxins and exposure to some of these chemicals, such as lead, are relatively common.[75] This is particularly alarming because research suggests that prenatal exposure to some of these chemicals can impair healthy fetal brain development[76] and can lead to behavioral problems later in life.[77]

To illustrate, Virginia Rauh and her colleagues were interested in exploring the effect of prenatal chlorpyrifos exposure on early child development.[78] Chlorpyrifos was one of the most widely used residential insecticides until it was banned by the Environmental Protection Agency (EPA) at the end of 2001. Rauh et al. examined chlorpyrifos levels in umbilical cord blood in a sample of 254 babies. They then followed this sample over the next three years. When the children were 36 months old, they subjected them to a battery of tests that were designed to assess normal child development. The results of their analysis revealed that prenatal exposure to chlorpyrifos was associated with attention problems, ADHD, psychomotor development, and mental development. Importantly, additional studies have identified prenatal exposure to other industrial chemicals, such as manganese[79] and hexachlorobenzene (a chemical used in agriculture)[80], to be associated with behavioral problems during childhood.

Of all the industrial chemicals, lead is commonly pointed to as being the most applicable to the study of crime, violence, and aggression.[81] Lead is a neurotoxin that has been linked to variations in brain structure, including those regions of the brain that are responsible for executive functions.[82] Only recently, however, has research emerged showing a connection between prenatal lead exposure and criminal involvement in adulthood. In a groundbreaking study, John Wright and his colleagues at the University of Cincinnati assayed prenatal lead concentrations in a sample of 250 pregnant women.[83] The offspring were then followed longitudinally and official records were searched to determine the number of arrests that each subject accrued. The results of this study were truly amazing: prenatal lead levels were a statistically significant predictor of total number of arrests and total number of arrests for violent crime, even after taking into account a host of sociodemographics (e.g., poverty), maternal characteristics (e.g., highest level of education), and participant characteristics (e.g., drug use).

This study provides strong empirical evidence that lead is implicated in the development of violent crime.

Healthy prenatal environments are essential for normal fetal development, including normal brain development. It is no surprise to learn that toxins that cross the placenta and enter the fetus can lead to abnormal brain development, which may result in structural and functional deficits. These deficits, in turn, may confer an increased risk of maladaptive behaviors, including crime, delinquency, and violence. Although the preceding discussion focused on just three toxins—prenatal exposure to cigarettes, alcohol, and industrial chemicals—it should be noted that there are many other toxins that are known to interfere with brain development. Unfortunately, there is a scarcity of empirical research examining whether these other toxins relate to antisocial phenotypes.

Prenatal malnutrition. Prenatal nutrition is critical to healthy fetal development, including fetal brain development. With the help of prenatal vitamins, most pregnant women consume the necessary amount of vitamins, minerals, and other essential nutrients that are needed by the fetus. Sometimes, however, for a variety of reasons, ranging from extreme poverty to countrywide famines, pregnant mothers are unable to eat diets that contain adequate amounts of prenatal nutrients. The effects of prenatal malnutrition are wide and varied and depend, in large part, on the severity of malnutrition, where generally speaking, more serious malnutrition corresponds to more deleterious outcomes. Not surprisingly, prenatal malnutrition can also adversely affect fetal brain development[84], which can result in permanent damage to particular regions of the brain, including the hippocampus[85] and the cerebellum.[86] These brain regions have been tied to antisocial phenotypes (see Chapter 4) and, as a result, some scholars have posited that prenatal malnutrition may be associated with antisocial phenotypes via its adverse effects on certain brain regions.

One of the main problems with examining the effects of prenatal malnutrition on later life phenotypes is that prenatal malnutrition covaries with sociodemographics. To illustrate, pregnant women living in poverty are more likely to consume inadequate prenatal diets when compared to pregnant women not living in poverty. Poverty, as many criminologists point out, is a risk factor for delinquent and criminal behavior. So, if prenatal malnutrition was found to be related to antisocial behavior, it could really be due to the effect of sociodemographics (e.g., poverty) and not malnutrition per se. In other words, it is difficult to disentangle the effects of poverty (or any other potentially confounding measure, such as race, age, etc.) from the effects of prenatal malnutrition. One way to overcome this serious problem is by restricting the diets of all pregnant women, including the rich and the poor, the white and the nonwhite, and so on and so forth. Then the offspring who were malnourished in utero could be compared to the offspring who were not malnourished. Any phenotypic differences between these two groups would most likely be the result of prenatal malnutrition. While this type of experiment would be unethical, it would provide the most direct way to separate the effect of prenatal malnutrition from other confounding measures.

Researchers have searched for ways to isolate the influence of malnutrition on human development. They have discovered that famines can be used to study the effects of prenatal malnutrition. Famines are a type of naturally occurring experiment, where pregnant women from all walks of life have diets that are severely restricted. In this way, all other potentially confounding factors are presumably held constant. Two studies exist that test the relationship between famine and antisocial phenotypes. In the first study, Richard Neugebauer and colleagues examined the effect that prenatal exposure to famine had on subsequent adulthood antisocial personality disorder.[87] To do so, they analyzed a sample of Dutch males who were born from 1944 to 1946. Between 1944 and 1945 the German army blockaded the delivery of food to the Netherlands, which initially lead to moderate malnutrition, but ultimately resulted in severe malnutrition. Using birth dates and locations of birth, Neugebauer et al. identified a group of males who were not exposed to malnutrition in utero, a group of males who were exposed to moderate malnutrition in utero, and a group of males who were exposed to severe malnutrition in utero. The results of their study revealed that males who were exposed to severe malnutrition during the first and second trimesters of pregnancy had increased odds of antisocial personality disorder compared to males who were not exposed to such high levels of prenatal malnutrition. Exposure to moderate levels of prenatal malnutrition and exposure to severe malnutrition during the third trimester of pregnancy were both unrelated to antisocial personality disorder. This team of researchers concluded by calling attention to the possibility "that severe nutritional insults to the developing brain in utero may be capable of increasing the risk for antisocial behaviors in offspring."[88]

In the second study, Ernst Franzek et al. examined the effect that this same famine had on addictive behaviors in a sample of males and females.[89] They found that subjects who had been exposed to the famine during the first trimester were more likely to become addicted to substances during adulthood compared with subjects who were not exposed to famine during this trimester. Once again, the study authors concluded that severe prenatal malnutrition probably led to addiction via adversely affecting brain development in utero. The possibility that prenatal malnutrition is associated with antisocial phenotypes later in life remains an interesting line of inquiry, but given that only a handful of studies exist on this topic, much more research is needed before any definitive conclusions can be reached.

Prenatal exposure to stress. Maternal stress during pregnancy has been found to have effects on a number of cognitive and behavioral outcomes in offspring.[90] As with the other prenatal environments discussed so far, there is reason to believe that prenatal exposure to stress can alter fetal brain development. Studies conducted on non-human animals have found prenatal exposure to stress to result in modifications to limbic system structures[91], including the hippocampus[92], and to affect the structure of the prefrontal cortex.[93] These anatomical changes are probably the result of hormonal changes that occur in response to stress. Exposure to stressful stimuli is known to stimulate the release of stress hormones, such as cortisol (see Chapter 4 for a discussion of hypothalamic-pituitary-adrenal [HPA] axis), and these hormones are thought to affect the structure of the developing brain.

Given that research using humans has found that maternal stress during pregnancy increases levels of cortisol in utero[94], it is likely that maternal stress during pregnancy affects the developing brain (particularly the hippocampus) in humans.[95] If this is the case, then it is also feasible that maternal stress during pregnancy could relate to antisocial phenotypes later in life. Researchers have investigated this possibility and they have found some evidence that prenatal exposure to stress has adverse effects that begin to emerge during infancy and that are carried forward into adolescence. In infants, prenatal exposure to stress has been linked to negative affect[96], poor reactivity to distressful situations[97], and delayed motor and mental skills.[98] Exposure to stress in utero has also been found to increase the odds of ADHD[99] and externalizing problem behaviors[100] in children and impulsivity in adolescents.[101] Since all of these phenotypes are strong predictors of criminal involvement later in life, it is possible that prenatal exposure to stress may also affect the odds of engaging in crime during adolescence and adulthood. This remains pure speculation because criminologists have yet to examine this possibility.

Perinatal Environmental Influences

The previous section examined a number of different prenatal environments that are tied to the development of antisocial phenotypes. Technically speaking, the prenatal period spans from conception through about the sixth month of gestation, after which the perinatal period begins. The perinatal period runs from about the seventh month of gestation through about the first month after birth. During this time, the brain continues to develop and, consequently, is susceptible to environmental insults. Two of the more salient perinatal environments, at least in terms of their effects on the brain and being related to crime and delinquency, are birth complications and low birth weight. The following discussion will examine the potential relationship between these perinatal environments and subsequent antisocial phenotypes. Just remember that once again these environments are thought to exert their influence on behavior via altering brain structure and/or functioning.

Birth complications. A broad range of complications can occur at birth, some of which are relatively minor (e.g., a cesarean section) and some of which can be extremely severe (e.g., anoxia and meconium). Although minor birth complications do not likely result in any long-term deleterious effects, serious birth complications, such as anoxia (i.e., oxygen starvation), can result in permanent damage to the brain[102], including damage to the prefrontal cortex,[103] which, in turn, may cause executive dysfunctions.[104] Severe birth complications, therefore, are thought to be related to antisocial phenotypes via the damage they inflict on the brain.

There is a line of research that has examined the nexus between birth complications and criminal behaviors later in life. In a landmark study, Elizabeth Kandel and Sarnoff Mednick analyzed a sample of 216 adults to test for an association between birth complications and official measures of violent offending and property offending.[105] The results of their analysis indicated that birth complications were a significant predictor of violent offending, but not property offending.

This study provided some of the first empirical evidence that birth complications could affect the odds of involvement in later life violent offending. Subsequent researchers have built off this study and begun to examine not only the association between birth complications and criminal outcomes, but also whether certain environments interact with birth complications (i.e., a biosocial interaction between birth complications and environmental factors) to predict crime and delinquency. For example, Adrian Raine and his colleagues detected a biosocial interaction between birth complications and maternal rejection in the prediction of violent crime at the age of 18.[106] Other studies have found birth complications to interact with the family environment in the prediction of violent offending[107] and nonviolent offending.[108] It should be pointed out, however, that some studies have failed to detect this biosocial interaction.[109] Nonetheless, after reviewing the research examining biosocial interactions and their relation to crime, Adrian Raine concluded that "the best-replicated biosocial effect appears to consist of birth complications interacting with negative home environments in predisposing to adult violence … "[110]

Low birth weight. Approximately 8 percent of all babies are considered low-birth weight babies, meaning that they weigh below 5.5 pounds at birth. The causes of low birth weight are wide and varied but include preterm birth, prenatal exposure to cigarette smoke, inadequate maternal weight gain (perhaps leading to malnutrition in the fetus), and psychosocial factors (e.g., maternal stress).[111] Low birth weight serves as a visible indicator, at least in some cases, of the presence of one or more of these other risk factors. What is particularly interesting is that all of these other risk factors have been found to relate to abnormal brain development (see discussion above) and thus low birth weight is likely a (crude) indicator of neurological deficits. Babies who are born with a low birth weight face a number of difficulties that normal weight babies do not. For example, low birth weight babies, in comparison with babies of normal weight, have higher infant mortality rates, are more likely to display abnormal social development, have lower IQs, and are at risk for school failure.[112] There is also some evidence that low birth weight babies are at risk for engaging in serious antisocial phenotypes during adolescence and adulthood.

Studies have revealed, for example, that low birth weight babies are more likely than normal birth weight babies to have an early onset of criminal offending.[113] This is a particularly important finding because an early onset of offending is one of the strongest predictors of future violence, number of arrests accrued, and the persistence of crime into adulthood.[114] These reports should be tempered by the fact that a number of studies have failed to detect any association between low birth weight and antisocial outcomes.[115] One potential reason why some researchers have failed to detect an effect of low birth weight is because they have neglected to take into account the possible biosocial interactions between low birth weight and environmental risk factors. Stephen Tibbetts and Alex Piquero addressed this issue in a sample of 207 offenders.[116] The results of their statistical models indicated that low birth weight interacted with low socioeconomic status and with weak family structure to predict an early onset of offending. The results of this study, along with those of others[117], provide some evidence that low birth weight—especially when paired with criminogenic environments—is associated with serious violent offending.

Environmental Influences during Infancy and Early Childhood

The first three years of life represent a time of tremendous physical, emotional, and behavioral change. During this section of the life course, children learn to walk, to talk, and to form and sustain social relationships. Just as important as these outward physical changes, are the changes that are occurring in the brain. During infancy and childhood, the brain continues to form and develop at an astonishing rate by laying down new synaptic connections (i.e., connections between axons and dendrites) and eliminating existing ones in response to environmental stimuli. To grossly oversimplify, synaptic connections that are stimulated are retained (or built if not yet formed), while those synaptic connections that are not stimulated are pruned (or not built if not yet formed). This process is often referred to as "neural Darwinism" as only the strongest and most fit synapses survive (also captured with the "use-it-or-lose-it" slogan). In this way, the brain is partially a reflection of the social environment in which children are embedded.

For example, if a child is exposed to violence, abuse, and neglect on a daily basis, then their brain will develop differently than if they had been exposed to a loving, warm, and enriched environment. This is particularly important because it underscores the fact that environmental experiences early in life are integral in shaping the developing brain. And as Chapter 4 discussed, the brain is largely responsible for determining phenotypic outcomes. What this means is that early life environmental conditions may affect later life antisocial phenotypes by affecting the structure and functioning of the brain. Below we will explore three environments— exposure to toxins, exposure to malnutrition, and exposure to severe abuse and neglect—all of which have been found to affect brain development and have also been to antisocial phenotypes later in life.

Exposure to toxins. Infants and children are particularly vulnerable to toxins. Remember that the brain is maturing at a rapid rate during the first three years of life and, just as prenatal exposure to toxins can disrupt brain development, so too can exposure to toxins very early in life. What is particularly problematic is that young children engage in a host of behaviors (e.g., crawling, putting objects in their mouth, etc.) that places them in contact with chemicals and toxins (e.g., house dust, dirt, etc.). This is compounded by the fact that children, compared to adults, absorb toxins at greater rates whether it is by inhalation, by skin contact, or by oral absorption. And, relative to adults, children are also less able to detoxify (i.e., eliminate) these chemicals once they are absorbed.[118] Taken together, toxins represent a major threat to healthy brain development early in life because 1) the brain is in a major stage of critical development, 2) children come into contact with a wide range of toxins, 3) children are more likely than adults to absorb these toxins, and 4) children are less able than adults to detoxify these toxins from their body. Although hundreds of toxins have been identified as having particularly harmful effects[119], only two will be briefly discussed here: cigarette smoke and lead.

Exposure to environmental tobacco smoke (sometimes referred to as secondhand smoke) has become a major public health concern in the United States. With reports that environmental tobacco smoke increases the risk of cancer and other serious diseases[120], interest groups pressured companies, restaurants, universities, and large-scale corporations to prohibit smoking on their premises. These movements have been largely successful and rates of secondhand exposure have dropped in the public domain. Infants and children, however, continue to be exposed to second-hand smoke at alarming rates. For example, conservative estimates indicate that about 11 percent of all children under the age of six are exposed to cigarette smoke *in their home* on a regular basis, which translates into about three million children.[121] These exposure rates are particularly important because research has revealed that early life exposure to cigarette smoke interferes with brain development[122] and produces reduced cognitive abilities.[123] There is also mounting evidence indicating that exposure to environmental tobacco smoke early in life is associated with maladaptive behaviors, including antisocial behavior, attention problems, conduct disorder, externalizing behavioral problems, and hyperactivity.[124] The results of these studies hint at the very real possibility that exposure to cigarette smoke during the first few years of life might be a contributing factor to subsequent behavioral problems.

In addition to environmental tobacco smoke, lead is another toxin that children regularly come into contact with. Approximately three percent of all children under the age of six are exposed to high levels of lead. These rates of lead exposure, however, vary considerably across different racial groups. For example, when looking at children under the age of six, nearly 9 percent of African Americans, 5.5 percent of Hispanics, and 2 percent of whites have elevated blood lead levels (i.e., blood lead levels > $10\mu g/dL$). Similar to the effects of environmental tobacco smoke, exposure to lead during childhood also appears to interfere with brain development, including regions of the brain that are responsible for executive functions[125], and to confer an increased risk to antisocial behaviors later in life.[126]

Studies have reported a link between elevated childhood blood lead levels and criminal arrests, including arrests for violent crimes[127] and juvenile delinquency, including both self-reported delinquency[128] and official delinquency.[129] These associations remain even after controlling for a host of confounders, such as SES and neighborhood disadvantage.[130] Additional evidence of the effect that lead has on criminal outcomes comes from macro-level research. Some studies have shown, for example, that part of the reason for why crime rates, including homicide rates, vary from country to country is because of country-to-country variations in rates of childhood lead exposure.[131] In general, there is a positive association between exposure to lead and violent crime rates, where crime rates tend to be higher in countries with higher rates of lead exposure. The consistency with which studies find a connection between lead exposure and antisocial phenotypes points to the very real possibility that lead plays an important role in the development of violence specifically and crime more generally.[132]

Exposure to malnutrition. A healthy diet consists of vitamins, minerals and other nutrients that are essential in supporting early childhood development. Although nutrition is known to affect the brain, including cognitive processes and abilities[133], and although a handful of studies have found a link between certain nutritional deficiencies and behavior[134], there is only one well-designed study that has examined the association between childhood malnutrition and subsequent antisocial behaviors. This study, conducted by Jianghong Liu and colleagues, employed a large birth cohort (N = 1,795) and included measures of malnutrition (at age 3), neurocognitive deficits, and antisocial and aggressive behaviors.[135] A total of 353 subjects were identified as being malnourished and they were compared to subjects who were not malnourished. The malnourished children, in comparison with unaffected children, were rated as more aggressive at the age of eight, they had more externalizing problem behaviors at the age of 11, and they had more symptoms of conduct disorder at the age of 17. Moreover, their analysis also revealed that the degree of malnutrition mattered—that is, behavioral problems were worse among those children who were the most malnourished.

Liu et al. were interested in trying to uncover the mechanism(s) that accounted for the link between malnourishment and antisocial phenotypes. To do so, they examined whether measures of neurocognitive deficits were associated with malnutrition and with the behavioral outcomes. They found that neurocognitive impairments mediated the relationship between malnutrition and antisocial behavior, meaning that childhood malnutrition led to neurocognitive deficits and neurocognitive deficits led to antisocial phenotypes. The study authors interpreted their findings by opining "that early malnutrition negatively affects brain growth and development and that brain impairments predispose to antisocial and violent behavior by affecting cognitive functions."[136] While this study provides strong evidence of a link between early malnutrition and later life behavioral problems, more research is needed to determine the consistency with which this effect might be observed.

Exposure to severe abuse and neglect. Rearing-environments can be arranged along a continuum, where the worst rearing-environments are found at one end of the continuum and the best rearing-environments are found at the other end of the continuum (see Figure 5.3). For example, rearing-environments that provide children with love and affection are probably considered by most people to be better than rearing-environments that fail to provide children with love and affection. Even though rearing-environments vary (and they can vary quite drastically) most are sufficient enough to promote normal human development. What this means is that most children are exposed to rearing-environments that fall within the normal range of variation and thus they all receive the necessary stimulation to live, develop, and mature normally. It is only a relatively small percentage of all children who are reared in environments that lack love, affection, and warmth, while concomitantly being subjected to physical, sexual, and/or physical abuse and other forms of maltreatment *on a regular basis*. These types of environments are labeled as "criminogenic rearing-environments" in Figure 5.3. All of the rearing-environments to the right of the criminogenic rearing-environments would be considered rearing-environments that fall within the normal range of variation.

There is little doubt that the criminogenic rearing-environments described above are associated with various forms of maladjustment and perhaps even antisocial phenotypes.[137] But, what is controversial is that it is unlikely that any of the rearing-environments that fall within the normal range of variation (i.e., above the criminogenic threshold) have any affect on the development of antisocial phenotypes.[138] Most criminological research, however, examines whether variations in normal rearing-environments are associated with antisocial phenotypes and fails to include samples with a sufficient number of respondents who were exposed to criminogenic rearing-environments (as defined above). Perhaps this methodological shortcoming may explain why parenting measures have such weak and inconsistent effects on adolescent delinquency and adult criminal behavior.[139] With that said, research has revealed that children who are raised in criminogenic environments are at greater risk for displaying antisocial behaviors later in life when compared to non-abused children.[140] (It should be noted, however, that most children who were abused, including being sexually abused, mature into prosocial adolescents and adults.) Exposure to severe neglect and abuse early in life has been linked with a number of structural modifications to the brain, including regions of the brain that have been tied to antisocial phenotypes (see Chapter 4).[141]

Chronic exposure to stressful situations causes the body to release steroid hormones called glucocorticoids (one of which is cortisol) and when these hormones are present in large quantities for prolonged periods of time, they can

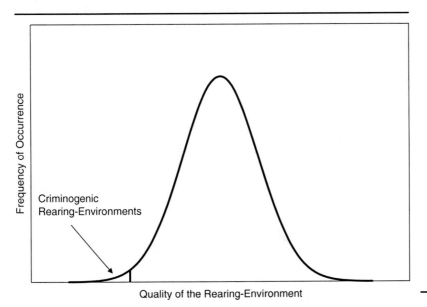

Criminogenic
Rearing-Environments

Frequency of Occurrence

Quality of the Rearing-Environment

Figure 5.3
The distribution in the quality of rearing-environments.

affect the central nervous system, including the brain.[142] Since the brain is still developing during childhood, early life exposure to stress has the greatest potential to affect and alter brain maturation. Neuroscience research has revealed, for example, that severe abuse and neglect in childhood is associated with disruptions to the neocortex and the hippocampus[143], while the amygdala and the corpus callosum[144] have been found to be smaller in abused children when compared to non-abused children.[145]

Some of the best evidence linking early exposure to abuse/neglect and brain alterations comes from studies conducted on Romanian orphans. In Romania during the 1980s more than 65,000 children were sent to be raised in orphanages. The conditions of these orphanages were horrific: the child-to-caregiver ratio was about 10-to-1 for infants and they spent upwards of 20 hours a day alone in their cribs. The situation was no better for older children, where the child-to-caregiver ratio was 20-to-1 for children over the age of three. These children were reared in severe deprivation where they were exposed to unsanitary conditions, infectious diseases, and were generally reared in hellish conditions. Then with the fall of the Ceauçescu regime in 1990, these orphanages were exposed and, since that time, many of the orphans have been adopted worldwide.

Some of the Romanian orphans were subjected to a battery of tests at the time of their adoption and they were found to have severe mental and developmental deficits as well as behavioral problems.[146] To examine whether these phenotypes were the result of neurological damage, researchers have used brain-imaging techniques (see Chapter 4) to examine the structure and function of the Romanian orphans' brains. These neuroimaging studies have found the prefrontal cortex, the amygdala, the hippocampus, and other brain regions to differ significantly between the orphans and control subjects.[147] These are many of the same brain regions that are tied to aggression, violence, and other antisocial phenotypes.

The neuroimaging studies conducted on the Romanian orphans have provided strong evidence that early life exposure to abusive and neglectful environments can shape the developing brain.[148] Perhaps this is one of the reasons for why criminological research has found childhood exposure to abuse to be a risk factor for involvement in crime and delinquency. Unfortunately, criminologists have yet to examine the interrelationships among early abuse, brain development, and later life crime.

Summary

This chapter described the environmental factors that biosocial criminologists have identified as particularly important to the development of antisocial phenotypes. Although many other environmental conditions are also implicated in the etiology of criminal outcomes, this chapter reviewed those that met two requirements. First, the environment had to be a nonshared environment. Second, the environment had to be known to affect brain development. With these two criteria in place, three groups of environments were identified: prenatal environments, perinatal environments, and environments in infancy and early childhood. The current chapter presented evidence discussing how these environments affect the developing brain and how these neurological disruptions are ultimately responsible for the production of antisocial phenotypes.

Key Points

- For biosocial criminologists, the environment refers to any non-genetic factors.

- Environments affect phenotypes by affecting the developing brain.

- The brain is developing at an astonishing rate during pregnancy and during the first three years of life.

- Higher levels of prenatal testosterone result in more "male-like" behaviors.

- The 2D:4D ratio is an indirect way to measure prenatal exposure to testosterone.

- Lower 2D:4D ratios reflect greater exposure to testosterone in utero and so, on average, males have lower 2D:4D ratios than females.

- Lower 2D:4D ratios are associated with more violence and aggression.

- Prenatal exposure to cigarette smoke, alcohol, industrial chemicals, malnutrition, and stress are all associated with subsequent antisocial phenotypes.

- The interaction between a biological risk factor (e.g., low birth weight) and an environmental risk factor (e.g., an adverse home environment) is known as a biosocial interaction.

- Biosocial interactions tend to have stronger effects on phenotypes when compared to the main effect of the biological or environmental risk factor.

- Prenatal exposure to lead is a strong risk factor for serious violence during adolescence and adulthood.

- Perinatal environments, including birth complications and low birth weight, are associated with later life antisocial phenotypes.

- Environmental influences during infancy and childhood, such as exposure to toxins, malnutrition, and severe abuse/neglect, are all related to involvement in antisocial phenotypes later in life.

1. Sociological criminologists typically study what types of environments?

   a) shared environments
   b) environments that affect the brain
   c) nonshared environments
   d) all of the above

2. Exposure to testosterone in utero _____ the fetal brain.

   a) feminizes   c) harms
   b) masculinizes   d) none of the above

3. Girls with congenital adrenal hyperplasia (CAH) display a variety of phenotypes that are typical of _____.

   a) females   b) males   c) adults   d) adolescents

4. The 2D:4D ratio is a(n) _____ measure of prenatal exposure to testosterone.

   a) direct
   b) unreliable
   c) indirect
   d) none of theabove

5. In general, a lower 2D:4D ratio corresponds with _____ antisocial behavior.

   a) more
   b) less
   c) equal
   d) none of theabove

6. Prenatal exposure to toxins has been found to interfere with
_____.

    a) marital quality   c) brain development
    b) athletic abilities   d) none of the above

7. Approximately _____ percent of all pregnant women smoke
cigarettes.

    a) zero
    b) one
    c) fifty
    d) none of the above

8. Prenatal exposure to lead has relatively _____ and
_____ effects on later life involvement in crime and
delinquency.

    a) small, inconsistent   c) large, inconsistent
    b) small, consistent   d) large, consistent

9. Two perinatal environments that have been found to affect antisocial
behaviors later in life are _____ and _____.

    a) birth complications, hospitals
    b) birth weight, hospitals
    c) birth complications, birth weight
    d) none of the above

10. The brain stops developing _____.

    a) in utero
    b) at birth
    c) at the age of three
    d) none of the above

1. Discuss the differences between the environments studied by most sociological criminologists and the environments studied by biosocial criminologists.

2. Describe what is meant by a biosocial interaction. Provide an example of a biosocial interaction.

3. Researchers have consistently found a relationship between prenatal exposure to cigarette smoke and subsequent antisocial behavior. Discuss two alternative explanations for this association. (Hint: think about spuriousness and think about the brain.)

4. Identify one prenatal environment that is associated with antisocial behaviors later in life. Describe how the prenatal environment you chose ultimately produces the antisocial behavior.

5. It is generally accepted that abuse/neglect early in life is a risk factor for criminal outcomes during adolescence and adulthood. Provide an explanation of how abuse/neglect creates these antisocial phenotypes.

Further Reading

Baron-Cohen, S., Lutchmaya, S., & Knickmeyer, R. (2004). *Prenatal testosterone in mind: Amniotic fluid studies.* Cambridge, MA: MIT Press.

Cohen, D. B. (1999). *Stranger in the nest: Do parents really shape their child's personality, intelligence, or character?* New York: John Wiley and Sons.

Karr-Morse, R., & Wiley, M. S. (1997). *Ghosts from the nursery: Tracing the roots of violence.* New York: Atlantic Monthly Press.

Manning, J. T. (2002). *Digit ratio: A pointer to fertility, behavior, and health.* Piscataway, NJ: Rutgers University Press.

Martin, R. P., & Dombrowski, S. C. (2008). *Prenatal exposures: Psychological and educational consequences for children.* New York: Springer.

Rowe, D. C. (1994). *The limits of family influence: Genes, experience, and behavior.* New York: Guilford Press.

Shonkoff, J. P., & Phillips, D. A. (2000). *From neurons to neighborhoods: The science of early childhood development.* Washington, DC: National Academy Press.

Shore, R. (1997). *Rethinking the brain: New insights into early development.* New York: Families and Work Institute.

End Notes

1. This is not to say that environments are free of genetic influences; rather, almost all environments are at least partially influenced by genetic factors (see Chapter 2). The environments explored in the current chapter are no exception.

2. Beaver, K. M., Wright, J. P., & DeLisi, M. (2007). Self-control as an executive function: Reformulating Gottfredson and Hirschi's parental socialization thesis. *Criminal Justice and Behavior, 34*, 1345–1361.

3. Breedlove, S. M. (1994). Sexual differentiation of the human nervous system. *Annual Review of Psychology, 45*, 389–418.

4. Brizendine, L. (2006). *The female brain.* New York: Morgan Road Books.

5. Mazur, A. (2005). *Biosociology of dominance and deference.* Lanham, MD: Rowman and Littlefield.

6. Collaer, M. L., & Hines, M. (1995). Human behavioral sex differences: A role for gonadal hormones during early development? *Psychological Bulletin, 118*, 55–107.

7. American Academy of Pediatrics: Section on Endocrinology and Committee on Genetics. (2000). Technical report: congenital adrenal hyperplasia. *Pediatrics, 106*, 1511–1518.

8. Ehrhardt, A. A., & Baker, S. W. (1974). Fetal androgens, human central nervous system differentiation, and behavior sex differences. In Friedman, R. C., Richart, R. M., & van de Wiele, R. L. (Eds.), *Sex differences in behavior.* New York: Wiley.

9. Hines, M., & Kaufman, F. R. (1994). Androgen and the development of human sex-typical behavior: Rough-and-tumble play and sex of preferred playmates in children with congenital adrenal hyperplasia (CAH). *Child Development, 65*, 1042–1053.

10. Hines, M., Brook, C., & Conway, G. S. (2004). Androgen and psychosexual development: Core gender identity, sexual orientation and recalled childhood gender role behavior in women and men with congenital adrenal hyperplasia (CAH). *Journal of Sex Research, 41*, 75–81.

11. Fausto-Sterling, A. (1992). *Myths of gender.* New York: Basic Books; Quadagno, D. M., Briscoe, R., & Quadagno, J. S. (1977). Effect of perinatal gonadal hormones on selected non-sexual behavior patterns: A critical assessment of the nonhuman and human literature. *Psychological Bulletin, 84*, 62–80.

12. Pasterski, V. L., Geffner, M. E., Brain, C., Hindmarsh, P., Brook, C., & Hines, M. (2005). Prenatal hormones and postnatal socialization by parents as determinants of male-typical toy play in girls with congenital adrenal hyperplasia. *Child Development, 76*, 264–278.

13. Cohen-Bendahan, C. C. C., van de Beek, C., & Berenbaum, S. A. (2005). Prenatal sex hormone effects on child and sex-typed behavior: Methods and findings. *Neuroscience and Biobehavioral Reviews, 29*, 353–384.

14. Brizendine, L. (2006). *The female brain.* New York: Morgan Road Books; Moir, A., & Jessel, D. (1992). *Brain sex: The real difference between men and women.* New York: Dell Publishing; Rhoads, S. E. (2004). *Taking sex differences seriously.* San Francisco, CA: Encounter Books.

15. Ehrhardt, A. A., & Baker, S. W. (1974). Fetal androgens, human central nervous system differentiation, and behavior sex differences. In Friedman, R. C., Richart, R. M., & van de Wiele, R. L. (Eds.), *Sex differences in behavior.* New York: Wiley; Ehrhardt, A. A., Epstein, R., & Money, J. (1968). Fetal androgens and female gender identity in the early-treated adrenogenital syndrome. *Johns Hopkins Medical Journal, 122*, 165–167; Money, J., & Schwartz, M. (1976). Fetal androgens in the early treated adrenogenital syndrome of 46 XX hermaphroditism: Influence on assertive and aggressive types of behavior. *Aggressive Behavior, 2*, 19–30.

16. Pasterski, V., Hindmarsh, P., Geffner, M., Brook, C., Brain, C., & Hines, M. (2007). Increased aggression and activity level in 3- to 11-year-old girls with congenital adrenal hyperplasia (CAH). *Hormones and Behavior, 52*, 368–374.

17. Berenbaum, S. A., & Resnick, S. M. (1997). Early androgen effects on aggression in children and adults with congenital adrenal hyperplasia. *Psychoneuroendocrinology, 22*, 505–515.

18. Pasterski, V., Hindmarsh, P., Geffner, M., Brook, C., Brain, C., & Hines, M. (2007). Increased aggression and activity level in 3- to 11-year-old girls with congenital adrenal hyperplasia (CAH). *Hormones and Behavior, 52*, 368–374.

19. Pasterski, V., Hindmarsh, P., Geffner, M., Brook, C., Brain, C., & Hines, M. (2007). Increased aggression and activity level in 3- to 11-year-old girls with congenital adrenal hyperplasia (CAH). *Hormones and Behavior, 52*, 368–374,p. 371.

20. Cohen-Bendahan, C. C. C., van de Beek, C., & Berenbaum, S. A. (2005). Prenatal sex hormone effects on child and sex-typed behavior: Methods and findings. *Neuroscience and Biobehavioral Reviews, 29*, 353–384.

21. Manning, J. T. (2002). *Digit ratio: A pointer to fertility, behavior, and health.* Piscataway, NJ: Rutgers University Press.

22. Kondo, T., Zakany, J., Innis, J. W., & Duboule, D. (1997). Of fingers, toes, and penises. *Nature, 390*, 29.

23. Manning, J. T., & Taylor, R. P. (2001). Second to fourth digit ratio and male ability in sport: Implications for sexual selection in humans. *Evolution and Human Behavior, 22,* 61–69.

24. Manning, J. T., Baron-Cohen, S., Wheelwright, S., & Sanders, G. (2001). The 2nd to 4th digit ratio and autism. *Developmental Medicine and Child Neurology, 43,* 160–164.

25. Sluming, V. A., & Manning, J. T. (2000). Second to fourth digit ratio in elite musicians: Evidence for musical ability as an honest signal of male fitness. *Evolution and Human Behavior, 21,* 1–9.

26. Cohen-Bendahan, C. C. C., van de Beek, C., & Berenbaum, S. A. (2005). Prenatal sex hormone effects on child and sex-typed behavior: Methods and findings. *Neuroscience and Biobehavioral Reviews, 29,* 353–384; Rahman, Q., & Wilson, G. D. (2003). Sexual orientation and the 2nd to 4th finger length ratio: Evidence for organizing effects of sex hormones or developmental instability? *Psychoneuroendocrinology, 28,* 288–303; Williams, T. J., Pepitine, M. E., Christensen, S. E., Cooke, B. M., Huberman, A. D., Breedlove, N. J., Breedlove, T. J., Jordan, C. L., & Breedlove, S. M. (2000). Finger length ratio and sexual orientation. *Nature, 404,* 455–456.

27. Williams, J. H. G., Greenhalgh, K. D., & Manning, J. T. (2003). Second to fourth finger ratio and possible precursors of developmental psychopathology in preschool children. *Early Human Development, 72,* 57–65.

28. Austin, E. J., Manning, J. T., McInroy, K., & Mathews, E. (2002). A preliminary investigation of the associations between personality, cognitive ability and digit ratio. *Personality and Individual Differences, 33,* 1115–1124.

29. McIntyre, M. H., Barrett, E. S., McDermott, R., Johnson, D. D. P., Cowden, J., & Rosen, S. (2007). Finger length ratio (2D:4D) and sex differences in aggression during a simulated war game. *Personality and Individual Differences, 42,* 755–764.

30. Millet, K., & Dewitte, S. (2007). Digit ratio (2D:4D) moderates the impact of an aggressive music video on aggression. *Personality and Individual Differences, 43,* 289–294.

31. Benderlioglu, Z., & Nelson, R. J. (2004). Digit length ratios predict reactive aggression in women, but not in men. *Hormones and Behavior, 46,* 558–564.

32. Bailey, A. A., & Hurd, P. L. (2005). Finger length ratio (2D:4D) correlates with physical aggression in men but not in women. *Biological Psychiatry, 68,* 215–222.

33. Hampson, E., Ellis, C. L., & Tenk, C. M. (2008). On the relation between 2D:4D and sex-dimorphic personality traits. *Archives of Sexual Behavior, 37,* 133–144.

34. Cohen-Bendahan, C. C. C., van de Beek, C., & Berenbaum, S. A. (2005). Prenatal sex hormone effects on child and sex-typed behavior: Methods and findings. *Neuroscience and Biobehavioral Reviews, 29*, 353–384.

35. Hines, M., Golombok, S., Rust, J., Johnston, K. J., Golding, J., & the Avon Longitudinal Study of Parents and Children Study Team. (2002). Testosterone during pregnancy and gender role behavior of preschool children: A longitudinal population study. *Child Development, 73*, 1678–1687.

36. Jacklin, C. N., Maccoby, E. E., & Doering, C. H. (1983). Neonatal sex-steroid hormones and timidity in 6- to-18-month-old boys and girls. *Developmental Psychobiology, 21*, 567–574.

37. Udry, J. R. (2000). Biological limits of gender construction. *American Sociological Review, 65*, 443–457; Udry, J. R. (1994). The nature of gender. *Demography, 31*, 561–573.

38. Kondo, T., Zakany, J., Innis, J. W., & Duboule, D. (1997). Of fingers, toes, and penises. *Nature, 390*, 29.

39. Blanchard, R. (2004). Quantitative and theoretical analyses of the relation between older brothers and homosexuality in men. *Journal of Theoretical Biology, 230*, 173–187; Blanchard, R., & Bogaert. (1996). Homosexuality in men and number of older brothers. *American Journal of Psychiatry, 153*, 27–31.

40. Ellis, L. (2005). A theory explaining biological correlates of criminality. *European Journal of Criminology, 2*, 287–315.

41. Cnattingius, S., Lindmark, G., & Meirik, O. (1992). Who continues to smoke while pregnant? *Journal of Epidemiology Community Health, 46*, 218–221; Haug, K., Aaro, L. E., & Fugelli, P. (1992). Smoking habits in early pregnancy and attitudes towards smoking cessation among pregnant women and their partners. *Family Practice, 9*, 494–499; Nishimura, B. K., Adams, K. E., Melvin, C. L., Merritt, R. K., Tucker, P. J., Stuart, G., & Rivera, C. C. (2006). *Prenatal data smoking book*. Washington, DC: Center for Disease Control, Reproductive Health.

42. Smith, B., Martin, J., & Ventura, S. (1999). *Births and deaths: Preliminary data for July 1997-June, 1998*. Hyattsville, MD: National Center for Health Statistics.

43. Slotkin, T. A., Seidler, F. J., Qiao, D., Aldridge, J. E. et al. (2005). Effects of prenatal nicotine exposure on primate brain development and attempted amelioration with supplemental choline or vitamin c: Neurotransmitter receptors, cell signaling and cell development biomarkers in fetal brain regions of rhesus monkeys. *Neuropsychopharmacology, 30*, 129–144.

44. Abreu-Villaça, Y., Seidler, F. J., & Slotkin, T. A. (2004). Does prenatal nicotine exposure sensitize the brain to nicotine-induced neurotoxicity in adolescence? *Neuropsychopharmacology, 29*, 1440–1450.

45. Muneoka, K., Ogawa, T., Kamei, K., Muraoka, S. et al. (1997). Prenatal nicotine exposure affects the development of the central nervous system as well as the dopaminergic system in rat offspring: Involvement of route of drug administrations. *Developmental Brain Research, 102*, 117–126.

46. Cigarettes contain thousands of chemicals. As a result, it is impossible in non-experimental studies (which is what is used with human subjects) to isolate the effect of nicotine from all of these other chemicals. Stated differently, if prenatal exposure to cigarettes is associated with phenotypic outcomes, it is not possible to say with certainty that the effect is due to nicotine versus some other chemical. It is commonly assumed, however, that nicotine is the active agent in cigarettes that adversely affects the developing fetus. Nonetheless, this section will talk in terms of prenatal exposure to cigarettes as opposed to nicotine.

47. Rivkin, M. J., Davis, P. E., Lemaster, J. L. et al. (2008). Volumetric MRI study of brain in children with intrauterine exposure to cocaine, alcohol, tobacco, and marijuana. *Pediatrics, 121*, 741–750.

48. Rizwan, S., Manning, J. T., & Brabin, B. J. (2007). Maternal smoking during pregnancy and possible effects of in utero testosterone: Evidence from the 2D:4D finger length ratio. *Early Human Development, 83*, 87–90.

49. Sexton, M., Fox, N. L., & Hebel, J. R. (1990). Prenatal exposure to tobacco: II. Effects on cognitive functioning at age three. *International Journal of Epidemiology, 19*, 72–77.

50. Martin, R. P., Dombrowski, S. C., Mullis, C., Wisenbaker, J., & Huttunen, M. O. (2006). Smoking during pregnancy: Association with childhood temperament, behavior, and academic performance. *Journal of Pediatric Psychology, 31*, 490–500.

51. Huijbregts, S. C., Séguin, J. R., Zoccolillo, M., Boivin, M., & Tremblay, R. E. (2007). Associations of maternal prenatal smoking with early childhood physical aggression, hyperactivity-impulsivity, and their co-occurrence. *Journal of Abnormal Child Psychology, 35*, 203–215.

52. Gatzke-Kopp, L. M., & Beauchaine, T. P. (2007). Direct and passive prenatal nicotine exposure and the development of externalizing psychopathology. *Child Psychiatry and Human Development, 38*, 255–269.

53. Wakschlag, L., S., Pickett, K. E., Cook, E., Benowitz, N. L., & Leventhal, B. L. (2002). Maternal smoking during pregnancy and severe antisocial behavior in offspring: A review. *American Journal of Public Health, 92*, 966–974.

54. Gibson, C. L., Piquero, A. R., & Tibbetts, S. G. (2000). Assessing the relationship between maternal cigarette smoking during pregnancy and age at first police contact. *Justice Quarterly, 17*, 519–541; McGloin, J. M., Pratt, T. C., & Piquero, A. R. (2006). A life-course analysis of the criminogenic effects of maternal cigarette smoking during pregnancy: A research note on the

mediating impact of neuropsychological deficit. *Journal of Research in Crime an Delinquency, 43,* 412–426; Piquero, A. R., Gibson, C. L., Tibbetts, S. G., Turner, M. G., & Katz, S. H. (2002). Maternal cigarette smoking during pregnancy and life-course-persistent offending. *International Journal of Offender Therapy and Comparative Criminology, 46,* 231–248.

55. Gibson, C. L., Piquero, A. R., & Tibbetts, S. G. (2000). Assessing the relationship between maternal cigarette smoking during pregnancy and age at first police contact. *Justice Quarterly, 17,* 519–541; Gibson, C. L., & Tibbetts, S. G. (2000). A biosocial interaction in predicting early onset of offending. *Psychological Reports, 86,* 509–518.

56. Brennan, P. A., Grekin, E. R., & Mednick, S. (1999). Maternal cigarette smoking during pregnancy and adult male criminal outcomes. *Archives of General Psychiatry, 56,* 215–219; Piquero, A. R., Gibson, C. L., Tibbetts, S. G., Turner, M. G., & Katz, S. H. (2002). Maternal cigarette smoking during pregnancy and life course persistent offending. *International Journal of Offender Therapy and Comparative Criminology, 46,* 231–248.

57. Pratt, T. C., McGloin, J. M., & Fearn, N. E. (2006). Maternal cigarette smoking during pregnancy and criminal/deviant behavior. *International Journal of Offender Therapy and Comparative Criminology, 50,* 672–690.

58. Gibson, C. L., & Tibbetts, S. G. (2000). A biosocial interaction in predicting early onset of offending. *Psychological Reports, 86,* 509–518.

59. See also: Turner, M. G., Hartman, J. L., & Bishop, D. M. (2007). The effects of prenatal problems, family functioning, and neighborhood disadvantage in predicting life-course-persistent offending. *Criminal Justice and Behavior, 34,* 1241–1261.

60. Raine, A. (2002). Biosocial studies of antisocial and violent behavior in children and adults: A review. *Journal of Abnormal Child Psychology, 30,* 311–326.

61. Boutwell, B. B., Beaver, K. M., & Gibson, C. L. (2008). Maternal smoking during pregnancy and childhood externalizing behavioral problems: A propensity score matching approach. Unpublished manuscript.

62. It is also interesting to note that maternal smoking during pregnancy might increase levels of testosterone prenatally. If this is the case, then part of the relationship between prenatal nicotine exposure and antisocial phenotypes could be accounted for by testosterone. See: Rizwan, S., Manning, J. T., & Brabin. (2007). Maternal smoking during pregnancy and possible effects of in utero testosterone: Evidence from the 2D:4D finger length ratio. *Early Human Development, 83,* 87–90.

63. Maughan, B., Taylor, A., Caspi, A., & Moffitt, T. E. (2004). Prenatal smoking and early childhood conduct problems: Testing genetic and environmental explanations of the association. *Archives of General Psychiatry, 61,* 836–843.

64. D'Onofrio, B. M., van Hulle, C. A., Waldman, I. D., Rodgers, J. L., Harden, K. P., Rathouz, P. J., & Lahey, B. B. (2008). Smoking during pregnancy and offspring externalizing problems: An exploration of genetic and environmental confounds. *Development and Psychopathology, 20,* 139–164.

65. Flynn, H. A., Marcus, S. M., Barry, K. L., & Blow, F. C. (2003). Rates and correlates of alcohol use among pregnant women in obstetrics clinics. *Alcoholism: Clinical and Experimental Research, 27,* 81–87.

66. Jacobson, J. L., & Jacobson, S. W. (1994). Prenatal alcohol exposure and neurobehavioral development: Where is the threshold? *Alcohol Health and Research World, 18,* 30–36.

67. Mattson, S. H., Schoenfeld, A. M., & Riley, E. P. (2001). Teratogenic effects of alcohol on brain and behavior. *Alcohol Research and Health, 25,* 185–190.

68. Kodituwakku, P. W., Kalberg, W., & May, P. A. (2001). The effects of prenatal alcohol exposure on executive functioning. *Alcohol Research and Health, 25,* 192–198.

69. Linnet, K. M., Dalsgaard, S., Obel, C., Wisborg, K. et al. (2003). Maternal lifestyle factors in pregnancy risk of attention deficit hyperactivity disorder and associated behaviors: Review of the current evidence. *American Journal of Psychiatry, 160,* 1028–1040K; O'Malley, K. D., & Nanson, J. (2002). Clinical implications of a link between fetal alcohol spectrum disorder and attention-deficit hyperactivity disorder. *Canadian Journal of Psychiatry, 47,* 349–354.

70. Mattson, S. H., Schoenfeld, A. M., & Riley, E. P. (2001). Teratogenic effects of alcohol on brain and behavior. *Alcohol Research and Health, 25,* 185–190.

71. Kelly, S., J., Day, N., & Streissguth, A. P. (2000). Effects of prenatal alcohol exposure on social behavior in humans and other species. *Neurotoxicology and Teratology, 22,* 143–149.

72. Kelly, S., J., Day, N., & Streissguth, A. P. (2000). Effects of prenatal alcohol exposure on social behavior in humans and other species. *Neurotoxicology and Teratology, 22,* 143–149; Sood, B., Delaney-Black, V., Covington, C., Nordstrom-Klee, B., Ager, J., Templin, T., Janisse, J., Martier, S., & Sokol, R. J. (2001). Prenatal alcohol exposure and childhood behavior at age 6 to 7 years: I. Dose-response effect. *Pediatrics, 108,* e34.

73. Sood, B., Delaney-Black, V., Covington, C., Nordstrom-Klee, B., Ager, J., Templin, T., Janisse, J., Martier, S., & Sokol, R. J. (2001). Prenatal alcohol exposure and childhood behavior at age 6 to 7 years: I. Dose-response effect. *Pediatrics, 108,* e34.

74. D'Onofrio, B., van Hullen, C. A., Waldman, I. D., Rodgers, J. L., Rathouz, P. J., & Lahey, B. B. (2007). Causal inferences regarding prenatal alcohol exposure and childhood externalizing problems. *Archives of General Psychiatry, 64,* 1296–1304.

75. Grandjean, P., & Landrigan, P. J. (2006). Developmental neurotoxicity of industrial chemicals. *The Lancet, 368*, 2167–2178.

76. Martin, R. P., & Dombrowski, S. C. (2008). *Prenatal exposures: Psychological and educational consequences for children.* New York: Springer.

77. Grandjean, P., & Landrigan, P. J. (2006). Developmental neurotoxicity of industrial chemicals. *The Lancet, 368*, 2167–2178.

78. Rauh, V. A., Garfinkel, R., Perera, F. P., Andrews, H. F. et al. (2006). Impact of prenatal chlorpyrifos exposure on neurodevelopment in the first 3 years of life among inner-city children. *Pediatrics, 118*, e1845–e1859.

79. Ericson, J. E., Crinella, F. M., Clarke-Stewart, K. A., Allhusen, V. D., Chan, T., & Robertson, R. T. (2007). Prenatal manganese levels linked to childhood behavioral disinhibition. *Neurotoxicology and Teratology, 29*, 181–187.

80. Ribas-Fitó, N., Torrent, M., Carrizo, D., Júlvez, J., Grimalt, J. O., & Sunyler, J. (2007). Exposure to hexachlorobenzene during pregnancy and children's social behavior at 4 years of age. *Environmental Health Perspectives, 115*, 447–450.

81. Denno, D. W. (1990). *Biology and violence: From birth to adulthood.* New York: Cambridge University Press.

82. Cecil, K. M., Brubaker, C. J., Adler, C. M., Deitrich, K. N., Altaye, M. et al. (2008). Decreased brain volume in adults with childhood lead exposure. *PLoS Medicine, 5*, 0741–0750.

83. Wright, J. P., Dietrich, K. N., Ris, M. D., Hornung, R. W., Wessel, S. D., Lanphear, B. P., Ho, M., & Rae, M. N. (2008). *PLoS Medicine, 5*, 0732–0740.

84. Morgane, P. J., Austin-LaFrance, R., Bronzino, J., Tonkiss, J., Díaz,-Cintra, S., Cintra, L., Kempr, T., & Galler, J. R. (1993). Prenatal malnutrition and development of the brain. *Neuroscience and Biobehavioral Reviews, 17*, 91–128.

85. Morgane, P. J., Mokler, D. J., & Galler, J. R. (2002). Effects of prenatal protein malnutrition on the hippocampal formation. *Neuroscience and Biobehavioral Reviews, 26*, 471–483.

86. Levitsky, D. A., & Strupp, B. J. (1995). Malnutrition and the brain: Changing concepts, changing concerns. *Journal of Nutrition, 125*, 2212S–2220S.

87. Neugebauer, R., Hoek, H. W., & Susser, E. (1999). Prenatal exposure to wartime famine and development of antisocial personality disorder in early adulthood. *Journal of the American Medical Association, 281*, 455–462.

88. Neugebauer, R., Hoek, H. W., & Susser, E. (1999). Prenatal exposure to wartime famine and development of antisocial personality disorder in early adulthood. *Journal of the American Medical Association, 281*, 455–462, p. 455.

89. Franzek, E. J., Sprangers, N., Janssesn, A. C. J. W., van Duijn, V., & van de Wetering, B. J. M. (2008). Prenatal exposure to the 1944–45 Dutch 'hunger winter' and addiction later in life. *Addiction, 103*, 433–438.

90. Laplante, D. P., Barr, R. G., Brunet, A., Galbaud de Fort, G. et al. (2004). Stress during pregnancy affects general intellectual and language functioning in human toddlers. *Pediatric Research, 56*, 400–410.

91. Kofman, O. (2002). The role of prenatal stress in the etiology of developmental behavioural disorders. *Neuroscience and Biobehavioral Reviews, 26*, 457–470.

92. Lemaire, V., Koehl, M., Le Moal, M., & Abrous, D. N. (2000). Prenatal stress produces learning deficits associated with an inhibition of neurogenesis in the hippocampus. *Proceedings of the National Academy of Sciences, 97*, 11032–11037.

93. Michelsen, K. A., van den Hove, D. L. A., Schmitz, C., Segers, O., Prickaerts, & Steinbusch, H. W. M. (2007). Prenatal stress and subsequent exposure to chronic mild stress influence dendritic spine density and morphology in the rat medial prefrontal cortex. *BMC Neuroscience, 8*, 107.

94. Gitau, R., Fisk, N. M., Teixeira, J. M., Cameron, A., & Glover, V. (2001). Fetal hypothalamic-pituitary-adrenal stress responses to invasive procedures are independent of maternal responses. *Journal of Clinical Endocrinology and Metabolism, 86*, 104–109.

95. Kofman, O. (2002). The role of prenatal stress in the etiology of developmental behavioural disorders. *Neuroscience and Biobehavioral Reviews, 26*, 457–470.

96. Huot, R. L., Brennan, P. A., Stowe, Z. N., Plotsky, P. M., & Walker, E. F. (2004). Negative affect in offspring of depressed mothers is predicted by infant cortisol levels at 6 months and maternal depression during pregnancy, but not postpartum. *Annals of the New York Academy of Sciences, 1032*, 234–236.

97. Möhler, E., Parzer, P., Brunner, R., Wiebel, A., & Resch, F. (2006). Emotional stress in pregnancy predicts human infant reactivity. *Early Human Development, 82*, 731–737.

98. Huizink, A. C., Robles de Medina, P. G., Mulder, E. J. H., Visser, G. H. A., & Buitelaar, J. K. (2003). Stress during pregnancy is associated with developmental outcome in infancy. *Journal of Child Psychology and Psychiatry, 44*, 810–818.

99. Linnet, K. M., Dalsgaard, S., Obel, C., Wisborg, K. et al. (2003). Maternal lifestyle factors in pregnancy risk of attention deficit hyperactivity disorder and associated behaviors: Review of the current evidence. *American Journal of Psychiatry, 160*, 1028–1040; Rodriguez, A., & Bohlin, G. (2005). Are maternal smoking and stress during pregnancy related to ADHD symptoms in children? *Journal of Child Psychology and Psychiatry, 46*, 246–254.

100. Van den Bergh, B. R. H., & Marcoen, A. (2004). High antenatal maternal anxiety is related to ADHD symptoms, externalizing problems, and anxiety in 8- and 9-year-olds. *Child Development, 75*, 1085–1097.

101. Van den Bergh, B. R. H., Mennes, M., Oosterlaan, J., Stevens, V., Stiers, P., Marcoen, A., & Lagae, L. (2005). High antenatal maternal anxiety is related to impulsivity during performance on cognitive tasks in 14- and 15-year-olds. *Neuroscience and Biobehavioral Reviews, 29*, 259–269.

102. Raine, A. (2002). Biosocial studies of antisocial and violent behavior in children and adults: A review. *Journal of Abnormal Child Psychology, 30*, 311–326.

103. Brake, W. G., Sullivan, R. M., & Gratton, A. (2000). Perinatal distress leads to lateralized medial prefrontal cortical dopamine hypofunction in adult rats. *The Journal of Neuroscience, 20*, 5538–5543; Cannon, T. D., van Erp, T. G. M., Rosson, I. M., Huttunen, M. et al. (2002). Fetal hypoxia and structural brain abnormalities in schizophrenic patients, their siblings, and controls. *Archives of General Psychiatry, 59*, 35–41.

104. Beaver, K. M., & Wright, J. P. (2005). Evaluating the effects of birth complications on low self-control in a sample of twins. *International Journal of Offender Therapy and Comparative Criminology, 49*, 450–471.

105. Kandel, A., & Mednick, S. A. (1991). Perinatal complications predict violent offending. *Criminology, 29*, 519–530; See also: Cannon, M., Huttunen, M. O., Tanskanen, A. J., Arseneault, L., Jones, P. B., & Murray, R. M. (2002). Perinatal and childhood risk factors for later criminality and violence in schizophrenia. *British Journal of Psychiatry, 180*, 496–501.

106. Raine, A., Brennan, P., & Mednick, S. A. (1994). Birth complications combined with early maternal rejection at age 1 year predispose to violent crime at age 18 years. *Archives of General Psychiatry, 51*, 984–988; See also: Raine, A., Brennan, P., & Mednick, S. A. (1997). Interaction between birth complications and early maternal rejection in predisposing individuals to adult violence: Specificity to serious, early-onset violence. *American Journal of Psychiatry, 154*, 1265–1271.

107. Piquero, A. R., & Tibbetts, S. (1999). Arsenuault, L., Tremblay, R. E., Boulerice, B., & Saucier, J.-F. (2002). Obstetrical complications and violent delinquency: Testing two developmental pathways. *Child Development, 73*, 496–508; The impact of pre/perinatal disturbances and disadvantaged familial environment in predicting criminal offending. *Studies on Crime and Crime Prevention, 8*, 52–70.

108. Hodgins, S., Kratzer, L., & McNeil, T. F. (2001). Obstetric complications, parenting, and risk of criminal behavior. *Archives of General Psychiatry, 58*, 746–752.

109. Beaver, K. M., & Wright, J. P. (2005). Evaluating the effects of birth complications on low self-control in a sample of twins. *International Journal of Offender Therapy and Comparative Criminology, 49,* 450–471; Cannon, M., Huttunen, M. O., Tanskanen, A. J., Arseneault, L., Jones, P. B., & Murray, R. M. (2002). Perinatal and childhood risk factors for later criminality and violence in schizophrenia. *British Journal of Psychiatry, 180,* 496–501.

110. Raine, A. (2002). Biosocial studies of antisocial and violent behavior in children and adults: A review. *Journal of Abnormal Child Psychology, 30,* 311–326, p. 322.

111. Ricketts, S. A., Murray, E. K., & Schwalberg, R. (2005). Reducing low birthweight by resolving risks: Results from Colorado's Prenatal Plus Program. *American Journal of Public Health, 95,* 1952–1957.

112. Hack, M., H., Taylor, G., Klein, N., Eiben, R., Schatschneider, C., & Mercuri-Minich, N. (1995). Long-term developmental outcomes of low birth weight infants. *The Future of Children: Low Birth Weight (Center for the Future of Children), 5,* 176–196.

113. Gibson, C. L., Piquero, A. R., & Tibbetts, S. G. (2000). Assessing the relationship between maternal cigarette smoking during pregnancy and age at first police contact. *Justice Quarterly, 17,* 519–542; McGloin, J. M., & Pratt, T. C. (2003). Cognitive ability and delinquent behavior among inner-city youth: A life-course analysis of main, mediating, and interaction effects. *International Journal of Offender Therapy and Comparative Criminology, 47,* 253–271.

114. DeLisi, M. (2005). *Career criminals in society.* Thousand Oaks, CA: Sage.

115. Cannon, M., Huttunen, M. O., Tanskanen, A. J., Arseneault, L., Jones, P. B., & Murray, R. M. (2002). Perinatal and childhood risk factors for later criminality and violence in schizophrenia. *British Journal of Psychiatry, 180,* 496–501; McGloin, J. M., Pratt, T. C., & Piquero, A. R. (2006). A life-course analysis of the criminogenic effects of maternal cigarette smoking during pregnancy: A research note on the mediating impact of neuropsychological deficit. *Journal of Research in Crime and Delinquency, 43,* 412–426; Piquero, A. R., Gibson, C. L., Tibbetts, S. G., Turner, M. G., & Katz, S. H. (2002). Maternal cigarette smoking during pregnancy and life-course-persistent offending. *International Journal of Offender Therapy and Comparative Criminology, 46,* 231–248.

116. Tibbetts, S. G., & Piquero, A. R. (1999). The influence of gender, low birth weight, and disadvantaged environment in predicting early onset of offending: A test of Moffitt's interactional hypothesis. *Criminology, 37,* 843–878.

117. Gibson, C. L., Piquero, A. R., & Tibbetts, S. G. (2000). Assessing the relationship between maternal cigarette smoking during pregnancy and age at first police contact. *Justice Quarterly, 17,* 519–542.

118. Ginsberg, G., Hattis, D., & Sonawane, B. (2004). Incorporating pharmacokinetic differences between children and adults in assessing children's risks to environmental toxicants. *Toxicology and Applied Pharmacology, 198*, 164–183.

119. Grandjean, P., & Landrigan, P. J. (2006). Developmental neurotoxicity of industrial chemicals. *The Lancet, 368*, 2167–2178.

120. United States Department of Health and Human Services. (2006). *The health consequences of involuntary exposure to tobacco smoke: A report of the surgeon general.* Washington, DC: United States Department of Health and Human Services.

121. United States Environmental Protection Agency. (1992). *Fact sheet: National survey on environmental management of asthma and children's exposure to environmental tobacco smoke.* Washington, DC: Office of Research and Development, Office of Health and Environmental Assessment.

122. Slotkin, T. A. (2004). Cholinergic systems in brain development and disruption by neurotoxicants: Nicotine, environmental tobacco smoke, and organophosphates. *Toxicology and Applied Pharmacology, 198*, 132–151.

123. Yolton, K., Dietrich, K., Auinger, P., Lanphear, B. P., & Hornung, R. (2005). Exposure to environmental tobacco smoke and cognitive abilities among U.S. children and adolescents. *Environmental Health Perspectives, 113*, 98–102.

124. Eskenazi, B., & Castorina, R. (1999). Association of prenatal maternal or postnatal child environmental tobacco smoke exposure and neurodevelopmental and behavioral problems in children. *Environmental Health Perspectives, 107*, 991–1000.

125. Cecil, K. M., Brubaker, C. J., Adler, C. M., Deitrich, K. N., Altaye, M. et al. (2008). Decreased brain volume in adults with childhood lead exposure. *PLoS Medicine, 5*, 0741–0750; Lidsky, T. I., & Schneider, J. S. (2003). Lead neurotoxicity in children: Basic mechanisms and clinical correlates. *Brain, 126*, 5–19.

126. Wright, J. P., Dietrich, K. N., Ris, M. D., Hornung, R. W., Wessel, S. D., Lanphear, B. P., Ho, M., & Rae, M. N. (2008). *PLoS Medicine, 5*, 0732–0740.

127. Wright, J. P., Dietrich, K. N., Ris, M. D., Hornung, R. W., Wessel, S. D., Lanphear, B. P., Ho, M., & Rae, M. N. (2008). *PLoS Medicine, 5*, 0732–0740.

128. Dietrich, K. N., Ris, D. M., Succop, P. A., Berger, O. G., & Bornschein, R. L. (2001). Early exposure to lead and juvenile delinquency. *Neurotoxicology and Teratology, 23*, 511–518.

129. Needleman, H. L., McFarland, C., Ness, R. B., Fienberg, S. E., & Tobin, M. J. (2002). Bone lead levels in adjudicated delinquents: A case control study. *Neurotoxicology and Teratology, 24*, 711–717.

130. Wright, J. P., Dietrich, K. N., Ris, M. D., Hornung, R. W., Wessel, S. D., Lanphear, B. P., Ho, M., & Rae, M. N. (2008). *PLoS Medicine, 5,* 0732–0740.

131. Nevin, R. (2000). How lead exposure relates to temporal changes in IQ, violent crime, and unwed pregnancy. *Environmental Research, 83,* 1–22; Nevin, R. (2007). Understanding international crime trends: The legacy of preschool lead exposure. *Environmental Research, 104,* 315–336; Stretsky, P B., & Lynch, M. J. (2001). The relationship between lead exposure and homicide. *Archives of Pediatric Adolescent Medicine, 155,* 579–582.

132. Denno, D. W. (1990). *Biology and violence: From birth to adulthood.* New York: Cambridge University Press.

133. Gómez-Pinilla, F. (2008). Brain foods: The effects of nutrients on brain function. *Nature Reviews Neuroscience, 9,* 568–578.

134. Breakey, J. (1997). The role of diet and behaviour in childhood. *Journal of Pediatrics and Child Health, 33,* 190–194.

135. Liu, J., Raine, A., Venables, P. H., & Mednick, S. A. (2004). Malnutrition at age 3 years and externalizing behavior problems at ages 8, 11, and 17 years. *American Journal of Psychiatry, 161,* 2005–2013.

136. Liu, J., Raine, A., Venables, P. H., & Mednick, S. A. (2004). Malnutrition at age 3 years and externalizing behavior problems at ages 8, 11, and 17 years. *American Journal of Psychiatry, 161,* 2005–2013, p. 2011.

137. Lykken, D. T. (2000). The causes and costs of crime and a controversial cure. *Journal of Personality, 68,* 559–605.

138. Harris, J. R. (1998). *The nurture assumption: Why children turn out the way they do.* New York: Touchstone; Harris, J. R. (2000). The outcome of parenting: What do we really know? *Journal of Personality, 68,* 625–637; Rowe, D. C. (1994). *The limits of family influence: Genes, experience, and behavior.* New York: The Guilford Press.

139. Wright, J. P., & Beaver, K. M. (2005). Do parents matter in creating self-control in their children? A genetically informed test of Gottfredson and Hirschi's theory of low self-control. *Criminology, 43,* 1169–1202.

140. Connor, D. F. (2002). *Aggression and antisocial behavior in children and adolescents: Research and treatment.* New York: Guilford Press.

141. Teicher, M. H., Andersen, S. L., Polcari, A., Anderson, C. M., Navalta, C. P., & Kim, D. M. (2003). The neurobiological consequences of early stress and childhood maltreatment. *Neuroscience and Biobehavioral Reviews, 27,* 33–44.

142. Gunnar, M. R., Fisher, P. A., & The Early Experience, Stress, and Prevention Network. (2006). Bringing basic research on early experience and stress neurobiology to bear on preventive interventions for neglected and

maltreated children. *Development and Psychopathology, 18*, 651–677; López, J. F., Akil, H., & Watson, S. J. (1999). Neural circuits mediating stress. *Biological Psychiatry, 46*, 1461–1471; McEwen, B., & Sapolsky, R. (1995). Stress and cognitive function. *Current Opinions in Neurobiology, 5*, 205–211.

143. Bremner, J. D., Randall, P., Vermetten, E. Staib, L. et al. (1997). Magnetic resonance imaging-based measurement of hippocampal volume in posttraumatic stress disorder related to childhood physical abuse and sexual abuse—A preliminary report. *Biological Psychiatry, 41*, 23–32; Sapolsky, R. M. (2000). Glucocorticoids and hippocampal atrophy in neuropsychiatric disorders. *Archives of General Psychiatry, 57*, 925–935.

144. Seckfort, D. L., Paul, R., Grieve, S. M., Vandenberg, B., Bryant, R. A. et al. (2008). Early life stress on brain structure and function across the lifespan: A preliminary study. *Brain Imaging and Behavior, 2*, 49–58.

145. Teicher, M. H., Andersen, S. L., Polcari, A., Anderson, C. M., Navalta, C. P., & Kim, D. M. (2003). The neurobiological consequences of early stress and childhood maltreatment. *Neuroscience and Biobehavioral Reviews, 27*, 33–44.

146. Marcovitch, S., Goldberg, S., Gold, A., Washington, J. et al. (1997). Determinants of behavioural problems in Romanian children adopted in Ontario. *International Journal of Behavioral Development, 20*, 17–31; Rutter, M. (1998). Developmental catch-up, and deficit, following adoption after severe global early privation. *Journal of Child Psychology and Psychiatry, 39*, 465–476.

147. Chugani, H. T., Behen, M. E., Muzik, O., Juhász, C., Nagy, F., & Chugani, D. C. (2001). Local brain functional activity following early deprivation: A study of post-institutionalized Romanian orphans. *NeuroImage, 14*, 1290–1301.

148. López, J. F., Akil, H., & Watson, S. J. (1999). Neural circuits mediating stress. *Biological Psychiatry, 46*, 1461–1471.

Biosocial
Prevention and Treatment Strategies

Introduction

One of the main criticisms leveled against the biosocial perspective is that it does not provide any guidance on how to prevent antisocial behaviors or how to rehabilitate criminals. According to this line of reasoning, criminal behavior is controlled by genes, and since genes are immutable, then criminal behavior is not preventable nor is it treatable. Some biosocial opponents even go so far as to argue that biosocial criminology can only lead to "lock-them-up-and-throw-away-the-key" crime control polices, where criminals are identified through genetic testing and then incarcerated for the remainder of their life. Criminals, in other words, are "born bad" and thus are impervious to prevention and treatment strategies.

The critics who set forth this argument (or some variant thereof) are engaging in pure rhetoric. No biosocial criminologist believes that genes are the end-all-be-all to antisocial phenotypes. In fact, and as the previous chapters have made clear, biosocial criminologists draw attention to the complexity of human behavior and argue that a confluence of genetic, biological, and environmental factors produce antisocial behaviors. Most importantly, all of these factors work *interactively* and are *co-dependent* on each other. What this means is that the effects of genetic factors are dependent on the presence of environmental factors and vice versa. This has particular relevance to prevention and treatment strategies because genes do not have to be physically altered in order to alter their effects; *genetic effects can be altered by altering the environment.* It is also narrow thinking to assume that biosocial criminologists always examine genetic factors. This simply is not the case. Chapter 5 described a number of different environmental factors that may exert an effect on the development of antisocial phenotypes, independent of genotype. Many of these environments, such as prenatal exposure to cigarette smoke, can be eliminated without having to worry about genotype.

The goal of the current chapter is to use the information that was presented in the previous chapters as an anchor for providing a rough sketch of how the biosocial perspective can be used in the prevention and treatment of antisocial behaviors. In so doing, this chapter will be divided into two halves. The first half will be devoted to exploring how biosocial research can inform crime prevention strategies. Emphasis will be placed on altering those environmental factors that were discussed in Chapter 5. The second half of the chapter will examine how biosocial research can inform strategies designed to rehabilitate criminals.

Biosocial Prevention Strategies

Before moving into a discussion of biosocial prevention strategies, it is essential to make the distinction between prevention programs and treatment programs. Prevention programs are designed to impede antisocial behaviors from ever surfacing, while treatment programs (sometimes referred to as rehabilitation programs) are designed to reduce future criminal involvement among criminals. Although both of these programs can be effective at reducing criminal involvement, the general consensus is that prevention programs are better able to reduce crime than are treatment programs. To see why this is the case, let's take a quick look at when antisocial phenotypes begin to emerge and how they relate to later life involvement in crime and delinquency.

Generally speaking, behavioral problems begin to emerge during childhood or even earlier. For the most part, childhood antisocial behavior is just a phase and by the time most children enter into school, their behavior improves markedly. But for a small group of children—especially those who are the "worst of the worst"—their antisocial behavior persists.[1] What this means is that these children will eventually grow into adolescents who engage in acts of serious violence and, as adults, they will become hardened criminals, wracking up long rap sheets, accruing multiple arrests, and spending a considerable amount of time incarcerated.[2] Because the majority of adult criminals have long histories of antisocial conduct, usually dating back to childhood, it is common to hear that the best predictor of future misbehavior is past misbehavior. In academic terms, this means that antisocial behavior is highly stable across the life course, where the way someone acts as a child is a harbinger of how they will act as an adult. The most effective prevention programs thus must be implemented in childhood (or earlier) in order to prevent antisocial behaviors from emerging.

To quell the emergence of antisocial phenotypes, prevention programs are frequently based on what is known as the "risk factor prevention paradigm."[3] To understand this paradigm, it is first necessary to introduce what is meant by a risk factor.[4] A risk factor is any factor that when present increases the odds of displaying antisocial phenotypes. Associating with delinquent peers is a risk factor for delinquency because if an adolescent is exposed to antisocial friends then they are more likely to become delinquent than if they had not been exposed to antisocial friends. Some risk factors, such as delinquent peers and low levels of self-control, have strong effects on delinquency and thus are potent risk factors, while others, such as poverty and low socioeconomic status, have small effects on antisocial behaviors and thus are weak risk factors.[5] Risk factors that are associated with crime, delinquency, or some other antisocial outcome are often referred to as criminogenic risk factors or crime-producing risk factors.

Not all criminogenic risk factors are *causes* of antisocial phenotypes; some are only correlates.[6] To understand this, think back to the discussion of spurious associations where we discussed the interrelationships among ice cream sales, temperature, and violent crime. Remember that although ice cream sales and violent crime were positively correlated, this correlation disappeared after taking into account temperature. If we use this example again, we could identify ice cream sales as a criminogenic risk factor for violent crime. Of course you would not identify ice cream sales as a *causal* criminogenic risk factor, but it is a risk factor nonetheless. When using the risk factor approach in the prevention of crime, the goal is to identify causal criminogenic risk factors, not risk factors that are spuriously related to crime. Although it is impossible to establish causality, it is not impossible to establish spuriousness. Prevention programs should focus on those risk factors that have not yet been found to be spurious.

There are, in general, two main types of risk factors: static risk factors and dynamic risk factors. Static risk factors are those risk factors that cannot be changed. Gender is an example of a static risk factor because although being a male is a potent criminogenic risk factor it cannot be altered. Dynamic risk factors, in contrast, are those risk factors that can be changed. Associating with delinquent peers is an example of a dynamic risk factor because a youth's peer group can be changed (e.g., they could shed their delinquent peers and begin to associate with prosocial friends). When working from a biosocial perspective, the distinction between static risk factors and dynamic risk factors often becomes muddied. For example, is a genetic polymorphism that confers an increased risk to aggression a static risk factor or a dynamic risk factor? On the one hand, it is a static risk factor because it is not possible to physically alter the gene. But, on the other hand, it is a dynamic risk factor because the *effects* of many genetic polymorphisms are contingent on the presence of certain environments; changing the environment will change the *effect* of the gene. So when considering whether a gene is a static risk factor or a dynamic risk factor it is imperative to examine how the effect of the particular gene waxes and wanes in response to environmental conditions.

In addition, some biosocial risk factors are dynamic risk factors at one point in time, but become static risk factors at another point in time. Consider, for instance, prenatal exposure to cigarette smoke. Prenatal exposure to cigarette smoke is a dynamic risk factor prior to or during pregnancy. Why? Because it is possible to alter whether a pregnant mother smokes cigarettes. After birth, however, prenatal exposure to cigarette smoke changes from a dynamic risk factor into a static risk factor. Why? Because it is impossible to undo any harmful effects that exposure to cigarette smoke had on the developing fetus. Time, therefore, matters when considering whether some biosocial risk factors are dynamic or static.

Risk factors work probabilistically. What this means is that the presence of a criminogenic risk factor *increases the likelihood* of antisocial behavior; however, not all people who have a particular criminogenic risk factor will become antisocial and some people without a particular criminogenic risk factor will become antisocial. Let's explore this in a little greater detail. Suppose that we could assign probabilities to each risk factor, such that the probability equaled the odds of criminal involvement. Pretend that one risk factor, let's call it risk factor X, had a probability of .20, while another risk factor, risk factor Z, had a probability of .10. If we ignored all of the other risk factors, and looked just at X and Z, we could determine the probability that someone would become a criminal. For example, the probability of someone becoming a criminal if they had risk factor X would be .20, while the probability of becoming a criminal for someone with risk factor Z would be .10. These risk factors clearly increase the probability of becoming a criminal, but they do not determine with 100 percent accuracy who will and who will not become an offender.

Given that criminogenic risk factors are associated with the development of antisocial phenotypes, the key to preventing crime is to suppress these risk factors from emerging or, if they have already emerged, eliminate them before they can have an effect. To do so, prevention (and treatment) efforts are most interested in identifying causal criminogenic risk factors that are potent and dynamic. Potent risk factors are targeted because they are the risk factors that have the strongest effects. Presumably this means that if potent risk factors are eliminated, then the odds of future antisocial behavior will also drop. If we return to the previous example with risk factors X and Z, we can see that it would make more sense to target risk factor X instead of risk factor Z. Why? Because if risk factor X is successfully eliminated, then the odds of antisocial behavior should decrease by .20, while successfully eliminating risk factor Z would only decrease the odds of antisocial behavior by .10.

Dynamic risk factors are targeted because they can be altered. It would not make any sense to focus on static risk factors (no matter how potent they are) because they cannot be changed. For example, pretend that having blue eyes was a potent risk factor for criminal involvement. While this surely would be important information to know, it would not be particularly relevant when trying to prevent crime because it is not a modifiable risk factor. The effectiveness of prevention programs hinges on the ability to identify potent dynamic risk factors.

Prevention efforts often target families that are at-risk for having children who will become involved in crime and delinquency. These at-risk families can be identified using a variety of different methods, but typically risk factors are used. For example, children born into families that are poor, that are headed by single mother and that are located in disadvantaged neighborhoods would be considered at-risk for delinquency. Other risk factors beyond those just listed could also be used to identify at-risk children. Once these at-risk families have been selected, then prevention programs can be employed to prevent the emergence of criminogenic risk factors (e.g., helping women to quit smoking prior to becoming pregnant) or to eliminate the existing criminogenic risk factors (e.g., informing parents about the dangers of abuse and neglect). For prevention programs to be effective, they must successfully change or modify potent dynamic risk factors.

The most difficult task is figuring out which risk factors to target and how to alter them. Part of the reason that some prevention programs have not been very successful is because they focus on changing the wrong risk factors. For example, sociological criminologists often point to negative parental socialization as a criminogenic risk factor that prevention programs should target.[7] According to this logic, children are molded into behaving or misbehaving depending on how they are socialized by their parents. But as was discussed in previous chapters (Chapters 1, 2, and 5), and contrary to popular belief, parental socialization is not a strong criminogenic risk factor. Consequently prevention programs that focus narrowly on altering the way a parent parents most likely will not be very successful at reducing antisocial behaviors. This is exactly what research has revealed.

For example, in a large-scale study, Harriet Hiscock and colleagues implemented a randomized experiment to determine whether decreasing harsh parenting would reduce childhood behavioral problems.[8] To do so, they split the sample into two groups: an experimental group that received the parent-training program and a control group that did not. Prior to the parenting intervention, the two groups were identical in terms of the child's behavioral problems and parent's harsh parenting—in other words, there were not any preexisting differences between the two groups. After the parent-training class, the parents from the experimental group were significantly less likely to use harsh discipline in comparison with parents from the control group—initial evidence that the program worked. There was a catch, however: the behavioral problems for the children from the two groups remained identical. In other words, although parenting improved for the experimental group, this improvement did not correspond with an improvement in the child's behavior.

This study highlights the fact that effective prevention programs must be successful in identifying potent criminogenic risk factors. If the wrong risk factors are targeted (e.g., parental socialization), then the odds of future criminal involvement will be unaffected. There are certainly hundreds of risk factors that can be used by prevention programs, but the ones that appear to be among the most salient are biosocial risk factors. Of all the biosocial risk factors, those that adversely affect brain development, such as prenatal risk factors, perinatal risk factors, and risk factors in infancy and childhood, appear to be the most applicable to early life crime prevention strategies. Presented below are three main ways that these biosocial risk factors can be targeted by prevention programs.

1. Prevention programs should educate parents-to-be, especially mothers-to-be, on the importance of a healthy pregnancy.

One of the keys to reducing antisocial behavior is promoting healthy fetal brain development. Too often, however, normal fetal brain development is compromised—either knowingly or unknowingly—by the actions of the mother. Pregnant mothers who smoke, consume alcohol, or use other types of drugs may cause irreversible damage to their unborn child. Although it may seem like common knowledge that these substances may adversely affect the fetus, not all women are aware of the effects that these drugs have on the developing fetus. There is some evidence to indicate, however, that educating women about the deleterious effects that these substances have on the fetus may actually reduce rates of use.[9] This is why prevention programs need to educate expectant mothers on the dangers of using tobacco, alcohol, and illegal drugs during pregnancy.

Fathers can also be a major culprit in exposing the fetus to toxins. To see how this could be the case, consider that research has shown that pregnant mothers who are exposed to second-hand smoke have offspring who are at-risk for behavioral problems.[10] A major source of exposure to second-hand smoke for pregnant mothers is their spouse or significant other. As a result fathers also need to be educated by prevention programs on how their behaviors can place the developing fetus in jeopardy.

2. Prevention programs should provide parents with adequate prenatal healthcare.

Although educating parents-to-be about the importance of a health pregnancy is vitally important to fetal development, it is not a substitute for prenatal healthcare coverage. Routine checkups can be used to provide information to mothers about their pregnancy, including what to do (e.g., eat properly) and what not to do (e.g., consume alcohol). Regular doctor visits are also needed in order to monitor the pregnancy, including both the mother and the fetus. Many problems that arise during pregnancy (e.g., gestational diabetes) do not pose a threat to the fetus as long as they are tracked closely by a doctor. This is especially true near the end of pregnancy, where the fetus is monitored to ensure it is not in distress and to ensure it is delivered within a normal time frame. Unfortunately, not all pregnant women have access to healthcare, a problem that disproportionately affects single, unmarried women living in poverty. Prevention programs should thus provide free prenatal healthcare coverage to those families that cannot afford it.

3. Prevention programs should offer free post-birth classes that are designed to inform new parents about early childhood development.

Many parents are woefully ignorant about early childhood development, including how early-life experiences, such as abuse, may lead to later life behavioral problems. There is often a misconception that if the child is too young to remember the event (e.g., abuse) they will not be affected by it. This is not true, and as Chapter 5 explained, abuse, neglect, and trauma very early in the life course (even before the formation of memories) can have lasting effects by interrupting brain development. Likewise, parents often lack a full appreciation of the important role that nutrition has on brain development and behavioral problems later in life. Prevention programs should thus educate parents about early childhood development, especially about how the brain can be affected by early-life experiences. This information would likely prove useful in fostering healthy brain development and preventing behavioral problems.

The Nursing-Family Partnership: A model biosocial prevention program. One prevention program that follows many of the recommendations set forth above is the Nursing-Family Partnership (NFP) developed by David Olds. The NFP was developed to improve the developmental outcomes of children born into high-risk families, where high-risk families were defined as pregnant teens who were unmarried and who were of low socioeconomic status. (Children born to mothers with these characteristics are at high-risk for a range of maladaptive outcomes, including antisocial phenotypes.) Once identified, the pregnant women were randomly assigned to either an experimental group where they received the NFP or to a control group where they received "comparison" services.

Women who were enrolled in the NFP were provided with a range of different services that began before the birth of their child. As Olds explains:

> During pregnancy, the nurses helped women complete 24-hour diet histories on a regular basis and plot weight gains at every visit; they assessed the women's cigarette smoking and use of alcohol and illegal drugs and facilitated a reduction in the use of these substances through behavioral change strategies. They taught women the signs and symptoms of pregnancy complications, encouraged women to inform the office-based staff about those complications, and facilitated compliance with treatment. They gave particular attention to urinary tract infections, sexually transmitted diseases, and hypertensive disorders of pregnancy (conditions associated with poor birth outcomes). They coordinated care with physicians and nurses in the office and measured blood pressure when needed.[11]

The NFP thus targets many of the prenatal and perinatal environments (e.g., prenatal exposure to cigarette smoke, diet/nutrition, and birth complications) that were identified in Chapter 5 as having some of the strongest effects on brain development and antisocial phenotypes. But, the NFP did not end here; the nursing visits continued from birth until the child was about two years old. During these visits, parents were educated about how to care for their child, how to understand their child, the importance of parent-child interactions, the consequences of abuse and neglect, and other skills needed to promote healthy development. Overall, then, the NFP focused resources on two time periods: pregnancy and the first two years of life. Olds summarized the NFP in the following way:

> The Nurse-Family Partnership (NFP) is different from most mental-health, substance-abuse, and crime-prevention interventions tested to date in that it focuses on improving *neuro-developmental, cognitive*, and behavioral functioning of the child by improving prenatal health, reducing child abuse and neglect, and enhancing family functioning and economic self-sufficiency in the *first two years of the child's life*. These early alterations in biology, behavior, and family context are expected to shift the life-course trajectories of children living in highly disadvantaged families and neighborhoods away from psychopathology, substance use disorders, and risky sexual behaviors. *Part of the program effect is now thought to be accomplished by moderating environmental risks that interact with genetic variations to increase the risk for poor child health and development.*[12] [emphasis added]

So the NFP targets many of the criminogenic risk factors that biosocial criminologists point to as particularly salient, but the real pressing question is whether the NFP was effective? Be your own judge. In comparison with the control group, women who participated in the NFP smoked fewer cigarettes while pregnant, had better prenatal diets, and had fewer kidney infections during pregnancy.[13] After birth, NFP women, in comparison with the control group, were less likely to abuse and neglect their children.[14] Clearly, the criminogenic risk factors targeted by the NFP were successfully altered, but did modifying these risk factors result in a concomitant decrease in offspring antisocial phenotypes? Without a doubt. Children from the NFP, when compared to children from the control group, were less likely to run away from home, had fewer arrests, had fewer convictions, had fewer sexual partners, smoked fewer cigarettes, consumed less alcohol, and had fewer alcohol- or drug-related behavioral problems.[15] These substantial reductions in antisocial behavior—reductions that are rare among crime prevention programs—are testimony to the fact that biosocial criminology has the potential to guide the development of successful crime prevention programs.

Biosocial Treatment Strategies

Although prevention programs that are implemented very early in life are the most effective way to prevent antisocial phenotypes, there are numerous obstacles with using such programs. For example, it is not possible to identify all at-risk families; some at-risk families may decline to participate in the program; and there may not be programs available in certain areas. Even among children who participate in these programs, a substantial number will still develop into adolescent delinquents or adult criminals. As a result, treatment programs are needed to help rehabilitate offenders into law-abiding citizens. Unfortunately recidivism rates are extremely high—even among offenders who successfully complete rehabilitation programs. But, there are at least four ways that the findings from biosocial criminological research can be used to improve the success rates of treatment programs.

1. Treatment programs should assess each offender's genetic risk to determine their eligibility in the program.

Not all offenders are equally likely to benefit from participating in a rehabilitation program. What is particularly interesting to learn is that treatment programs are the most effective for high-risk offenders, not low-risk offenders.[16] In fact, there is even some empirical research showing that low-risk offenders who complete treatment programs have higher recidivism rates when compared to low-risk offenders who did not participate in such programs.[17] As a result, many of the leading rehabilitation scholars advocate assessing each offender's risk level.[18] This is typically accomplished by using some type of actuarial tool that measures antisocial personality traits, antisocial cognitions, and other criminogenic risk factors (but not biosocial criminogenic risk factors). If the assessment indicates that the offender is high-risk, then they are funneled into a rehabilitation program, while offenders who are not high-risk are not placed into treatment programs. Again, it is important to reiterate that treatment programs are most effective at reducing recidivism among high-risk offenders.

Although risk assessment has become commonplace among rehabilitation programs, there is virtually no discussion of assessing offenders based on their genetic risk. Even though critics of biosocial criminology would argue that genetic testing is unconstitutional, dangerous, and evil, it should be pointed out that it is quite possible that treatment programs would be most beneficial to offenders with high genetic risk, not low genetic risk. In other words, genetic testing could be used as a way of delineating those who are the most likely to benefit from the program versus those who are the least likely to benefit from the program. That is precisely what the current risk assessments are designed to do, but instead of looking at genetic polymorphisms, they look at other criminogenic risk factors.

No study has explored the possibility that genetic risk may be related to success rates for criminals. There is, however, one study that examined the association among parenting skills training courses, cortisol levels (remember, cortisol is secreted in response to stressful situations), and DRD4 in a sample of children with externalizing behavioral problems.[19] The results of the study indicated that the parent-training class was associated with decreased levels of cortisol for children with high genetic risk (as measured by the 7R allele of DRD4), but not for children with low genetic risk. This single study, while only suggestive, provides empirical evidence that genetic risk level may be an important factor in determining the effectiveness of rehabilitation programs. Given the potential importance of this topic, future clinicians should begin to entertain the possibility of assessing genetic risk prior to shuffling offenders into treatment programs.

2. Treatment programs should consider the possibility that genetic factors moderate the effectiveness of the program.

It is widely recognized that individual-level characteristics are highly influential in structuring how offenders respond to treatment programs. Characteristics, such as age, gender, IQ, and even some biological factors, such as neurocognitive skills[20], may moderate the effectiveness of the rehabilitation program. To illustrate, males may be less likely than females to recidivate after completing treatment program A, while females may be less likely than males to recidivate after completing treatment program B. What this means is that in order to achieve the highest rates of success, rehabilitation programs need to be individually tailored to the offenders' characteristics.

Although a host of individual-level characteristics have been identified as potentially moderating program effectiveness, genetic factors have, once again, been overlooked. This is a serious oversight because as Chapter 3 discussed, genetic factors often interact with or condition the effects of environmental factors. This has direct application to rehabilitation programs because the program's effectiveness may depend on genotype. For example, people with one particular genotype may respond well to a particular treatment, but people with a different genotype may respond better to a different treatment. By taking into account genotype, rehabilitation programs can be individually tailored to each person giving them the highest chance of success (i.e., non-recidivism).

The importance of genotype to treatment response, while not investigated by criminologists, has been recognized in other fields of study. The medical community, in particular, has long recognized the possibility that genes may be implicated in how people respond to drugs. Known as pharmacogenomics, this field of study has shown that certain drugs are effective for people with particular genotypes, while these same drugs are ineffective or produce harmful side effects for people with different genotypes.[21] There is no reason why rehabilitation programs could not engage in this same practice, a view originally pointed out by the renowned scholar Richard Tremblay when he stated:

> Drug companies are developing a new research field which has been labeled 'pharmacogenomics.' Its aim is to create the knowledge which will enable the creation of pharmaceutical products meant to match the genetic makeup of an individual. It is easy to imagine that we can do the same with psychosocial interventions: match the intervention to the genetic profile of the client.[22]

Although rehabilitation programs have yet to use genotype as a way to construct personalized rehabilitation programs, the NFP program is taking this possibility seriously. According to David Olds: "We are beginning to conduct genotyping of the mothers and children in our samples in order to understand more precisely those groups who benefit from the intervention, and those who do not, and why."[23] Hopefully other programs will follow the lead of Olds' NFP and begin to genotype their clients. If this becomes standard practice, then the effectiveness of rehabilitation programs will likely increase.

3. Treatment programs should use brain-imaging techniques to monitor each offender's progress through the program.

A wide range of treatment modalities have been employed in attempts to rehabilitate criminals. Some of these modalities, such as those involving acupuncture, have bordered on the ridiculous and have not, in any way, shape, or form, been effective at curbing recidivism. Others, such as those that emphasize interpersonal skills, have been relatively successful at reducing recidivism. But overall, the most effective treatment programs are those that use cognitive behavioral therapy. Very briefly, cognitive behavioral therapy focuses on changing what offenders think and how offenders think. To do so, cognitive behavioral programs are grounded in social learning theories, where change is encouraged by modeling prosocial cognitions, practicing these newly acquired cognitive skills, and being rewarded for using them correctly. Programs that use cognitive behavioral therapy have been found to reduce recidivism by as much as 50 percent.[24]

Why are cognitive behavioral programs so effective at reducing recidivism? To answer this question, remember that some criminals have brain abnormalities, where certain regions of their brains (e.g., the prefrontal cortex, the amygdala, etc.) function differently than non-criminals (see Chapter 4). That is particularly important because cognitive behavioral programs have been found to alter brain activity in clinical samples. For example, Kimberly Goldapple and her colleagues examined the association between brain functioning and cognitive behavioral therapy in a sample of depressed patients.[25] This team of researchers used neuroimaging techniques to determine whether the cognitive behavioral program changed brain activity in the sample. The results indicated that cognitive behavioral therapy was associated with changes in the limbic system and the frontal cortex. Similar findings were reported in another study that examined the association between cognitive behavioral therapy and brain functioning in a sample of patients with posttraumatic stress disorder.[26] In this research, the application of cognitive behavioral therapy reduced activity levels in the amygdala. The results of these studies, along with others[27], indicate that the most effective treatment programs are the ones that alter brain functioning.

These findings point to the likelihood that cognitive behavioral programs are effective at reducing recidivism because they change brain functioning. Unfortunately no study has ever tested this possibility on samples of criminals and so it remains to be seen whether cognitive behavioral programs alter brain functioning in offenders. To the extent that they do, then it would be possible to monitor progress through rehabilitation programs by examining brain functioning. Prior to release, offenders could be subjected to brain scans to determine whether they are ready to be released. If the brain scan reveals appropriate changes to the brain, then they would be released; if not, they would have to remain in the program for an extended period of time. By using neuroimaging techniques, practitioners would be provided with an empirically based and objective way to determine whether the offender has been rehabilitated.

4. Treatment programs should begin to take seriously the possibility that epigenetic therapies may be a powerful way to reduce antisocial behaviors.

There is growing recognition that diseases and disorders, such as cancer, that are strongly influenced by genetic factors may be treated with epigenetic drugs (sometimes referred to as pharmacoepigenetics).[28] Recall that epigenetic modifications refer to alterations in gene activity (e.g., genes being switched "on" or "off") without alterations to the DNA (see Chapter 3). To see how knowledge about epigenetics can be used to treat disorders, pretend that a particular gene, say gene C, is a cause of a particular disorder, say disorder D. Let's also pretend that gene C is the only cause of disorder D, meaning that persons with gene C will always develop disorder D. Now let's suppose that a certain drug could be used to "silence" or "turn off" gene C via epigenetic modifications. In theory, it would be possible to erase disorder D through epigenetic changes to gene C that result from taking epigenetic drugs.

All of this may sound a bit like science fiction, but it's not. Researchers are beginning to identify certain drugs that affect epigenetic processes, and these drugs are potentially important in the treatment of certain diseases, especially cancer. Although it is much too early to determine how effective these drugs are in the fight against cancer, initial results indicate high levels of success.[29]

So epigenetic drugs may be useful when treating disorders and diseases, but would they have any application to preventing crime or rehabilitating criminals? The short answer is that we do not know; there is not any research conducted on humans that has examined whether epigenetic drugs could change antisocial behaviors. There are two main reasons why it makes logical sense to think that epigenetic drugs could be used as a way to reduce antisocial phenotypes. First, it is known that genetic factors account for at least 50 percent of the variance in antisocial phenotypes. In addition, a number of genetic polymorphisms have been identified that are associated with delinquent and criminal involvement. Thus, if it was possible to somehow "silence" these genes, then it would stand to reason that criminal involvement should decrease. Of course, the human genome and the human epigenome are much too complex to predict in advance how epigenetic drugs may work on criminals, but it is a line of inquiry that needs to be explored.

The second reason to suspect that epigenetic drugs may be effective at reducing crime and delinquency is because these phenotypes are influenced, in part, by early abuse, neglect, and maltreatment. These criminogenic environments likely exert part of their influence by producing epigenetic modifications. To illustrate, remember Chapter 3 presented a study conducted by Ian Weaver and colleagues where they examined maternal nurturing among rats.[30] Recall that the rats that were nurtured by their mothers were relatively calm and passive, while the rats that were not nurtured by their mothers were anxious and not adaptive. The differences between these two groups of rats were tied to differences in epigenetics, where rats that were nurtured had different epigenetic patterns when compared to rats that were not nurtured by their mothers. One of the more fascinating aspects of this study was that if the rats that were not nurtured were administered a drug, their epigenetic patterns were reversed and resembled the epigenetic patterns of the nurtured rats. What's more is that after the epigenetic patterns had been reversed by the drug, the rat pups' behavior changed; no longer were they anxious, but they were more passive and docile just like the rat pups that were nurtured their mothers. This study hints at the possibility that epigenetic drugs may be able to erase—at least partially—the deleterious effects of certain adverse environments.

Given that the study of epigenetics and how it relates to human phenotypes remains in its infancy, much of what is known about epigenetic therapies remains pure speculation. Even so, the possibility that epigenetic drugs could potentially be used to treat criminals should be taken seriously be criminologists and clinicians alike.

Summary

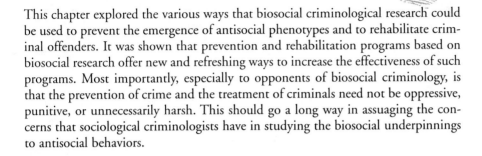

This chapter explored the various ways that biosocial criminological research could be used to prevent the emergence of antisocial phenotypes and to rehabilitate criminal offenders. It was shown that prevention and rehabilitation programs based on biosocial research offer new and refreshing ways to increase the effectiveness of such programs. Most importantly, especially to opponents of biosocial criminology, is that the prevention of crime and the treatment of criminals need not be oppressive, punitive, or unnecessarily harsh. This should go a long way in assuaging the concerns that sociological criminologists have in studying the biosocial underpinnings to antisocial behaviors.

Key Points

- Antisocial behaviors are stable over long periods of time.
- One of the best predictors of future misbehavior is a history of past misbehavior.
- Prevention programs are designed to prevent antisocial behaviors from emerging.
- Treatment (rehabilitation) programs are designed to reduce future criminal involvement among offenders.
- Biosocial criminology can guide the development of prevention programs and rehabilitation programs.
- Criminogenic risk factors are factors that when present increase the odds of criminal involvement.
- Prevention programs should educate parents-to-be on the importance of a healthy pregnancy.
- Prevention programs should provide parents with adequate prenatal healthcare.
- Prevention programs should offer free post-birth classes that are designed to inform new parents about early childhood development.
- David Olds' Nurse-Family Partnership is a model biosocial prevention program that has achieved considerable success.
- Treatment programs should assess each offender's genetic risk to determine their eligibility in the program.
- Treatment programs should consider the possibility that genetic factors moderate the effectiveness of the program.

- Treatment programs should use brain-imaging techniques to monitor each offender's progress through the program.

- Treatment programs should take seriously the possibility that epigenetic therapies may be a powerful way to reduce antisocial behaviors.

Mini Quiz

1. Genetic effects on antisocial behaviors _____ be altered.

    a) can always   c) can never
    b) can sometimes   d) none of the above

2. The general consensus is that _____ programs are better able to reduce criminal involvement than are _____programs.

    a) rehabilitation, prevention   c) treatment, rehabilitation
    b) rehabilitation, treatment   d) prevention, rehabilitation

3. _____ risk factors can be changed, while _____ risk factors cannot be changed.

    a) Static, dynamic   c) Criminogenic, dynamic
    b) Dynamic, static   d) Static, criminogenic

4. Many prevention programs are not very effective at reducing future anti-social behaviors because _____.

    a) they target criminogenic risk factors
    b) they target dynamic risk factors
    c) they target weak criminogenic risk factors
    d) all of the above

5. David Olds' Nurse-Family Partnership is effective at reducing antisocial behaviors. What types of risk factors does this program target?

    a) sociological risk factors only
    b) biological risk factors only
    c) biological and sociological risk factors
    d) none of the above

6. There is good reason to believe that genetic risk factors _____ the effectiveness of rehabilitation programs.

    a) are unrelated to   c) both a and b

    b) condition   d) neither a nor b

7. _____ offenders are more likely to benefit from rehabilitation programs than are _____ offenders.

    a) Low-risk, high-risk   c) High-risk, low risk

    b) High-risk, career criminals   d) none of the above

8. Cognitive behavioral therapies have been found to _____.

    a) modify genetic effects

    b) modify environmental conditions

    c) modify epigenetics

    d) modify brain functioning

9. Researchers are exploring the way that certain drugs may actually alter the expression of genes. What process is at work here?

    a) pharmacological   c) epigenetics

    b) non-pharmacological   d) all of the above

10. Even though genes are immutable, the effects of genes can sometimes be changed by changing _____.

    a) other genes   c) the environment

    b) the brain   d) none of the above

1. Describe David Olds' Nurse-Family Partnership. Identify the main reasons that it is so effective at reducing antisocial behaviors.

2. Based on everything that you have learned about biosocial criminology, describe how this perspective could be used to develop an effective prevention program.

3. Suppose someone was arguing that biosocial criminology could only lead to oppressive and inhumane crime-control policies. How would you explain to this critic that their view is unfounded?

4. Discuss why it is important to target biological, genetic, and environmental criminogenic risk factors when attempting to reduce criminal involvement.

Further Reading

Beauchaine, T. P., Neuhaus, E., Brenner, S. L., & Gatze-Kopp, L. (2008). Ten good reasons to consider biological processes in prevention and intervention research. *Development and Psychopathology, 20*, 745–774.

Farrington, D. P., & Coid, J. W. (2003). *Early prevention of adult antisocial behaviour*. Cambridge, UK: Cambridge University Press.

Fishbein, D. H. (2000). The importance of neurobiological research to the prevention of psychopathology. *Prevention Science, 1*, 89–106.

Fishbein, D. H. (2000). *The science, treatment, and prevention of antisocial behaviors: Applications to the criminal justice system*. Kingston, NJ: Civic Research Institute.

Nuffield Council on Bioethics. (2002). *Report on genetics and human behaviour: The ethical context*. London, UK: Nuffield Council on Bioethics. Available online at: http://www.nuffieldbioethics.org/fileLibrary/pdf/nuffieldgeneticsrep.pdf.

Olds, D. L. (2007). Preventing crime with prenatal and infancy support of parents: The Nurse-Family Partnership. *Victims and Offenders, 2*, 205–225.

Raine, A., & Liu, J.-L. (1998). Biological predispositions to violence and their implications for biosocial treatment and prevention. *Psychology, Crime, and Law, 4*, 107–125.

Rose, N. (2000). The biology of culpability: Pathological identity and crime control in a biological culture. *Theoretical Criminology, 4*, 5–34.

Tancredi, L. (2005). *Hardwired behavior: What neuroscience reveals about morality*. Cambridge, UK: Cambridge University Press.

van Goozen, S. H. M., & Fairchild, G. (2008). How can the study of biological processes help design new interventions for children with severe antisocial behavior? *Development and Psychopathology, 20*, 941–973.

1. Beaver, K. M., & Wright, J. P. (2007). The stability of low self-control from kindergarten through first grade. *Journal of Crime and Justice, 30*, 63–86; Loeber, R. (1982). The stability of antisocial and delinquent child behavior: A review. *Child Development, 53*, 1431–1446; Nagin, D., & Paternoster, R. (2000). Population heterogeneity and state dependence: State of the evidence and directions for future research. *Journal of Quantitative Criminology, 16*, 117–144; Olweus, D. (1979). Stability of aggressive reaction patterns in males: A review. *Psychological Bulletin, 86*, 852–875.

2. DeLisi, M. (2005). *Career criminals in society.* Thousand Oaks, CA: Sage.

3. Farrington, D. P. (2000). Explaining and preventing crime: The globalization of knowledge—the American Society of Criminology 1999 Presidential Address. *Criminology, 38*, 1–24.

4. I will not discuss protective factors here. For a discussion of protective factors see Farrington (2000).

5. Andrews, D. A., & Bonta, J. (2003). *The psychology of criminal conduct, 3rd edition.* Cincinnati, OH: Anderson.

6. Kazdin, A. E., Kraemer, H. C., Kessler, R. C., Kupfer, D. J., & Offord, D. R. (1997). Contributions of risk-factor research to developmental psychopathology. *Clinical Psychology Review, 17*, 375–406.

7. Lykken, D. T. (2000). The causes and costs of crime and a controversial cure. *Journal of Personality, 68*, 559–605.

8. Hiscock, H., Bayer, J. K., Price, A., Ukoumunne, O. C., Rogers, S., & Wake, M. (2008). Universal parenting programme to prevent early childhood behavioural problems: Cluster randomised trial. *British Medical Journal, 336*, 318–321.

9. Fang, W. L., Goldstein, A. O., Butzen, A. Y., Hartsock, S. A. et al. (2004). Smoking cessation in pregnancy: A review of postpartum relapse prevention strategies. *Journal of the American Board of Family Medicine, 17*, 264–275; Gebauer, C., Kwo, C.-Y., Haynes, E. F., & Wewers, M. E. (1998). A nurse-managed smoking cessation intervention during pregnancy. *Journal of Obstetric, Gynecologic, and Neonatal Nursing, 27*, 47–53.

10. Gatzke-Kopp, L. M., & Beauchaine, T. P. (2007). Direct and passive prenatal nicotine exposure and the development of externalizing psychopathology. *Child Psychiatry and Human Development, 38*, 255–269.

11. Olds, D. L. (2007). Preventing crime with prenatal and infancy support of parents: The Nurse-Family Partnership. *Victims and Offenders, 2*, 205–225, pp. 212–213.

12. Olds, D. L. (2007). Preventing crime with prenatal and infancy support of parents: The Nurse-Family Partnership. *Victims and Offenders, 2*, 205–225. pp. 212–213, p. 206.

13. Olds, D. L., Henderson, C. R., Kitzman, H. J., Eckenrode, J. J., Cole, R. E., & Tatelbaum, R. C. (1999). Prenatal and infancy home visitations by nurses: Recent findings. *The Future of Children, 9*, 44–65.

14. Eckenrode, J., Ganzel, B., Henderson, C. R., Smith, E., Olds, D. L., Powers, J., Cole, R., Kitzman, H., & Sidora, K. (2000). Preventing child abuse and neglect with a program of nurse home visitation: The limiting effects of domestic violence. *Journal of the American Medical Association, 284*, 1385–1391.

15. Olds, D., Henderson, C. R., Cole, R., Eckenrode, J., Kitzman, H., Luckey, D., Pettitt, L., Sidora, K., Morris, P., & Powers, J. (1998). Long-term effects of nurse home visitation on children's criminal and antisocial behavior: 15-year follow-up of a randomized controlled trial. *Journal of the American Medical Association, 280*, 1238–1244.

16. Andrews, D. A., Zinger, I., Hoge, R. D., Bonta, J., Gendreau P., & Cullen, F. T. (1990). Does correctional treatment work? A clinically relevant and psychologically informed meta-analysis. *Criminology, 28*, 369–404.

17. Lowenkamp, C. T., & Latessa, E. J. (2005). Increasing the effectiveness of correctional programming through the risk principle: Identifying offenders for residential placement. *Criminology and Public Policy, 4*, 263–290.

18. Andrews, D. A., Zinger, I., Hoge, R. D., Bonta, J., Gendreau P., & Cullen, F. T. (1990). Does correctional treatment work? A clinically relevant and psychologically informed meta-analysis. *Criminology, 28*, 369–404.

19. Bakermans-Kranenburg, M. J., van IJzendoorn, M. H., Mesman, J., Alink, L. R. A., & Juffer, F. (2008). Effects of an attachment-based intervention on daily cortisol moderated by dopamine D4: A randomized control trial on 1- to 3-year-olds screened for externalizing behavior. *Development and Psychopathology, 20*, 805–820.

20. Fishbein, D. H., Hyde, C., Coe, B., & Paschall, M. J. (2004). Neurocognitive and physiological prerequisites for prevention of adolescent drug abuse. *The Journal of Primary Prevention, 24*, 471–495; Fishbein, D. H., Hyde, C., Eldreth, D., Paschall, M. J., Hubal, R., Das, A., Tarter, R., Ialongo, N., Hubbard, S., & Yung, B. (2006). Neurocognitive skills moderate urban male adolescents' responses to preventive intervention materials. *Drug and Alcohol Dependence, 82*, 47–60.

21. Evans, W., & Relling, M. V. (1999). Pharmacogenomics: Translating functional genomics into rational therapeutics. *Science, 286*, 487–491; March, R. (2000). Pharmacogenomics: The genomics of drug response. *Yeast, 17*, 16–21.

22. Tremblay, R. E. (2005). Towards an epigenetic approach to experimental criminology: The 2004 Joan McCord Prize Lecture. *Journal of Experimental Criminology, 1, 397–415*, p. 407.

23. Olds, D. L. (2007). Preventing crime with prenatal and infancy support of parents: The Nurse-Family Partnership. *Victims and Offenders, 2*, 205–225. pp. 212–213, p. 210.

24. Landenberger, N. A., & Lipsey, M. W. (2005). The positive effects of cognitive-behavioral programs for offenders: A meta-analysis of factors associated with effective treatment. *Journal of Experimental Criminology, 1*, 451–476.

25. Goldapple, K., Segal, Z., Garson, C., Lau, M., Bieling, P., Kennedy, S., & Mayberg, H. (2004). Modulation of cortical-limbic pathways in major depression: Treatment-specific effects of cognitive behavior therapy. *Archives of General Psychiatry, 61*, 34–41.

26. Felmingham, K., Kemp, A., Williams, L., Das, P., Hughes, G., Peduto, A., & Bryant, R. (2007). Changes in anterior cingulated and amygdala after cognitive behavior therapy of posttraumatic stress disorder. *Psychological Science, 18*, 127–129.

27. Brody, A. L., Saxena, S., Stoessel, P., Gillies, L. A., Fairbans, L. A. et al. (2001). Regional brain metabolic changes in patients with major depression treated with either paroxetine or interpersonal therapy: Preliminary findings. *Archives of General Psychiatry, 58*, 631–640; Martin, S. D., Martin, E., Rai, S. S., Richardson, M. A., & Royall, R. (2001). Brain blood flow changes in depressed patients treated with interpersonal psychotherapy or venlafaxine hydrochloride. *Archives of General Psychiatry, 58*, 641–648.

28. Peedicayil, J. (2006). Epigenetic therapy–A new development in pharmacology. *Indian Journal of Medical Research, 123*, 17–24; Yoo, C. B., Cheng, J. C., & Jones, P. A. (2004). Zebularine: A new drug for epigenetic therapy. *Biochemical Society Transactions, 32*, 910–912.

29. Garcia-Manero, G., Kantarjian, H. M., Sanchez-Gonzalez, B., Yang, H. et al. (2006). Phase 1/2 study of the combination of 5-aza-2'-deoxycytidine with valproic acid in patients with leukemia. *Blood, 108*, 3271–3279; Issa, J.-P. J., Garcia-Manero, G., Giles, F. J., Mannari, R., Thomas, D. et al. (2004). Phase 1 study of low-dose prolonged exposure to schedules of the hypomethylating agent 5-aza-2'-deoxycytidine (decitabine) in hematopoietic malignancies. *Blood, 103*, 1635–1640.

30. Weaver, I. C. G., Cervoni, N., Champagne, F. A., D'Alessio, A. C., Sharma, S., Seckl, J. R., Dymov, S., Szyf, M., & Meaney, M. J. (2004). Epigenetic programming in maternal behavior. *Nature Neuroscience, 7*, 847–854.

Methodologies
In Biosocial Criminology

Introduction

Criminologists are typically well-trained in the methodological and statistical techniques that are needed to conduct social science research. At the same time, they have very little, if any, exposure to the types of methodologies that are employed by biosocial criminologists. This represents a major obstacle to criminologists who are interested in examining the biosocial correlates to antisocial phenotypes. Without knowing the appropriate ways to conduct biosocial research, criminologists are forced to continue analyzing data without taking into account genetic and biological factors. Fortunately there is a wealth of published materials discussing the statistical and methodological approaches used in behavioral genetic, molecular genetic, and biological research. Much of this literature, however, is written in statistical jargon, making it inaccessible to the beginning biosocial criminologist.

The purpose of this chapter is to present a very brief and non-technical overview of some basic biosocial methodologies. By no means is the current chapter designed to provide a detailed explanation of the complex methodologies used in biosocial research, but rather can be thought of as providing the "bare essentials" needed to work from a biosocial perspective. Toward this end, the proceeding discussion is divided into three main sections. First, the datasets that are often used by biosocial criminologists will be described. Second, the various ways of preparing the data for analyses will be covered. Third, the analytical techniques that are needed to carry out biosocial research will be reviewed. Readers interested in learning about these methodologies in greater detail should consult the books and articles listed in the "Further Readings" section at the end of this chapter.

Genetically Informative Datasets

Until relatively recently, it was nearly impossible for criminologists to conduct empirical research on the biological and genetic underpinnings to antisocial behaviors because most criminological datasets were not genetically informative. Now, however, many datasets—including a number of ones that are frequently used by criminologists—contain kinship pairs (e.g., twin pairs) or DNA markers (see Table 7.1). Even so, many criminologists are unaware of these available datasets, which is a major impediment to researchers who wish to explore the biosocial correlates to crime and delinquency. Below a brief overview of five datasets that are relevant to the study of crime and delinquency are discussed. Before doing so, it is important to point out that these are not the only—or even the "best"—datasets that are used by biosocial criminologists; they were chosen because they are analyzed regularly by sociological criminologists and because they are available to most researchers. It should also be noted that there are a number of other datasets that include biological variables (e.g., proxy measures for neuropsychological deficits, prenatal exposure to cigarette smoke, etc.), but the ones described below are unique in that they contain genetic information (e.g., twin pairs, DNA, etc.).

The National Longitudinal Study of Adolescent Health (Add Health). The National Longitudinal Study of Adolescent Health (Add Health) is a nationally representative and prospective study of American adolescents. Data collection began in 1994 when more than 90,000 seventh through twelfth grade students completed self-report questionnaires. To gain more detailed information about some of the students, follow-up interviews were conducted with a subsample of 20,745 youths and their primary caregiver. These follow-up interviews took place in the adolescent's home and included questions about their delinquent involvement, personality

Table 7.1 Genetically Informative Datasets

Dataset	Sample	Measures	Kinship Pairs	DNA
The National Longitudinal Study of Adolescent Health (Add Health)	Longitudinal and nationally representative sample; respondents followed from adolescence to early adulthood (N = 20,745)	Delinquency, crime, drug, alcohol and tobacco use, family environments, peer relationships, victimization, personality traits	Yes	Yes
The National Longitudinal Survey of Youth (NLSY)	Longitudinal sample; respondents followed from childhood into adulthood (N = 12,686)	Delinquency, cognitive skills, family environment, parental socialization, low self-control	Yes	No
The National Youth Survey Family Study (NYSFS)	Longitudinal sample; respondents followed from adolescence through adulthood (N = 1,725)	Delinquency, drug, alcohol, and tobacco use, family environments, social bonds, peer delinquency	No	Yes
Early Childhood Longitudinal Survey, Kindergarten Class (ECLS-K)	Longitudinal and nationally representative sample of children; respondents followed from kindergarten up through eighth grade (N~19,000)	Externalizing behavioral problems, low self-control, parent-child relationships, family environment, school environment, cognitive and motor skills	Yes	No
Early Childhood Longitudinal Survey, Birth Cohort (ECLS-B)	Longitudinal and nationally representative sample of children; respondents followed from birth through kindergarten (N = 10,700)	Aggression, peer rejection, cognitive and motor skills, birth complications, prenatal exposure to toxins, family environment, parent-child interactions	Yes	No

characteristics, social relationships, and home environment. Approximately one to two years later, the second wave of data was collected. Once again, a wide range of items were included on the survey instruments, including items pertaining to delinquency, victimization experiences, and family and peer relationships. The third wave of data was collected about seven years after the first wave of data when most of the respondents were young adults. The survey instruments at wave 3 included items germane to adults, such as employment status, childbearing history, lifetime contact with the criminal justice system, and many others. Altogether, more than 15,000 respondents were re-interviewed at wave 3. Efforts are currently underway to collect a fourth wave of data.[1]

Nested within the Add Health data is a sample of sibling pairs. During wave 1 in-school interviews, youths were asked to indicate whether they lived with a twin, a half-sibling, or an unrelated sibling (e.g., a stepsibling) who was between 11 and 20 years old. If they responded in the affirmative, then their sibling was added to the sample. In addition, a probability sample of regular siblings was also included in the sample. Altogether, 3,139 sibling pairs were contained in the Add Health study, including 783 twin pairs, 1,252 full-sibling pairs, 442 half-sibling pairs, and 662 unrelated sibling pairs.[2]

The Add Health data also contain a DNA sample. Only respondents who were part of the sibling pairs sample were eligible for inclusion in the DNA sample. Participants who met this criterion were asked to submit samples of their buccal cells to be genotyped. In total, 2,574 respondents were ultimately genotyped for a number of different genetic polymorphisms including those found in a dopamine transporter gene (DAT1), two dopamine receptor genes (DRD2, DRD4), a serotonin transporter gene (5-HTTLPR), and the monoamine oxidase A gene (MAOA). The Add Health research team plans on genotyping all of the respondents during wave 4 data collection.

Taken together, the Add Health data represents one of the richest sources of data available because it combines environmental and genotypic data in a unitary dataset. This is a particularly attractive sample to criminologists who are interested in studying the biosocial bases to antisocial phenotypes.

The National Longitudinal Survey of Youth (NLSY). The National Longitudinal Survey of Youth (NLSY79) commenced in 1979 when a nationally representative sample of 12,686 respondents, between the ages of fourteen and twenty-one, was selected to participate in the study. Follow-up interviews were conducted annually from 1979 through 1994 and biannually ever year since 1994. During data collection, participants were asked a broad range of questions pertaining to their educational achievements, employment status, economic well-being, delinquency, and drug use, among others.

The NLSY also extended their sample to include the children born to the NLSY79 females (i.e., the Child and Young Adult Supplement [CYAS] of the NLSY79).[3] In total, the NLSY79 included 6,283 females and 4,886 of them had had a child by 2002, resulting in 11,192 children. Beginning in 1986, the children and their mothers were interviewed biannually. Information about the child was collected in interviews with the child's mother and, when the child was between the ages of

10 and 14 years old, through self-reports. A diverse range of questions were asked about the child, including questions about the child's family life, their behaviors, their temperament, and many others. The richness of the NLSY data is evidenced by the fact that these data have been analyzed frequently by criminologists.

The NLSY can also be used in behavioral genetic research. To understand how this is the case, remember that children born to NSLY79 mothers were added to the sample. Mothers who had multiple children thus had more than one child included in the NLSY, which necessarily resulted in kinship pairs being embedded in the data. Unfortunately, the NLSY did not ask information as to the type of kinship pair (e.g., full sibling, DZ twin, MZ twin, etc.) making it seemingly impossible to determine the genetic relatedness of the sibling pairs. However, Joseph Rodgers and his colleagues overcame this limitation and constructed a linking algorithm that determined the genetic relatedness for the kinship pairs (N = 12,377 respondents).[4] This linking algorithm transforms the NLSY sample into a genetically sensitive dataset that can be used in behavioral genetic research.[5] Even so, criminologists have ignored the availability of the kinship pairs data and continued to analyze the NLSY without taking into account genetic factors. Criminologists need to begin to analyze the sibling pairs nested within the NLSY data as a way to examine the biosocial correlates to antisocial outcomes, including crime, delinquency, and low self-control.

The National Youth Survey Family Study (NYSFS). The National Youth Survey Family Study (NYSFS), formerly known as the National Youth Survey (NYS), is a longitudinal study based on a national probability sample of 1,725 youths who were born between 1959 and 1965. Initial interviews began in 1976 and were conducted every year between 1977 and 1981. The data collection procedure then changed and interviews were completed once every three years between 1984 and 1993. Then, during 2002, approximately 26 years after the first wave of data was collected, follow-up interviews were conducted with the respondents. Overall, the NYSFS includes measures that tap crime, delinquency, drug and alcohol use, social bonds, peer relationships, family conditions, and almost every other environmental measure of interest to criminologists. Against this backdrop, it is probably not too surprising that the NYSFS has been one of the most widely used criminological datasets to date.

Of particular interest is that during 2002 follow-up interviews, 1,007 respondents of the original NYS cohort submitted DNA samples for genotyping. Participants, for example, were genotyped for genes involved in neurotransmission, such as DRD2[6] and MAOA.[7] By adding genotypic information to the existing data, the NYSFS has become a very rich dataset that will most likely shed a great deal of light on the biosocial correlates to antisocial phenotypes. Importantly, other criminological and social science datasets could be enriched by following the lead of the NYSFS and genotyping study participants.

The Early Childhood Longitudinal Survey, Kindergarten Class (ECLS-K). The Early Childhood Longitudinal Survey, Kindergarten Class (ECLS-K) is a longitudinal and nationally representative study of kindergarteners. Approximately 19,000 children were included in the ECLS-K, making it the largest prospective sample of American children. Data collection efforts began in the fall of 1998 when the children first entered kindergarten. Since that time, additional waves of data have been collected in first grade, third grade, fifth grade, and eighth grade. Parents and teachers were interviewed and asked questions about the children, including questions pertaining to the child's temperament, behaviors, abilities, relationships, family life, and many others. In addition, the children were also subjected to a battery of standardized tests designed to measure their cognitive capabilities, language development, and motor skills, among others. Given the sheer number of children included in the study, the long time period that the children were followed, and the breadth of information collected, the ECLS-K is a rich source of data for exploring issues related to child development.

One of the unique aspects of the ECLS-K is that twins were oversampled. If the child indicated that they were part of a twin pair, then their co-twin was added to the study. Overall, a total of N = 155 twin pairs were included in the ECLS-K, a sample size large enough to support behavioral genetic research designs. As a result, biosocial criminologists have used the ECLS-K to examine genetic and biological factors that are related to early life antisocial phenotypes.[8]

The Early Childhood Longitudinal Survey, Birth Cohort (ECLS-B). The Early Childhood Longitudinal Survey, Birth Cohort (ECLS-B) is a longitudinal and nationally representative sample of American children born in 2001. So far, three waves of data have been collected: one when the child was nine months old, one when the child was 24 months old, and one when the child was enrolled in preschool. Information about the child was garnered from interviews with the child's mother, father, and childcare provider. Questions were asked about the child's antisocial behaviors, temperament, family life, and peer relationships, among others. Details about their birth, such as APGAR scores and birth weight, were extracted from their birthing files. Additionally, the child was also subjected to a series of standardized assessments to gauge their development early in life, such as their mental skills and motor skills. Altogether 10,700 children were included in the ECLS-B.

Like the ECLS-K, the ECLS-B also oversampled twins, a sampling process which netted N = 825 twin pairs. Given that the data have only been released relatively recently, biosocial criminologists have not yet employed the ECLS-B in empirical research. But since these data contain twins as well as questions pertaining to antisocial phenotypes, it is likely the ECLS-B will emerge as a particularly important dataset for biosocial criminologists interested in examining the development of aggression over the first few years of the life course.

Preparing Genetically Informative Data for Analysis

Most criminologists know how to prepare data for social science research, but not for biosocial research. In general, there are two main issues with preparing genetically informative data that most criminologists do not have experience with. First, in order to estimate behavioral genetic models, cross-twin correlations need to be calculated. Second, with molecular genetic research, the genetic polymorphism needs to be coded into a variable that can be used in statistical analyses. The following discussion will explain the steps that need to be taken in order to calculate cross-twin correlations and to code a genetic polymorphism.

Calculating cross-twin correlations. Virtually all behavioral genetic research that is interested in decomposing phenotypic variance uses samples of twin pairs. Recall from Chapter 2 that the cross-twin correlation for MZ twins is compared to the cross-twin correlation for DZ twins. By comparing the cross-twin correlation for MZ twins to the cross-twin correlation for DZ twins, researchers are able to estimate the relative effects of genetic factors, shared environmental factors, and nonshared environmental factors on a phenotype. One of the difficulties in calculating cross-twin correlations is setting up the data file for this type of analysis. Although cross-twin correlations can be estimated using a number of different statistical packages, one of the easiest ways to calculate them is by using SPSS.

Data in SPSS are typically arranged such that each row corresponds to a single case (i.e., one respondent) and each column corresponds to a single variable. This data structure is depicted in 7.2. As can be seen, each person in the sample occupies their own row, and their corresponding value for each variable is listed in that same row. For instance, the value for Variable #1 for Person #1 is 22, while the value for Variable #2 for Person #6 is 59. In social science research, the interest is usually in determining whether two (or more) variables are related. One way of testing this is by calculating a correlation coefficient (see Chapter 1) between the two variables of interest. Perhaps a researcher is interested in testing for an association (i.e., correlation) between Variable #1 and Variable #2. By using the point-and-click options in SPSS it is relatively easy to calculate the correlation between these two variables.

The key point to bear in mind is that criminologists are interested in calculating correlations for within-person variables—that is, where both variables are measured for the same person. But what happens if a researcher is interested in calculating correlations for between-person variables—that is, where the two variables are measured in two different people? To see what is meant by this,

Table 7.2 The default data file structure in SPSS where each row corresponds to a case

	Variable #1	Variable #2	Family ID	Twin #	Type of Twin
Person #1	22	54	10	1	.5
Person #2	28	59	10	2	.5
Person #3	27	52	11	1	1.0
Person #4	28	50	11	2	1.0
Person #5	26	55	12	1	.5
Person #6	21	59	12	2	.5

pretend that a researcher was interested in correlating Variable #1 for Person #1 with Variable #1 for Person #2. While it might seem somewhat odd to think that the variables for two different people would be correlated, this is exactly what behavioral genetic research does. For example, suppose Person #1 was the co-twin of Person #2. To calculate the cross-twin correlation for a particular phenotype, say Variable #1, Person #1's score on Variable #1 would need to be correlated with Person #2's score on Variable #1. SPSS, however, cannot be used to calculate cross-twin correlations when the data are structured as they are in Table 7.2.

In order to calculate cross-twin correlations the data need to be reformatted so that each row corresponds to a twin pair. If you take a close look at Table 7.2 you will be able to see that the data actually contain three pairs of twins. To see how this is the case, note that the Family ID variable represents the family that each person is from, such that persons from the same family have the same value for the Family ID variable. What this means is that Person #1 and Person #2 are from the same family (i.e., Family ID #10), Person #3 and Person #4 are from the same family (i.e., Family ID #11), and Person #5 and Person #6 are from the same family (i.e., Family ID # 12). Obviously, then, persons from the same family are siblings and this information can then be used to transform the data.

Recall that in order to calculate cross-twin correlations, each row must correspond to a twin pair. SPSS can be used to transform the data structure from one-person-per-row to one-twin-pair-per-row. To do so, two variables must be present in the data: a variable that represents the family that each twin is from (i.e., the Family ID variable) and a variable that differentiates each twin from each other (i.e., the Twin # variable). The latter variable can be constructed by randomly assigning one twin from each twin pair a value of "1"and the other twin from the twin pair a value of "2." Then the following steps need to be performed in SPSS in order to restructure the data file:

1. Click on the "Data" tab and select "Restructure."
2. A new box will emerge. Select the "Restructure selected cases into variables" option. Click "Next."
3. Another box will appear. This time, select the family identification variable (e.g., Family ID) as the "Identifier Variable" and select the variable that differentiates each twin (e.g., the Twin # variable) as the "Index Variable." Click "Next."
4. Another box will appear asking whether the data should be sorted by the identifier and index variables. Select "Yes" and click on "Next."
5. Another box will appear and at the top there will be two options: Select the option labeled "Group by index (for example: w1 h1, w2 h2, w3 h3)." Click "Next."
6. Another box will appear asking "What do you want to do?" Select "Restructure the data now." Click "Finish."

The data will now be restructured so that each row corresponds to one twin pair. As Table 7.3 shows, the variable labels will change somewhat in order to

Table 7.3 A restructured data file where each row corresponds to a twin pair

	Variable #1.1	Variable #2.1	Variable #1.2	Variable #2.2	Family ID	Type of Twin
Twin Pair #1	22	54	28	59	10	.5
Twin Pair #2	27	52	28	50	11	1.0
Twin Pair #3	26	55	21	59	12	.5

delineate the variables for Twin #1 and the variables for Twin #2. To see how this works, notice that the variables now have extension numbers (e.g., .1 or .2). The extension value indicates whether the variable is for Twin #1 or Twin #2. In Table 7.3, for example, Variable #1.1 corresponds to the value of Variable #1 for Twin #1, while Variable #1.2 corresponds to the value of Variable #1 for Twin #2. Comparing Tables 7.2 and 7.3 shows how the variables are rearranged when restructuring the data.

Now that the data have been restructured, it is possible to calculate cross-twin correlations. To do so, the variable for one twin is correlated with that same variable for their co-twin. For example, suppose we were interested in estimating the cross-twin correlation for Variable #2. This would be easily accomplished by correlating Variable #2.1 with Variable #2.2. The resulting correlation coefficient would be the cross-twin correlation. Remember, however, that we often are interested in comparing the cross-twin correlation for MZ twins to the cross-twin correlation for DZ twins. In our previous example, we pooled MZ and DZ twin pairs together. In order to gain separate estimates for MZ and DZ twins, we need to select certain cases using the "Type of Twin" variable, which indicates whether the twin pair is a MZ twin pair (represented with a value of "1.0" because they share 100 percent of their DNA) or whether the twin pair is a DZ twin pair (represented with a value of .5 because they share 50 percent of their DNA). As can be seen in Table 7.3, Twin Pairs #1 and #3 are DZ twin pairs, while Twin Pair #2 is a MZ twin pair.

It is relatively easy to calculate separate cross-twin correlations for MZ and DZ twin pairs in SPSS by performing the following steps:

1. Click on the "Data" tab and then select "Select Cases."
2. A new box will appear and click on the "If condition is satisfied" button. Click "If."
3. Another box will appear. Find the variable that corresponds to the type of twin pair (e.g., the Type of Twin variable). Move that variable into the equation box on the right hand side of the box.
4. After the type of twin pair variable is in the box, set it equal to .50 (e.g., Type of Twin = .50). This process selects only DZ twin pairs. Click "Continue."
5. Be sure that at the bottom of the box to select the "Filter out unselected cases" option.
6. Click "OK."

7. Calculate the DZ cross-twin correlation.
8. To calculate the MZ cross-twin correlation repeat these same steps except in Step #4 set the variable equal to 1.0 instead of .50 (this process selects only MZ twin pairs).

By following the steps above, the cross-twin correlations will first be estimated for DZ twin pairs and then for MZ twin pairs. These cross-twin correlations can then be used to begin to decompose phenotypic variance into a genetic component, a shared environmental component, and a nonshared environmental component.

Coding a genetic polymorphism. In datasets that include DNA markers, researchers are confronted with how the genetic polymorphism should be coded for statistical analyses. The very first step in coding a genetic polymorphism is to determine, based on empirical research, which allele(s) are the risk allele(s) and which allele(s) are the non-risk allele(s). (Remember that risk alleles are those alleles that confer an increased risk of developing a particular phenotype, such as an antisocial phenotype.) After the risk allele(s) have been identified, researchers then have the choice of three main ways to code the genetic variable: recessively, dominantly, or co-dominantly. To code a genetic polymorphism recessively, two groups are formed: one group consists of respondents who have two risk alleles and the other group consists of respondents who have one risk allele or zero risk alleles. The genetic variable can then be coded as a dichotomous dummy variable, where a value of "0" corresponds to the presence of zero or one risk alleles and a value of "1" corresponds to the presence of two risk alleles.

The second way to code a genetic variable is dominantly. With dominant coding, two groups are once again formed, but this time one group consists of respondents with one or two risk alleles and the other group consists of respondents with zero risk alleles. The genetic variable can then be coded as a dichotomous dummy variable, where a value of "0" corresponds to the presence of zero risk alleles and a value of "1" corresponds to the presence of one or two risk alleles.

The third way to code a genetic variable is co-dominantly. With co-dominant coding, three groups are formed: one group consists of respondents with zero risk alleles, one group consists of respondents with one risk allele, and one group consists of respondents with two risk alleles. The genetic variable is then coded as a trichotomous variable, where a value of "0" corresponds to the presence of zero risk alleles, a value of "1" corresponds to the presence of one risk allele, and a value of "2" corresponds to the presence of two risk alleles. In other words, with co-dominant coding the value of the variable indicates the number of risk alleles that each respondent possesses.

So, which of the three coding schemes should be employed? There is not a straightforward answer to this question; some research uses recessive coding, some research uses dominant coding, and some research uses co-dominant coding. Again, the best way to determine which coding scheme to use is to consult the existing studies that have examined the effects of that particular genetic polymorphism.

After the coding scheme has been selected, then the genetic variable can be analyzed to determine its relationship with phenotypic measures.

Analytical Techniques

After a dataset has been chosen and the data have been prepared, researchers are then faced with the decision of how to analyze the data. Obviously the choice of analytical techniques will largely be governed by the research question being studied. In biosocial research, however, there are three commonly used analytical techniques: biometric model fitting, DeFries-Fulker (DF) analysis, and genetic association designs. Each of these three analytical techniques will be briefly reviewed.

Biometrical model fitting. One of the issues central to biosocial criminology is the percentage of variance in a phenotype that is due to genetic factors (h^2), shared environmental factors (c^2), and nonshared environmental factors (e^2). Although estimates for h^2, c^2, and e^2 can be garnered by using the equations presented in Chapter 2 (equations 2.1–2.3), there is a more accurate and reliable way to estimate these effects: biometrical model fitting. To understand this modeling strategy, let's revisit and elaborate on some of what was discussed in Chapter 2. Recall that phenotypic variance can be due to genetic factors, environmental factors, or some combination of the two. More specifically, there are two types of genetic factors—additive genetic factors and dominance genetic factors—and there are two types of environmental factors—shared environmental factors and nonshared environmental factors. Although we have been using h^2 as the symbol for genetic factors, we need to somehow keep additive genetic factors separate from dominance genetic factors. This is accomplished relatively easily by using the symbol **A** for additive genetic factors and the symbol **D** for dominance genetic factors. The symbols for the environmental components also change slightly in the biometric model, where the symbol for the shared environment is **C** and the symbol for the nonshared environment is **E**. Putting this altogether, we know that the phenotypic variance (symbolized as **P**) is a function of these four components, such that

$$\mathbf{P} = \mathbf{A} + \mathbf{D} + \mathbf{C} + \mathbf{E} \qquad (7.1)$$

As Chapter 2 discussed, it is possible to employ twin data to estimate the effects of these different variance components. Figure 7.1 shows how twin data are used in the basic biometric twin model. A few comments about this model are in order. To begin with, the rectangular boxes represent the phenotype for Twin 1 and that same phenotype for their co-twin, Twin 2. The circles are latent factors that represent nonshared environmental effects (**E**), shared environmental effects (**C**), dominance genetic effects (**D**), and additive genetic effects (**A**). The double-headed arrows represent the correlations between twins on those latent factors. Let's explore this in a little greater detail by first looking at the nonshared environment. Remember nonshared environments are environments that are not shared between siblings. An example of a nonshared environment could be schools, where one sibling attends

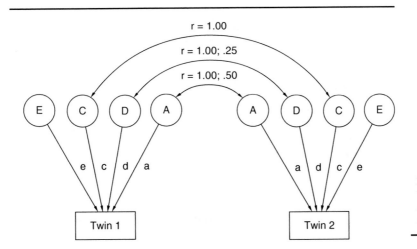

Figure 7.1
Univariate twin model (full ADCE model).

one school and their sibling attends another school. If this was the case, then the school environments between the siblings would be a nonshared environment and thus uncorrelated, which is precisely why there is not a double-headed error between the **E** latent factors. Now let's take a look at the shared environment. As can be seen, the correlation between the **C** factors for siblings is 1.00 because shared environments, by definition, are the same between siblings. And environments that are the same would be correlated at 1.00. Given that dominance effects (**D**) are not usually modeled, let's skip **D** for now and take a closer look at additive genetic factors (**A**). You will see that the correlation between the **A** factors can take on one of two values: 1.00 and .50. The reason for this is because MZ twins share 100 percent of their DNA, meaning that the correlation between the **A** factors for MZ twins is 1.00. DZ twins, in contrast, share, on average, 50 percent of their DNA, meaning that the correlation between the **A** factors for DZ twins is .50. The lower case letters in Figure 7.1—*e, c, d, a*—represent the path coefficients for each respective latent factor.

By using path tracing rules, it is also possible to derive the expected variance-covariance structure of the model presented in Figure 7.1. To see how this works, suppose that we were interested in determining the additive genetic covariance for MZ twins (**A**). In order to use path tracing rules, first place your finger on the rectangular box labeled Twin 1. Then, find the path coefficient for additive genetic effects (*a*). Move your finger from the rectangular box (i.e., Twin 1) up path *a* until you reach **A**. Next, move your finger across the correlation between the **A** latent factors (*r* = 1.00 for MZ twins). Last, move down path *a* until you reach the rectangular box labeled Twin 2. Now, write down each path that you traced: *a*, then *r* = 1.00, then *a*. According to path tracing rules, these three paths need to be multiplied together to gain the estimate of additive genetic covariance for MZ twins, which yields:

$$a * 1.00 * a = a^2$$

Now repeat this for DZ twins. Everything would remain the same except the correlation between the **A** factors would no longer be $r = 1.00$, but instead would be $r = .50$ yielding the following additive genetic covariance for DZ twins:

$$a * \frac{1}{2} * a = \frac{1}{2} a^2$$

Path tracing rules can be used to estimate the expected variances and covariances for the remaining latent factors. Doing so would produce the following expected variance-covariance matrix for MZ twins:

$$\begin{bmatrix} a^2 + d^2 + c^2 + e^2 & a^2 + d^2 + c^2 \\ a^2 + d^2 + c^2 & a^2 + d^2 + c^2 + e^2 \end{bmatrix}$$

And using path tracing rules would produce the following expected variance-covariance matrix for DZ twins:

$$\begin{bmatrix} a^2 + d^2 + c^2 + e^2 & \frac{1}{2}a^2 + \frac{1}{4}d^2 + c \\ \frac{1}{2}a^2 + \frac{1}{4}d^2 + c^2 & a^2 + d^2 + c^2 + e^2 \end{bmatrix}$$

Note that these are expected matrices, meaning that if the model in Figure 7.1 was reflective of reality then the observed data (i.e., the data that we actually collected) should approximate closely the variance-covariance matrices presented above. To see how this works, suppose that a particular phenotype has a variance of 24. Let's pretend that this variance was equally divided among the four variance components, so that a^2, d^2, c^2, and e^2 each explained one-fourth of the phenotypic variance. Essentially, the values for a^2, d^2, c^2, and e^2 would each be equal to 6. The expected variance-covariance matrix for MZ twins would thus become:

$$\begin{bmatrix} 6 + 6 + 6 + 6 & 6 + 6 + 6 \\ 6 + 6 + 6 & 6 + 6 + 6 + 6 \end{bmatrix} = \begin{bmatrix} 24 & 18 \\ 18 & 24 \end{bmatrix}$$

And the expected variance-covariance matrix for DZ twins would thus become:

$$\begin{bmatrix} 6 + 6 + 6 + 6 & \frac{6}{2} + \frac{6}{4} + 6 \\ \frac{6}{2} + \frac{6}{4} + 6 & 6 + 6 + 6 + 6 \end{bmatrix} = \begin{bmatrix} 24 & 10.5 \\ 10.5 & 24 \end{bmatrix}$$

The problem with this is example is that we are estimating expected variance-covariance values (i.e., values that we should obtain), but we are not actually estimating true variance-covariance values (i.e., values that we actually obtained). One way to estimate variance-covariance structures that are most likely to be true is by using biometrical model-fitting techniques. The goal of model-fitting techniques is to estimate expected variance-covariance matrices that are as similar as possible to the observed variance-covariance matrices. This is accomplished through an iterative process, where the expected matrix is compared to the observed matrix.

Then, based on the results, the expected matrix is recalculated to provide a closer "fit" to the observed matrix. Once again, the expected matrix is compared to the observed matrix. Depending on how well they match, the expected matrix may need to be re-estimated and compared again to the observed matrix. This process is repeated until the expected matrix represents the closest possible match to the observed matrix.

Suppose you were in charge of creating an expected variance-covariance matrix and comparing it to the observed variance-covariance matrix. Let us further suppose that you were presented with the following observed variance-covariance matrix for MZ twins:

$$\begin{bmatrix} 11.5 & 7.4 \\ 7.4 & 11.5 \end{bmatrix}$$

And the observed variance-covariance matrix for DZ twins is:

$$\begin{bmatrix} 13.2 & 6.8 \\ 6.8 & 13.2 \end{bmatrix}$$

What values would you start with to construct the expected variance-covariance MZ and DZ matrices? Perhaps you would choose $a^2 = 4$, $d^2 = .5$, $c^2 = 2.1$, and $e^2 = 4$. You could then enter these values into the expected variance-covariance matrix for MZ twins and you would arrive at:

$$\begin{bmatrix} 4 + .5 + 2.1 + 4 & 4 + .5 + 2.1 \\ 4 + .5 + 2.1 & 4 + .5 + 2.1 + 4 \end{bmatrix} = \begin{bmatrix} 10.6 & 6.6 \\ 6.6 & 10.6 \end{bmatrix}$$

And the expected variance-covariance matrix for DZ twins would be:

$$\begin{bmatrix} 4 + .5 + 2.1 + 4 & \dfrac{4}{2} + \dfrac{.5}{4} + 2.1 \\ \dfrac{4}{2} + \dfrac{.5}{4} + 2.1 & 4 + .5 + 2.1 + 4 \end{bmatrix} = \begin{bmatrix} 10.6 & 4.2 \\ 4.2 & 10.6 \end{bmatrix}$$

Note that the expected variance-covariance matrices are not identical to the observed variance-covariance matrices, but they are somewhat similar. Our goal is to produce a solution where the MZ and DZ matrices are very similar to each other. So, we would have to go back and choose a different set of values for a^2, d^2, c^2, and e^2 and then recalculate the matrices. We would keep doing this until we arrived at a solution that produced expected variance-covariance matrices that matched closely the observed variance-covariance matrices. Model-fit statistics are used to determine the solution that best fits the observed data.

Thus far we have discussed the fact that there are four different variance components that need to be estimated: **E**, **C**, **D**, and **A**. However, when analyzing data that consists solely of twin pairs, **E**, **C**, **D**, and **A** are confounded making it impossible to estimate the effects of each simultaneously. As a result, one of the latent factors must be removed from the model. Usually, most model-fitting studies drop **D**, and estimate what is known as an **ACE** model. By removing **D**, it is possible to

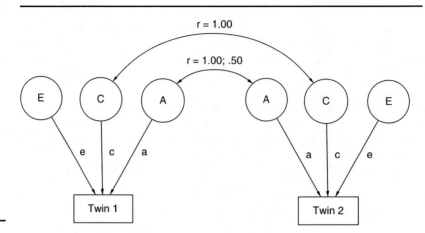

Figure 7.2
Univariate twin
model (standard ACE
model).

estimate **A**, **C**, and **E** simultaneously. This reduced biometric model is portrayed in Figure 7.2 and is the model most commonly estimated in behavioral genetic research.

One of the attractive qualities of the **ACE** model is that it produces only one "best" solution, meaning there are not multiple "best" solutions. This is important because it allows researchers to determine with confidence the estimates for **A**, **C**, and **E**. The **ACE** model can also be trimmed and estimated in reduced form. For example, it is common practice to set the effect of **C** equal to zero and estimate an **AE** model. Likewise, the effect of **A** could be set equal to zero and a **CE** model could be calculated. (Since **E** contains the effects of error, **E** is never set equal to zero.) These three models (i.e., **ACE**, **AE**, and **CE**) could be compared and, based on the model-fit statistics, the one that fits the observed data the best would be retained. Estimating all of these models is obviously complex and not feasible to carry out via hand calculations. Luckily, Michael Neale developed a freely downloadable statistical program, called *Mx*, that can be used to estimate behavioral genetic models, such as the **ACE** model.[9] More information about this statistical program can be found online at: http://www.vcu.edu/mx/. Overall, biometric model-fitting techniques are a powerful way of estimating the effects of genetic factors, shared environmental factors, and nonshared environmental factors on phenotypic variance.

DeFries-Fulker (DF) analysis. Another analytic technique that is used frequently in biosocial criminological research is DeFries-Fulker (DF) analysis.[10] The goal of DF analysis is the same as biometric model fitting: to estimate the percentage of phenotypic variance that is due to genetic and environmental factors. The mathematical equations underlying DF analysis, however, are quite different from those that were used when estimating the biometric model. Biometric model-fitting uses structural equation modeling with latent variables, while DF analysis is a regression-based statistic that takes the following form:

$$K_1 = b_0 + b_1 K_2 + b_2 R + b_3 (R * K_2) + e \qquad (7.2)$$

where K_1 is the phenotype for one twin, K_2 is the phenotype for their co-twin, R is a measure of genetic relatedness ($R = 1.0$ for MZ twins and $R = .5$ for DZ twins), and $R * K_2$ is an interaction term created by multiplying R and K_2. The interpretation of the coefficients in DF analysis is relatively straightforward: $b_0 =$ the constant and is not particularly important to the DF model, $b_1 =$ the proportion of variance in K_1 that is attributable to shared environmental factors, b_2 is not particularly important to the DF model, $b_3 =$ the proportion of variance in K_1 that is attributable to genetic factors, and $e =$ the proportion of variance in K_1 that is attributable to the nonshared environment and error. Note that in equation 7.2 the coefficients of interest are unstandardized coefficients (i.e., slopes); the standardized coefficients (i.e., Betas) are not particularly relevant to the DF model. Note also that b_1 is synonymous with **C** in the biometric model, b_3 is synonymous with the **A** in the biometric model, and e is synonymous with **E** in the biometric model.

The baseline DF formula has since been modified in order to overcome a number of problems.[11] This newly modified DF equation takes the following form:

$$K_1 = b_0 + b_1(K_2 - K_m) + b_2(R * (K_2 - K_m)) + e \qquad (7.3)$$

where K_1 is still the phenotype for one twin, K_2 is still the phenotype for the co-twin, and R is still is a measure of genetic relatedness. Equation 7.3 includes the term, K_m, which was not included in equation 7.2. $K_m =$ the mean of the phenotype for the co-twin—that is, the mean for K_2. What this means is that K_2 is being mean centered in equation 7.3, while in equation 7.2 it was not. The main effect of the measure of genetic relatedness (R) has also been removed from equation 7.3. Even with all of these modifications to the DF equation, the interpretation and substantive meaning of the unstandardized slopes remains unchanged: $b_1 =$ the proportion of variance in K_1 attributable to the shared environment, $b_2 =$ the proportion of variance in K_1 attributable to genetic factors, and $e =$ the proportion of variance in K_1 attributable to the nonshared environment plus error.

The DF model presented in equation 7.3 can also be expanded to include the effects of measured nonshared environments as shown in the following equation:[12]

$$K_1 = b_0 + b_1(K_2 - K_m) + b_2(R * (K_2 - K_m)) + b_4(ENVDIF) + e \quad (7.4)$$

The difference between equation 7.4 and equation 7.3 is that one additional term, *ENVDIF*, is included. *ENVDIF* is a measure of the nonshared environment that is estimated by taking the difference between twins on a particular measure. For example, one twin's score on a measure of delinquent peers could be subtracted from their co-twin's score on a measure of delinquent peers. The resulting new value, as indexed by *ENVDIF*, would capture the difference between twins on the measure of delinquent peers. This difference score (i.e., *ENVDIF*) is a measure of the nonshared environment. *ENVDIF* can then be introduced into equation 7.4 to estimate whether *ENVDIF* has an effect on the phenotype of interest.

Two additional comments about the DF model are warranted. First, prior to estimating the DF equations, the data file needs to be restructured such that each row corresponds to a twin pair. Second, it is not possible to introduce measures of the shared environment into the DF equation.[13] For example, suppose a criminologist was interested in determining whether the association between family poverty and delinquency was statistically significant after controlling for genetic factors. This type of research question cannot be answered using DF analysis; the only environmental measures that can be included are nonshared environmental factors (i.e., *ENVDIF* in equation 7.4). The DF model, however, is a robust statistical technique that has been used in a wide range research, including some biosocial criminological research.

Genetic association research designs. Biometric model-fitting techniques and DF analysis represent two important methodologies that can be employed to analyze samples consisting of kinship pairs. These methodologies are not, in general, used in genetic association studies, where a researcher is interested in examining the relationship between a genetic polymorphism and a phenotype. The methodologies used in genetic association studies are a simple extension to the methodologies frequently used by criminologists. For example, criminologists typically use some type of correlational analysis (e.g., ordinary least squares [OLS] regression) to test for an association between a particular independent variable, X, and a particular dependent variable, Y. X can be any measure of interest, but is often an environmental measure, such as parental socialization, while Y is usually some type of antisocial phenotype, such as a delinquency scale. In genetic association studies, the independent variable, X, is the genetic polymorphism variable. (Recall that genetic polymorphisms can be coded in three different ways, all of which can be entered into correlational analysis as an independent variable, X.) The analysis can then be calculated to determine whether the genetic polymorphism (X) is associated with the antisocial phenotype (Y). If there is a statistically significant association, then researchers typically conclude that the genetic polymorphism is related to the antisocial phenotype.

But as was discussed in Chapter 3, there is good reason to suspect that genetic polymorphisms have their strongest effects on a phenotype when they are paired with certain environments—that is, a gene X environment (GxE) interaction. GxEs can also be estimated by using correlational analysis, especially regression analysis. To see how this works, pretend that we were interested in calculating an OLS regression model to determine the effect that a genetic polymorphism (X) and that an environment (Z) had on an antisocial phenotype (Y). This equation would take the following form:

$$Y = \alpha_0 + b_1 X + b_2 Z + e \qquad (7.5)$$

where Y is the phenotype, α_0 is the intercept, b_1 is the unstandardized slope for the genetic polymorphism, b_2 is the unstandardized slope for the environment, and e is the error term. The unstandardized slopes for X and Z represent the independent and additive effects that the genetic polymorphism and the environment have on the phenotype, respectively.

Equation 7.5 can be altered to examine whether there is an interaction between the genetic polymorphism (X) and the environment (Z) in the prediction of the phenotype (Y). To do so, a two-step process must be undertaken. First, X and Z need to be multiplied together to create a multiplicative interaction term, XZ. Second, this new interaction term (XZ) along with the two main effect terms (X and Z) need to be entered into the equation predicting the phenotype (Y). This process would yield the following equation:

$$Y = \alpha_0 + b_1X + b_2Z + b_3XZ + e \qquad (7.6)$$

where Y is still the phenotype, α_0 is still the intercept, b_1 is still the unstandardized slope for the genetic polymorphism, b_2 is still the unstandardized slope for the environment, and e is still the error term. The coefficient for XZ (b_3) is of particular interest because it estimates that interaction between the genetic polymorphism and the environment; in other words, it is testing for a GxE. A GxE is detected when the interaction term (XZ) is a statistically significant predictor of the phenotype (Y).

Although equation 7.6 is often used to test for GxEs, it should be noted that interaction models (i.e., equation 7.6) can become unstable due to collinearity between the main effect terms (e.g., X and Z) and the interaction term (e.g., XZ). Harmful levels of collinearity often result in unstable parameter estimates, exploding standard errors, and biased tests of statistical significance for the coefficients. One way to reduce collinearity is to mean center the main effect terms (e.g., X and Z) prior to creating the interaction (e.g., XZ).[14] Then, the uncentered main effect terms and the interaction term (that was created by multiplying the mean centered main effect terms) are introduced into the model. This procedure often eliminates collinearity and allows unbiased tests of statistical significance for the coefficients. Although using a multiplicative interaction term in multivariate analysis remains the most common way of estimating a GxE between a measured genetic polymorphism and a measured environment, there are multiple different types of GxEs and some of these cannot be estimated with a multiplicative interaction term. Just bear in mind that statistical interactions are one way to test for GxEs, but they are not the only way.[15]

Summary

The purpose of this chapter was to provide beginning biosocial criminologists with a brief overview of the methodologies typically used in biosocial criminological research. This entailed discussing the available genetically informative datasets, the ways to prepare genetic data for analysis, and the analytical techniques commonly used by biosocial criminologists. All of these methodologies can be used by criminologists to begin to unpack the biosocial correlates to antisocial phenotypes.

Key Points

- There are a number of genetically informative datasets available to criminologists.
- Some genetically informative datasets include kinship pairs (e.g., NLSY), some include DNA markers (e.g., NYSFS), and some include kinship pairs and DNA markers (e.g., Add Health).

- Cross-twin correlations can be calculated in SPSS by restructuring the data.
- There are three main ways to code a genetic polymorphism for use in statistical analyses: dominantly, recessively, or co-dominantly.
- Biometric model-fitting techniques are used to estimate the proportion of variance in a phenotype that is due to additive genetic factors, dominance genetic factors, shared environmental factors, and nonshared environmental factors.
- DF analysis is a regression-based statistic that can be used to decompose phenotypic variance into a genetic component, a shared environmental component, and a nonshared environmental component.
- DF analysis can also be used to estimate the effect of measured nonshared environments on a phenotype.
- Genetic association research designs are used to test for an association between a particular genetic polymorphism and a phenotype.

1. The National Longitudinal Study of Adolescent Health (Add Health) contains _____.

    a) DNA markers

    b) kinship pairs

    c) both a and b

    d) neither a nor b

2. The National Longitudinal Survey of Youth (NLSY) contains _____.

    a) DNA markers

    b) kinship pairs

    c) both a and b

    d) neither a nor b

3. The National Youth Survey Family Study (NYSFS) contains _____.

    a) DNA markers

    b) kinship pairs

    c) both a and b

    d) neither a nor b

4. The Early Childhood Longitudinal Survey, Kindergarten Class (ECLS-K) contains _____.

    a) DNA markers

    b) kinship pairs

    c) both a and b

    d) neither a nor b

5. The Early Childhood Longitudinal Survey, Birth Cohort (ECLS-B) contains _____.

    a) DNA markers

    b) kinship pairs

    c) both a and b

    d) neither a nor b

6. What is a cross-twin correlation?

   a) A correlation between two different variables, both measured in the
      same twin
   b) A correlation among three different variables, both measured in the
      same twin
   c) A correlation between the same variables, measured in two
      different twins
   d) None of the above

7. If a genetic polymorphism is coded co-dominantly, then the value of the
   variable indicates the total number of _____.

   a) risk alleles   c) recessive alleles
   b) epigenetic effects   d) dominant alleles

8. An **ACE** model is used to estimate _____ on a phenotype.

   a) genetic influences
   b) shared environmental influences
   c) nonshared environmental influences
   d) all of the above

9. DeFries-Fulker (DF) analysis is a regression-based statistic that can be
   used to estimate _____ on a phenotype.

   a) genetic influences
   b) shared environmental influences
   c) nonshared environmental influences
   d) all of the above

10. Collinearity can be eliminated in some instances through
    _____.

    a) mean centering   c) collinearity diagnostics
    b) multiplicative interactions   d) none of the above

Discussion Questions

1. Briefly describe one dataset that criminologists could use if they were interested in testing for an association between a genetic polymorphism and an antisocial phenotype.

2. Briefly describe one dataset that criminologists could use if they were interested in estimating the genetic, shared environmental, and nonshared environmental effects on an antisocial phenotype.

3. Briefly discuss the standard **ACE** model.

4. Briefly discuss DF analysis.

5. Briefly describe how a biosocial criminologist could test for an association between a genetic polymorphism and an antisocial phenotype.

Further Reading

D'Onofrio, B. M., Turkheimer, E. N., Eaves, L. J., Corey, L. A., Berg, K., Solaas, M. H., & Emery, R. E. (2003). The role of the Children of Twins design in elucidating causal relations between parent characteristics and child outcomes. *Journal of Child Psychology and Psychiatry, 44*, 1130–1144.

DeFries, J. C., & Fulker, D. W. (1985). Multiple regression of twin data. *Behavior Genetics, 15*, 467–473.

Neale, B. M. Ferreira, M. A. R., Medland, S. E., & Posthuma, D. (2008). *Statistical genetics: Gene mapping through linkage and association.* New York: Taylor and Francis.

Neale, M. C., Boker, S. M., Xie, G., & Maes, H. H. (2002). *Mx: Statistical modeling* (6th ed.). Richmond: Virginia Commonwealth University, Department of Psychiatry.

Neale, M. C., & Cardon, L. R. (1992). *Methodology for genetic studies of twins and families.* Dordrecht, Netherlands: Kluwer.

Purcell, S. (2002). Variance components models for gene-environment interaction in twin analysis. *Twin Research, 5*, 554–571.

Purcell, S., Sham, P. (2002). Variance components models for gene-environment interaction in quantitative trait locus linkage analysis. *Twin Research, 5*, 572–576.

Rijsdijk, F. V., & Sham, P. C. (2002). Analytic approaches to twin data using structural equation models. *Briefings on Bioinformatics, 3*, 119–133.

Rodgers, J. L., Buster, M. A., & Rowe, D. C. (2001). Genetic and environmental influences on delinquency: DF analysis of NLSY kinship data. *Journal of Quantitative Criminology, 17*, 145–168.

Rodgers, J. L., & Kohler, H.-P. (2005). Reformulating and simplifying the DF analysis model. *Behavior Genetics, 35*, 211–217.

Rodgers, J. L., Kohler, H.-P., Kyvik, K. O., & Christensen, K. (2001). Behavior genetic modeling of human fertility: Findings from a contemporary Danish twin study. *Demography, 38*, 29–42.

Rodgers, J. L., Rowe, D. C., & Li, C. (1994). Beyond nature versus nurture: DF analysis of nonshared environmental influences on problem behaviors. *Developmental Psychology, 16*, 633–654.

Sham, P. (1998). *Statistics in human genetics.* New York: Oxford University Press.

Notes

1. Harris, K. M., Florey, F., Tabor, J., Bearman, P. S., Jones, J., & Udry, J. R. (2003). *The national longitudinal study of adolescent health: Research design.* http://www.cpc.unc.edu/projects/addhealth/design.

2. Jacobson, K. C., & Rowe, D. C. (1999). Genetic and environmental influences on the relationship between family connectedness, school connectedness, and adolescent depressed mood: Sex differences. *Developmental Psychology, 35,* 926–939.

3. For more information about the Child and Young Adult Supplement see: Chase-Lansdale, P. L., Mott, F. L., Brooks-Gunn, J., & Phillips, D. A. (1991). Children of the National Longitudinal Survey of Youth: A unique opportunity. *Developmental Psychology, 27,* 918–931.

4. Rodgers, J. L. (1996). *NLSY youth linking algorithm.* Unpublished manuscript.

5. See, for example: Rodgers, J. L., Buster, M., & Rowe, D. C. (2001). Genetic and environmental influences on delinquency: DF analysis of NLSY kinship data. *Journal of Quantitative Criminology, 17,* 145–168; Rodgers, J. L., Rowe, D. C., Buster, M. (1999). Nature, nurture, and first sexual intercourse in the USA: Fitting behavioural genetic models to the NLSY kinship data. *Journal of Biosocial Science, 31,* 29–41; Rodgers, J. L., Rowe, D. C., & Li, C. (1994). Beyond nature vs. nurture: DF analyses of nonshared influences on problem behaviors. *Developmental Psychology, 30,* 374–384; Rodgers, J. L., Rowe, D. C., & May, K. (1994). DF analysis of NLSY IQ/achievement data: Nonshared environmental influences. *Intelligence, 19,* 157–177.

6. Haberstick, B. C., Timberlake, D., Smolen, A., Sakai, J. T., Hopfer, C. J. et al. (2007). Between- and within-family association test of the dopamine receptor D2 TaqIA polymorphism and alcohol abuse and dependence in a general population sample of adults. *Journal of Studies on Alcohol and Drugs, 68,* 362–370.

7. Huizinga, D., Haberstick, B. C., Smolen, A., Menard, S., Young, S. E. et al. (2006). Childhood maltreatment, subsequent antisocial behavior, and the role of monoamine oxidase A genotype. *Biological Psychiatry, 60,* 677–683.

8. Beaver, K. M., DeLisi, M., Vaughn, M. G., Wright, J. P., & Boutwell, B. B. (2008). The relationship between self-control and language: Evidence of a shared etiological pathway. *Criminology.* Forthcoming; Beaver, K. M., Wright, J. P., & DeLisi, M. (2007). Self-control as an executive function: Reformulating Gottfredson and Hirschi's parental socialization thesis. *Criminal Justice and Behavior, 34,* 1345–1361; Wright, J. P., & Beaver, K. M. (2005). Do parents matter in creating self-control in their children? A genetically informed test of

Gottfredson and Hirschi's theory of low self-control. *Criminology, 43,* 1169–1202.

9. Neale, M. C., Boker, S. M., Xie, G., & Maes, H. H. (2002). *Mx: Statistical modeling* (6th ed.). Richmond: Virginia Commonwealth University, Department of Psychiatry.

10. DeFries, J. C., & Fulker, D. W. (1985). Multiple regression analysis of twin data. *Behavior Genetics, 15,* 467–473.

11. Rodgers, J. L., & Kohler, H.-P. (2005). Reformulating and simplifying the DF analysis model. *Behavior Genetics, 35,* 211–217.

12. Rodgers, J. L., Rowe, D. C., & Li, C. (1994). Beyond nature versus nurture: DF analysis of nonshared influences on problem behaviors. *Developmental Psychology, 30,* 374–384.

13. Purcell, S., & Koenan, K. C. (2005). Environmental mediation and the twin design. *Behavior Genetics, 35,* 491–498.

14. Aiken, L. S., & West, S. G. (1991). *Multiple regression: Testing and interpreting interactions.* Newbury Park, CA: Sage; Jaccard, J. R., Turrisi, R., & Wan, C. K. (1990). *Interaction effects in multiple regression.* Newbury Park, CA: Sage.

15. Rutter, M., & Silberg, J. (2002). Gene-environment interplay in relation to emotional and behavioral disturbance. *Annual Review of Psychology, 53,* 463–490.

Conclusions
And Future Directions

Introduction

The purpose of this book was to provide a primer on the emerging perspective known as biosocial criminology. In doing so, a broad range of interdisciplinary research was discussed showing that biosocial criminology is the most promising perspective to employ in the study of crime, criminality, and criminals. This final chapter summarizes the major themes of the book, provides some brief recommendations on how these themes can and should guide future criminological research, and concludes with a brief discussion of the future of biosocial criminology.

Major Findings from Biosocial Criminology

The previous chapters covered a lot of research that had examined the biosocial foundations to antisocial phenotypes. Much of the literature discussed was not published in criminology journals per se, but rather in psychological, psychiatric, genetic, biological, and neuroscience journals. Out of this work, five major findings directly relevant to biosocial criminological research are presented below. These findings are by no means the only ones that are of importance to biosocial criminologists, but they are some of the central tenets of the biosocial criminological perspective. Also, given that biosocial criminology is a relatively new line of inquiry among criminologists, recommendations for future research are also presented.

1. Genes matter, and they matter more than most criminologists think.

Perhaps the most apparent theme in this book was that genetic factors are extremely important to the study of crime. All of the previous chapters made clear that mounds upon mounds of rigorous, empirical-based research have revealed that genetic factors account for somewhere between 50 to 90 percent of the variance in antisocial phenotypes. With the mapping of the human genome, more recent genetic studies have examined whether certain genetic polymorphisms are associated with various antisocial phenotypes, such as aggression, violence, and drug use. The results of these studies have revealed that genes involved in neurotransmission are linked to antisocial outcomes.

Unfortunately, sociological criminologists have ignored all of this genetic research and have continued to focus narrowly on the association between environmental factors and criminal and delinquent behaviors.

Recommendation: It is imperative that criminologists begin to take into account genetic factors in their research. This can be accomplished relatively easily by analyzing datasets that are genetically informative. In addition, existing datasets should be converted into biosocial datasets by genotyping the study participants. This can be done relatively cheaply because DNA can be genotyped from cheek swabs (one way to collect DNA) for approximately 10 dollars per person. Furthermore, all future criminological datasets should over-sample sibling pairs (e.g., twins, full siblings, etc.), which will permit behavioral genetic research designs. With these types of biosocial datasets, criminologists will be able to explore the biosocial underpinnings to antisocial phenotypes and their research will thus be able to keep pace with the quality of research generated from the "hard sciences."

2. Standard social science methodologies (SSSMs) should be abandoned.

Almost all criminological research is conducted by using standard social science methodologies (SSSMs). With SSSMs, genetic effects on a phenotype are assumed to be uncorrelated with the environment and with the phenotype of interest. There is a great deal of research showing that these assumptions are false and that environments (e.g., parental socialization) and phenotypes (e.g., criminal involvement) are influenced heavily by genetic factors. What this means is that research, especially family socialization research, using SSSMs may be misspecified, resulting in biased results. Unfortunately, sociological criminologists continue to use SSSMs even though they are seriously flawed.

Recommendation: It is imperative that criminologists abandon SSSMs in favor of behavioral genetic research designs. With behavioral genetic research designs, criminologists would be able to hold genetic effects constant and then examine whether environmental factors have an effect on the phenotype.

3. Not all environments are created equal.

Environmental factors are critically important to criminological research, but criminologists rarely make the distinction between shared environments and nonshared environments. This is a serious mistake because a rich line of behavioral genetic research has shown that shared environments have very little effect on antisocial behaviors, while nonshared environments account for approximately 50 percent of the variance in antisocial phenotypes. Unfortunately, sociological criminologists have tended to focus their attention on shared environments.

Recommendation: It is imperative that criminologists begin to focus their resources on studying the nonshared environment and move away from studying the effects of the shared environment. In order to do so, criminologists will need to begin to analyze samples of kinship pairs because nonshared environments cannot be studied in samples that collect information about only one person per household.

4. The nature versus nurture debate is dead.

Criminologists and other social scientists continue to view the nature versus nurture debate as alive and well, with most arguing that genes are inconsequential and the environment is the dominant force. However, the nature versus nurture debate has been settled: all human phenotypes are the result of both genetic and environmental factors. Of particular importance is that emerging research has revealed that the effects of genes are contingent on the presence of certain environments and that the effects of environments are contingent on the presence of certain genetic polymorphisms. These types of interactions, known as gene X environment interactions (GxEs), are particularly relevant to criminologists because they show the interlocking effects of genetic and environmental factors in the production of antisocial phenotypes. Unfortunately, sociological criminologists, because they narrowly focus on the environment, have failed to examine GxEs in the etiology of criminal and delinquent behaviors.

Recommendation: It is imperative that criminologists abandon the nature versus nurture debate and begin to examine how antisocial phenotypes are shaped by interactions between genetic factors and environmental factors. To do so, criminologist will have to learn new methodologies and they will also have to analyze genetically sensitive datasets.

5. The brain is central to the study of antisocial phenotypes.

Particular regions of the brain, especially the prefrontal cortex and the amygdala, have been linked to violence and aggression. What this means is that variations in certain brain regions may actually be responsible for predisposing people to act criminally. Moreover, genetic and environmental criminogenic risk factors typically exert their effect on antisocial phenotypes indirectly by affecting the structure and function of certain regions of the brain. Unfortunately, sociological criminologists have largely neglected to study the brain and its relation to criminal and delinquent outcomes.

Recommendation: It is imperative that criminologists begin to examine directly the interrelationships among the brain, the environment, genetics, and antisocial phenotypes. To do so, datasets will need to include neurological information, as well as genotypic and phenotypic measures. This is certainly a challenge, but one that will increase exponentially what we know about the development of antisocial phenotypes. At the same time, it will also most likely produce a greater knowledge base from which to create newer and better prevention and intervention programs.

The Future of Biosocial Criminology

Although over the past decade much has been learned about the biosocial correlates to antisocial phenotypes, much still remains unknown. For example, only a handful of genetic polymorphisms have been found to be associated with aggression, violence, and other forms of antisocial behavior. Given that criminal behaviors are polygenic phenotypes, there are certainly many more genetic polymorphisms that confer a risk to offending behaviors. Moreover, much more needs to be learned about which genes interact with which environments to produce delinquent and criminal behaviors. And the exact ways in which the brain contributes to all types of antisocial behaviors remains a pressing research agenda. Ultimately the success of biosocial criminology will hinge on answering these and many other questions that are salient to understanding the origins of antisocial behaviors.

Perhaps one of the most important gaps in the biosocial criminological literature is the general paucity of biosocial theories. Biosocial criminology remains an empirical-based perspective that lacks a guiding theory. This is not too surprising because emerging perspectives often are grounded in research and then theories are developed based on the empirical regularities flowing from this research. There are, however, a scattering of biosocial criminological theories that are beginning to be developed.[1] They remain relatively untested, making it nearly impossible to ascertain the efficacy of them. But with more and more biosocial datasets becoming available, it is likely that these theories will be tested empirically and refined according to the study results.

Biosocial theories can also be developed by integrating genetic and biological concepts into existing criminology theories. Anthony Walsh, for example, has shown how findings from the biological sciences can be fused with traditional criminological theories, such as anomie/strain theories, control theories, and critical and feminist theories to create biosocial theories of crime.[2] Hopefully biosocial criminologists will follow the lead of Walsh and map out the various ways that extant criminological theories can be converted into biosocial theories. This type of theoretical modification will ultimately advance our understanding of the biosocial foundations to antisocial phenotypes.

Summary

The twenty-first century is an exciting time period to be a biosocial criminologist. It is an exciting time period because with the mapping of the human genome biosocial criminologists can now examine whether DNA markers are associated with antisocial phenotypes. It is an exciting time period because with the advent of neuroimaging machines, biosocial criminologists can now examine whether brain structure and brain functioning are associated with antisocial phenotypes. It is an exciting time period because with criminological datasets beginning to include kinship pairs biosocial criminologists can now estimate the environmental and genetic influences on antisocial phenotypes. But most of all it is an exciting time period because biosocial criminologists can now begin to map out the complex ways in which biological, genetic, and social factors interlock to produce antisocial phenotypes. While a daunting endeavor, biosocial criminologists are certainly up to the challenge.

Further Reading

Ellis, L. (2005). A theory explaining biological correlates of criminality. *European Journal of Criminology, 2,* 287–315.

Ellis, L., & Walsh, A. (1997). Gene-based evolutionary theories in criminology. *Criminology, 35,* 229–276.

Guo, G., Roettger, M. E., & Cai, T. (2008). The integration of genetic propensities into social-control models of delinquency and violence among male youths. *American Sociological Review, 73,* 543–568.

Robinson, M. B. (2004). *Why crime? An integrated systems theory of antisocial behavior.* Upper Saddle River, NJ: Prentice Hall.

Savage, J., & Vila, B. (2003). Human ecology, crime, and crime control: Linking individual behavior and aggregate crime. *Social Biology, 50,* 77–101.

Vila, B. J. (1994). A general paradigm for understanding criminal behavior: Extending evolutionary ecological theory. *Criminology, 32,* 311–360.

Walsh, A. (2000). Behavior genetics and anomie/strain theory. *Criminology, 38,* 1075–1108.

Wilson, E. O. (1998). *Consilience: The unity of knowledge.* New York: Alfred A. Knopf.

1. Ellis, L. (2005). A theory explaining biological correlates of criminality. *European Journal of Criminology, 2*, 287–315; Robinson, M. B. (2004). *Why crime? An integrated systems theory of antisocial behavior.* Upper Saddle River, NJ: Prentice Hall.

2. Walsh, A. (2000). Behavior genetics and anomie/strain theory. *Criminology, 38*, 1075–1108; Walsh, A. (2002). *Biosocial criminology: Introduction and integration.* Cincinnati, OH: Anderson.

About the Author

Kevin M. Beaver is an assistant professor in the College of Criminology and Criminal Justice at Florida State University, where he teaches biosocial criminology and statistics. He earned his doctorate in criminal justice from the University of Cincinnati in 2006 and was awarded the Graduate Research Fellowship from the National Institute of Justice. His current research examines the ways in which the environment intersects with biological and genetic factors to create antisocial phenotypes. He is the author of more than sixty publications which have appeared in a diverse range of journals, such as *American Journal of Public Health, Behavioral and Brain Functions, Criminal Justice and Behavior, Criminology, Journal of Adolescent Research, Journal of Genetic Psychology, Journal of Quantitative Criminology, Justice Quarterly, Sex Abuse,* and *Social Biology,* among others. Along with Anthony Walsh, he is co-editor of *Biosocial Criminology: New Directions in Theory and Research* (Routledge, 2009).